The Automated City

Seng W. Loke • Andry Rakotonirainy

The Automated City

Internet of Things and Ubiquitous Artificial Intelligence

 Springer

Seng W. Loke
Centre for Internet of Things Ecosystems
Research and Experimentation
(CITECORE), School of Information
Technology
Deakin University
Burwood, VIC, Australia

Andry Rakotonirainy
Centre for Accident Research and Road
Safety Queensland (CARRS-Q)
Queensland University of Technology
Kelvin Grove, QLD, Australia

ISBN 978-3-030-82320-7   ISBN 978-3-030-82318-4   (eBook)
https://doi.org/10.1007/978-3-030-82318-4

This Springer imprint is published by the registered company Springer Nature Switzerland AG
The registered company address is: Gewerbestrasse 11, 6330 Cham, Switzerland

The first author dedicates this book to his one and only princess YC.
The second author dedicates this book to all past, present and future sentient beings who grace him with their unconditional love.

Imagination is more important than knowledge.

- Albert Einstein

Through wisdom a house is built;
by understanding it is established;
by knowledge the rooms are filled
with all rare and beautiful treasure.

- Proverbs 24:3-4 (WEB)

Sapientia urbs conditur
(In English: A city is built on wisdom)

- Motto of the University of Nottingham

Preface

We see, in the smartphone of today, a convergence of technologies, many drawing on decades of advances across many different areas of engineering and computing, including mobile and distributed computing, sensors, wireless networking, human-computer interaction, computer graphics, artificial intelligence, software engineering, operating systems, programming tools, and computer hardware design. As developments in smart city technologies continue, we also see a convergence of technologies in urban development, and in what we see every day in the city, such as vehicles and transportation systems. We wanted to capture in one place the excitement of computing technologies for the city of today and tomorrow.

We initially wanted to write a short book summarizing our current review of work in the areas of smart cities and automation in cities, with a focus on networked "physical agents" in the city such as urban robots, automated vehicles, and drones, biased towards our interests in the Internet of Things and transport (especially, road safety). We think such a book would be useful to researchers, innovators, and students researching and studying smart cities, Internet of Things, smart vehicles, smart things, artificial intelligence, robotics, drones, and other related areas, or anyone interested in these topics and their inter-connections, and wanting a "quick" overview, in one book.

But as we explored related technologies and their convergence, and the many perspectives on the smart city, we found many emerging and exciting ideas worthy of discussion. We take a broad and integrated perspective instead of piecemeal description of urban robots, automated vehicles, and drones in cities, thereby widening the scope, and with the publisher encouraging us to write a full-length book, this book is as it is now. We try to be comprehensive, but cannot be exhaustive, as there would be a wide range of links among different areas, technical, social, and ethical. The book can also be read by interested non-technical readers—we do not dwell into algorithmic or technical details, keeping the book largely readable by a broad audience, or at least an audience with an interest in technology and how they might be used in cities of the future. Also, this book can be a starting point for those who would like an introductory overview of the areas and how they connect. Some of the topics in this book we have only briefly touched on—for the reader keen to go into technical details, we provide numerous references from the scientific peer-reviewed and grey literature.

Also, an aim of this book is to identify, highlight, and define the notion of the Automated City, as it continues to take shape and evolve among the many perspectives on the smart city. We also discuss metaphors and ways of thinking about the Automated City, at least from the technological perspective.

It must be said from the start that the book does not attempt to forecast or envision all aspects of the future city—this would be too difficult a task and prone to error. After all, who knows really what the future will bring. (However, we note that Alan Kay's maxim "the best way to predict the future is to invent it" is perhaps one way to see, at least, some aspect of the future—that is, the part which we invent.)

Instead, the book attempts a review of topics related to the notion of the smart city, with a particular focus on technology areas that we have worked on and have an interest in. We attempted to highlight what we call the Automated City, in the context of other work (and perspectives) in the smart city area, e.g., work on the Participatory City and the Data-Centric City. At certain points, we do try to extrapolate from current developments to consider how things can develop, and ask "what-if" questions, and discuss issues that would arise as a result. There are many places in the book where we used "can" and "could" to point out possibilities, about what can happen, and what could happen, not necessarily what will happen (we try not to pretend we can predict the future there, as we certainly cannot!). One might consider some aspects of the book as rather speculative, but we, as researchers, are trying to be exploratory, and write about possibilities. The book discusses opportunities and issues that can arise with the use of certain technologies for the Automated City, not so much a book of solutions. We also introduce some of our own ideas for the Automated City, such as massive cooperation of smart things in the city, and the issues therein. If forced to choose between problem solvers and problem creators, we would be largely problem identifiers in this book. Hence, the book might be of interest to someone looking for challenges to address! In Chap. 1 of this book, we provide an overview of technology trends, many of which have or are being applied to make cities "smarter". As we embarked on the book, the COVID-19 pandemic happened, which had an enormous social, mental, and economical impact on lives throughout the world. Over a year later, it is still not over as we pen the conclusion of this book. A question then arises is how the Automated City could help in a pandemic-stricken world. One could think of how automation could help keep certain important functions in the city going, from food supply chain to waste management, but answering this question is a much broader and bolder ambition than what this book can achieve (and certainly not the intent of this book). Instead, we devote a whole section in this chapter to exploring how people have used technology in the city during the pandemic situation. Many of the ideas and technologies we discuss are prototype deployments and pioneering, and some are more mature. While not an exhaustive review of technology use for the pandemic, the book highlights examples of automation and how they can help in pandemic situations— while not a water-tight argument for the importance of automation in the city, our review illustrates possibilities and suggests some technology directions in the city that could outlive the pandemic. Finally, the chapter provides a brief overview of conceptualizations of the smart city, introducing the theme of the book, which is the Automated City—it is not intended to be a theme that should supersede other perspectives, but only one perspective among many for looking at the smart city concept.

Chapter 2 discusses the concept of the Automated City in detail and introduces a number of metaphors for the Automated City. We first consider the automation of large-scale city systems, the availability of data enabling proactive and reactive cities, self-repairing cities, and urban robots. Then, we consider the metaphor of the Automated City as partner, as host and as art, in relation to its inhabitants. The metaphors highlight the collection of autonomous entities (from vehicles to robots) in the city, taken as a whole, on one side, and the human inhabitants, on the other side, and consider how they relate. The metaphors act as "lenses" through which one can view the Automated City concept. We conclude the chapter by providing a definition of the Automated City.

Chapter 3 takes a deep dive into three types of technologies, namely, automated vehicles, drones (or UAVs, short for unmanned aerial vehicles), and urban robots. We discuss their potential benefits and applications, and their issues and limitations. We choose these three technologies mainly because we have been active in some aspects of their development, and they are easily visible (and tangible) technologies that illustrate how the Automated City could develop. These technologies could, if they proliferate, occupy a large part of the public physical space in the city and are often easily noticeable. While we see their potential and look forward to their future development, we try to provide a balanced view of both their promises and issues (even their perils!).

After the focus on specific technologies, Chap. 4 takes a step back and considers the broader concerns of the development of a city. We review visions of future cities and point out issues of the governance of automation and the automation of governance. We briefly discuss new business models, city transportation, sustainability, real-time tracking, and urban edge computing. Finally, we also discuss the challenges of massive cooperation and the broad range of issues of trust and ethics in relation to the use of AI and smart devices (in private or public) in the city.

Finally, in Chap. 5, we conclude on a more philosophical and reflective note.

Melbourne, VIC, Australia   Seng W. Loke

Brisbane, QLD, Australia   Andry Rakotonirainy
June 2021

Acknowledgements

We thank our home universities for the environment which allowed this book to happen. In particular, the first author thanks Deakin University and the Queensland University of Technology (QUT), for the opportunity to spend a sabbatical at QUT, though it was spent virtually, due to COVID-19 travel restrictions. We also thank the publisher for being patient with us.

Contents

1 An Overview of Technology Trends Towards Smarter Cities 1
  1.1 The Rise of Automation 1
  1.2 The Rise of Smart Cities 2
  1.3 Technology in Cities in the Midst of a Pandemic 4
    1.3.1 Robots Helping to Deal with Infectious Diseases 5
    1.3.2 Delivery Robots 6
    1.3.3 Delivery Drones 7
    1.3.4 Drones, Robots, AI and Wireless Signals for
         Monitoring and Enforcement 7
    1.3.5 Mobile App for Social Contact Tracing and
         Location-Based Visualizations............................... 9
    1.3.6 Government Health Notifications and Advice via
         Smartphones 10
    1.3.7 Data Analytics for the City 10
    1.3.8 Smart Public Transport Stations 12
    1.3.9 Discussion 13
  1.4 An Overview of Trends in Technology 17
    1.4.1 Internet of Things (IoT), Ubiquitous Computing 17
    1.4.2 Artificial Intelligence (AI) and Robotics 22
    1.4.3 Platforms, Sharing Economy, Urban Apptivism,
         and City Operating Systems 26
    1.4.4 Digital Tools for Participation, Human
         Coordination, and Hackable Smart Cities 30
    1.4.5 Intelligent Transport Systems (ITS) and Automated
         Vehicles (AVs).. 32
  1.5 Conceptualisations of the Smart City 34
    1.5.1 Smart City Standards... 34
    1.5.2 Three Focus Areas of Technology in Smart Cities.......... 37
  1.6 Towards Smarter Cities.. 38
  References 39

2   The Automated City: Concept and Metaphors 43
   2.1   The Automated City in Relation to Current and Emerging
         Technologies: Concept 43
         2.1.1   Automation of Large Scale City Systems 43
         2.1.2   Predictive and Proactive Cities, and the Availability of Data 44
         2.1.3   Robots Everywhere 44
         2.1.4   Self-Repairing Cities, Self-Organizing Cities and
                 Self-Regenerating Cities 45
         2.1.5   The Automated City as a "Living" Machine 45
   2.2   The Automated City in Relation to its Inhabitants: Metaphors 46
         2.2.1   Machines as Partners: Machines Living in Human
                 Environments 46
         2.2.2   Machines as Hosts: Humans Living Inside Machines 54
         2.2.3   Machines as Art: Machines as Expressions of
                 Human Living 61
         2.2.4   The Humane Automated City 64
   2.3   The Automated City: A Working Definition 65
   References 67

**3   Automated Vehicles, Urban Robots and Drones: Three
     Elements of the Automated City** 69
   3.1   Introduction 69
   3.2   Automated Vehicles (AVs) 70
         3.2.1   The Potential of Automated Vehicles 73
         3.2.2   Issues and Limitations 75
         3.2.3   Summary on Automated Vehicles 81
   3.3   Urban Robots 81
         3.3.1   The Potential of Urban Robots 85
         3.3.2   Issues and Limitations 86
         3.3.3   Summary on Urban Robots 96
   3.4   Urban Drones 96
         3.4.1   The Potential of Urban Drones 99
         3.4.2   Issues and Limitations 101
         3.4.3   Summary on Urban Drones 103
   3.5   Summary of Chapter 103
   References 104

**4   The Future of the Automated City: Social, Technical and
     Ethical Perspectives** 109
   4.1   Visions of Future Cities 109
         4.1.1   The Walkable City and Urban Hubs 110
         4.1.2   Trees, Energy, the Green City and Sustainability 112
         4.1.3   Other Visions of the Future City 114
         4.1.4   Impacts of Technology on Citizens and
                 Workforce—What Do We Want City Inhabitants to
                 Become? 114

        4.1.5   Which Vision? 115
        4.1.6   The Evolution of Cities: Bottom-Up or Top-Down? 116
   4.2 Governance 117
        4.2.1   Policies.. 117
        4.2.2   Governance by Algorithms 119
   4.3 New Business Models 120
   4.4 Urban Transportation 123
   4.5 Real-Time Tracking 126
   4.6 Urban Edge Computing 127
   4.7 Blockchain for Smart Cities 129
   4.8 Massive Cooperation 130
        4.8.1   Platforms for Massive Cooperation............................ 132
        4.8.2   Cooperative Intelligent Transport Systems (Coop-ITS) 134
        4.8.3   Cooperative Vehicles and Applications 136
        4.8.4   Cooperative-By-Design 137
        4.8.5   Cooperative Internet of Things 142
   4.9 Trust and Ethics in AI and the Automated City 143
        4.9.1   Trusting Machines... 143
        4.9.2   Can AI and the Automated City be Dangerous? 145
        4.9.3   Ethical Algorithms in the Automated City 146
        4.9.4   Ethical Algorithmic Behaviour for Smart
                Connected Things 147
   4.10 Summary of Chapter... 150
   References 151

5 Conclusion 157
   5.1 The City in Physical Space and in Cyber Space 157
   5.2 What Use Will the Automated City Have? Reflections on
        the Post-Pandemic City... 157
   5.3 Its Not All About the Technology 160
   References 161

Index... 163

About the Authors

Professor Seng W. Loke received his BSc (First Class Hons.) degree in computer science from the Australian National University and PhD degree in computer science from the University of Melbourne, Australia, in 1994 and 1998, respectively. He is currently professor in computer science within the School of Information Technology at Deakin University, Australia. He currently co-directs the Platforms and Applications Lab, in the Centre for Internet of Things ECOsystems Research and Experimentation (CITECORE) at Deakin's School of Information Technology. His research interests include the Internet of Things, cooperative vehicles, mobile computing, crowd computing, smart city, and social impacts of information technology. He authored *Context-Aware Pervasive Systems: Architectures for a New Breed of Applications* published by Auerbach (CRC Press), Dec 2006, and more recently authored Crowd-Powered Mobile Computing and Smart Things published by Springer in 2017.

Professor Andry Rakotonirainy received his PhD degree in computer science from Sorbonne University and INRIA (French National Institute for Research in Digital Science and Technology) in 1995. He is currently the director of the Centre for Accident Research and Road Safety Queensland (CARRS-Q) and founder of its Intelligent Transport Systems (ITS) human factors research program. He has 25 years' research and management experience in computer science, road safety, and ITS design and implementation. He is currently a member of the Australian Research Council (ARC) College of Experts and is a regular member of EU-funded research projects' advisory boards. Professor Rakotonirainy's research has been recognised both nationally and internationally. He has proactively investigated the use of existing and emerging ITS from multiple disciplines such as computer science, mathematics, human factors, engineering, psychology, and sociology.

Chapter 1
An Overview of Technology Trends Towards Smarter Cities

Abstract The chapter discusses the rise of technology usage in cities, and how the recent COVID-19 crisis provided an opportunity for technologists to meaningfully consider how their technologies could be useful in cities. We also provide an overview of current technology trends such as AI and robotics, Internet of Things, Intelligent Transport Systems, Automated Vehicles, City Platforms, as well as their applications to smart cities. The chapter provides an integrative overview of Information and Communication Technologies (ICT) related to making cities smarter. Against the backdrop of the technology trends, this chapter positions the concept of the Automated City within current conceptualisations of the Smart City, including smart city standards and participatory and data-centric views of the smart city.

1.1 The Rise of Automation

A fundamental human need is arguably to be happy. We all need a comfortable shelter and social setting where we can fulfil our needs and reach our potential. Cities are increasingly attracting newcomers as they promise stable environments offering basic food and shelter for families as well as rich infrastructure and services to satisfy emotional needs and the desire for comfort. Etymologically speaking, the word *city* originated from the Latin *civitas*. Civitas refers to the legal status of a citizen belonging to a community and the territory occupied by this community.

Cities are places of belonging for many, with their construction and lives aided by increasingly sophisticated machinery. Contrary to common belief, automation is not a concept from the industrial revolution. It dates back to ancient Greek mythology. Hephaestus (in Homer's *Illiad*), the Greek god of invention, constructed automatons crafted out of metal to help him in his workshop in order to perform various tasks. Conceptually, they can be viewed as self-operating machines or robots. Indeed, as reviewed by Mayor in [32], automata, ideas of Artificial Intelligence, and human enhancements, have been envisioned in ancient Greek, Indian, Roman, and Chinese mythology.

© The Author(s), under exclusive license to Springer Nature Switzerland AG 2021   1
S. W. Loke, A. Rakotonirainy, *The Automated City*,
https://doi.org/10.1007/978-3-030-82318-4_1

Automation refers to man-made machines, such as computers or robots, that have been programmed to carry out tasks to assist humans or on behalf of humans. It is important to note that the assistive mission of robots, no matter how advanced the automation, there is always a human or a team behind it (e.g., the developer, or controller).

Our contemporary use of *Automated City* covers how the citizens of a city are assisted by automation and how citizens' daily life change as a result. It does not refer to a completely roboticized city emptied of its humane nature. Indeed, the role of automation is to make cities *better for* humans, not to constrain humans or make cities *without* humans.

The Automated City is the intersection of urbanity and ingenuity brought about by automated technology to empower its citizens.

Over the centuries, the development of technology, which incidentally also has its etymology in the Greek *tekhnologia* for "systematic treatment of an art, craft, or technique",[1] especially information technology, is bringing ancient visions into reality (even if not intentionally so).

1.2   The Rise of Smart Cities

Today, the world is largely urban, and will be increasingly so. About 55% of the world today live in urban areas and this is projected to rise to 70% in the coming three decades.[2] Australia, in particular, despite its large geographical size, has over 65% of its population living in capital cities and 23% in other urban areas, that is, over 88% of its population live in urban areas.[3]

Urbanisation itself takes different forms, with different sizes of cities, and different characteristics, growing not just outwards (e.g., the urban sprawl) and upwards (e.g., the skyscrapers of increasing heights), but also inwards with changes within. As noted by Batty in [6], there are waves of development (also called the *Kondratieff wave*, named after a Soviet economist) when considered from the Industrial Revolution onwards, the first wave from around 1775 based on the invention of steam power and combustion engines, the second wave based on rail power and large-scale manufacturing in the 1800s, the third wave was the age of the electricity till the early 1900s, the fourth wave was marked by the automobile, aircraft, and the early stages of computing till 1975, the fifth wave from 1975 onwards is characterised by global communications and the pervasiveness of computing as we see today, and as argued by Batty, the sixth wave will be:

---

[1] https://www.etymonline.com/word/technology [last accessed: 30/6/2020].

[2] https://www.un.org/development/desa/en/news/population/2018-revision-of-world-urbanization-prospects.html [last accessed: 30/6/2020].

[3] https://www.abs.gov.au/websitedbs/D3310114.nsf/home/Interesting+Facts+about+Australia%E2%80%99s+population [last accessed: 30/6/2020].

strongly associated with digital technologies applied to cities, medicine, security, and many other aspects of everyday life, notwithstanding the massive automation that will define society from now on.

Batty goes on to say that this sixth wave is "the age of the smart city."

The association of smart city with technology is not surprising, given its history.[4] Cities continue to be areas of rapid development as large cities get larger, so that problems of congestion and resource management persist, while cities continue to allow increasing opportunities and attract newcomers.[5] There is then the increasing need for cities and its citizens to get smarter, not only in the use of resources but also in managing city issues and in increasing the quality of city life; a collection of solutions and technological tools (e.g., smart apps) rooted in the rapid developments of information technology and communications have become a common approach. For example, to consider just four application areas, taken from [62], we have the following smart city application areas:

- *security*: example applications include "predictive policing", "real-time crime mapping", "gunshot detection", "smart surveillance", "emergency response optimization", "body-worn cameras", "disaster early-warning systems", "personal alert applications", "home security systems", "data-driven building inspections", "crowd management";
- *mobility*: example applications include "real-time public transit information", "digital public transit payment", "autonomous vehicles", "predictive maintenance of transportation infrastructure", "intelligent traffic signals", "congestion pricing", "demand-based microtransit", "smart parking", "e-hailing (private and pooled)", "car sharing", "bike sharing", "integrated multimodal information", "real-time road navigation", "parcel load pooling", "smart parcel lockers";
- *waste management*: we have "digital tracking and payment for waste disposal", and "optimization of waste collection routes"; and
- *water management*: we have "water consumption tracking", "leakage detection and control", "smart irrigation", and "water quality monitoring".

Other application areas include health, energy, community engagement and housing, with technologies for in-home care, air-quality monitors, digital services apps, technologies used for smart energy monitoring, building automation and smart street-lighting. Not every smart city employs all of such tools; and there are other listings of such smart city tools and applications.[6] But they are suggestive of the rise of technologies in managing cities. Such tools have benefits and have provided some improvements in urban life. We will look at some of the above technologies (e.g., for mobility) in greater depth later in the book.

---

[4]https://www.verdict.co.uk/smart-cities-timeline/ [last accessed: 30/6/2020].

[5]https://www.forbes.com/sites/deborahtalbot/2018/09/12/why-cities-get-the-best-jobs/#
33710b821492 [last accessed: 30/6/2020].

[6]Also, see the list of smart city tools at https://smartcitiescouncil.com/taxonomy/term/558 [last accessed: 30/6/2020].

While smart cities are generally characterised by the heavy use of information and computing technologies in an increasing number of aspects of city life, smart cities are not merely collections of applications. As noted by Halegoua in [20]:

> ...technology alone will not fundamentally transform urban governance or necessarily improve quality of life for all residents. ...Technological solutions are not wholly capable of fixing underlying conditions that lead to urban inequalities and inadequate service provisions.

Social inclusion is among the fundamental properties that smart cities need to uphold. Smart environments such as ubiquitous computing and new innovative services have been used to encourage and facilitate inclusion where the city turns into a digital platform imbued with a sense of citizen engagement.

Later in the book, we will explore and discuss further different conceptualisations of smart cities.

1.3 Technology in Cities in the Midst of a Pandemic

However, just in the midst of flourishing, as we started on this book, many cities around the world were hit by the COVID-19 pandemic, and many countries were responding to it in drastic ways.

The pandemic is a shock to all of us. However, the uncertainty caused by COVID-19 generated a larger, unprecedented shock-wave disrupting all layers of our society. Such uncertainty raises the question of how to sustain city life.

We observed an unprecedented increasing uptake of technology at work, education, governance, medical care, and a wide range of businesses migrated online, albeit some only temporarily, in a massive way. Elderly citizens who had no need to use particular technology would now employ Zoom to talk to their family members who could not visit them in-person due to social distancing restrictions. Children normally used to in-person classrooms have to resort to tablets and iPads for their educational needs. Cloud computing companies and online meeting providers enjoyed a tremendous growth in uptake during this time, while the travel industry (and related industries) suffered. Life seemed to be happening more in cyberspace than in physical space, in a "new normal". In a way, in a short time, cities had undertaken a transformation into being more technologically supported or dependent, perhaps at a pace faster than typical (which one might say is already fast), facilitated by computing and information technology as well as increasing connectivity. This sudden leap to technology adoption has surpassed the wildest expectations of researchers and developers who have been working on technology acceptance for years.

One might wonder if such technology is an important ingredient for providing the capability of a city to adapt to sudden changes such as COVID-19.

For technologists, the challenging times also called for an answer to the question of how the many exciting fairly recent developments in computing and related fields, from the Internet of Things (IoT) to Artificial Intelligence (AI), and their convergence, can be used to help the COVID-19 pandemic situation. The question is relevant beyond the context of COVID-19, i.e. the question of the the the impact of such technologies in society, in general. The answer is, in fact, multifaceted, and not without wide-ranging societal implications.

Automation alone, it must be noted, will not spontaneously improve our city life, but COVID-19 has accelerated the adoption of various kinds of technologies, including video conference technology. Microsoft's CEO Satya Nadella noted that we have achieved in two months what it would have taken two years to happen:[7] "We've seen two years' worth of digital transformation in two months. From remote teamwork and learning, to sales and customer service, to critical cloud infrastructure and security—we are working alongside customers every day to help them adapt and stay open for business in a world of remote everything." However, it seems that we have missed the opportunity to use other technologies, such as Automated Cars, to help people cope with some aspects of COVID-19 on a large scale (as the technology and regulations are still maturing).

Nevertheless, given the impact and scale of COVID-19 in cities around the world, we consider some technological applications that have been seen in popular press[8] in the following subsections.

1.3.1   Robots Helping to Deal with Infectious Diseases

At the Providence Regional Medical Center, a robot suitably equipped with a camera, stethoscope and microphone was used by doctors to interact with quarantined people—the robot is moved around by nursing staff and is not completely autonomous.[9] At the Wuchang field hospital, 5G-powered bots are used to take patients' temperatures, deliver meals and disinfect the facility.[10] Robots for cleaning areas include the germ-zapping robot Xenex[11] and robots for cleaning aeroplane cabins such as the UV-C Light system.[12] A robot developed by MIT used a custom

---

[7]https://www.microsoft.com/en-us/microsoft-365/blog/2020/04/30/2-years-digital-transformation-2-months/ [last accessed: 2/10/2020].

[8]Many are highlighted in https://www.linkedin.com/pulse/amazing-ways-robots-drones-helping-fight-covid-19-bernard-marr/ and in
https://economictimes.indiatimes.com/news/science/coronavirus-fighting-robots-and-drones/sanitizing-toilet/slideshow/75656015.cms [last accessed: 30/6/2020].

[9]https://www.medicaldevice-network.com/features/coronavirus-robotics/   [last   accessed:
30/6/2020].

[10]https://nypost.com/2020/03/10/coronavirus-hospital-ward-staffed-by-robots-opens-in-wuhan-to-protect-medics/ [last accessed: 30/6/2020].

[11]https://www.xenex.com/our-solution/lightstrike/ [last accessed: 30/6/2020].

[12]https://www.ainonline.com/aviation-news/aerospace/2020-04-27/uv-c-light-system-eliminates-covid-19-aircraft-cabins [last accessed: 30/6/2020].

UV-C light to disinfect the Greater Boston Food Bank.[13] A Beijing technology company produced small sidewalk sweepers and delivery robots for tasks too dangerous to be done by humans.[14]

1.3.2 Delivery Robots

In 2019, JD.com launched two smart delivery stations in China with 50% operation by delivery robots and 50% by humans, with an aim towards full automation.[15] In the midst of lockdowns, similar robots have been deployed in Wuhan to deliver medical supplies and groceries[16] and robots delivered food to those in quarantine[17] and there are robots for "non-contact restaurants".[18] Robots played a role in hotels housing mildly sick COVID-19 patients in Japan, mainly playing meet and greet roles.[19] It was also reported that the Jacksonville Transportation Authority tested the use of autonomous vehicles for delivering COVID-19 tests to processing labs[20] and the Nuro startup used robots to deliver goods for healthcare workers in California.[21] In Milton Keynes, Starship Technologies[22] have been deploying six-wheeled small robots moving on pathways for deliveries even before the pandemic.[23] China's Keenon Robotics has deployed robots to serve food in restaurants to reduce contact of food with persons.[24]

---

[13] http://news.mit.edu/2020/csail-robot-disinfects-greater-boston-food-bank-covid-19-0629 [last accessed: 30/6/2020].

[14] https://www.voanews.com/episode/robots-do-covid-19-jobs-too-dangerous-humans-4236651 [last accessed: 30/6/2020].

[15] https://www.techrepublic.com/article/ces-2019-chinas-e-commerce-giant-jd-launches-smart-delivery-stations-for-drones-and-robots/ [last accessed: 30/6/2020].

[16] https://www.techinasia.com/chinas-ecommerce-robots-delivery [last accessed: 30/6/2020].

[17] https://thespoon.tech/robots-deliver-food-to-people-quarantined-in-china-hotel/ [last accessed: 30/6/2020].

[18] https://syncedreview.com/2020/03/21/chinas-autonomous-delivery-vehicles-navigate-the-coronavirus-outbreak/ [last accessed: 30/6/2020].

[19] https://www.usatoday.com/story/travel/hotels/2020/05/01/coronavirus-hotel-robots-japan-debuts-tech-overflow-patients/3065881001/ [last accessed: 30/6/2020].

[20] https://www.techinasia.com/chinas-ecommerce-robots-delivery [last accessed: 30/6/2020].

[21] See https://www.techtimes.com/articles/249079/20200422/california-uses-delivery-robots-for-health-workers-fighting-covid-19.htm, https://www.theverge.com/2020/4/22/21231466/nuro-delivery-robot-health-care-workers-food-supplies-california [last accessed: 30/6/2020].

[22] https://www.starship.xyz/ [last accessed: 30/6/2020].

[23] https://industryeurope.com/sectors/automationandrobotics/the-robots-delivering-food-during-coronavirus-lockdown/ [last accessed: 30/6/2020].

[24] https://thespoon.tech/just-in-time-for-a-contactless-world-keenon-robotics-has-6000-food-server-robots-already-in-action/ [last accessed: 30/6/2020].

1.3.3 Delivery Drones

Especially for harder to reach places, drones can provide delivery services—e.g., rural areas in Canada, US and Australia can use drones for delivering supplies.[25] Drones have been used to deliver COVID-19 test-kits in Africa[26] and to do medical deliveries in Rwanda and Ghana;[27] a range of projects using drones for delivery have been noted around the world.[28]

1.3.4 Drones, Robots, AI and Wireless Signals for Monitoring and Enforcement

Besides delivery, in China, drones have been used for temperature checking, disinfecting affected areas via sprays, and broadcasting messages.[29] Coupled with computer vision technology, drones have been deployed and are being developed for a range of COVID-19 related applications[30]—for example, it is mentioned that drones equipped with sensors, including normal light cameras, microphones, thermal cameras, and temperature sensors, can provide information about respiratory and heart rates, body temperature, blood pressure, skin tone and movement and skin colour changes, enabling potential tracking of cases in a crowd of people.[31] Indoors, robots can be used to efficiently detect people with high temperatures—for example, it was reported that, in China, the Cruzr robot can track the temperature of two hundred people in a minute, notifying medical staff when needed.[32]

As cameras can be set up with Machine Learning (or Computer Vision) algorithms to track people and to monitor if people are following social distancing

---

[25] https://360.here.com/coronavirus-contactless-drone-delivery [last accessed: 30/6/2020].

[26] https://www.kidsnews.com.au/technology/aussie-company-making-drones-that-deliver-covid19-test-kids/news-story/e171f0b1f014e74bc2d3c4d2c51dca1e [last accessed: 30/6/2020].

[27] https://www.weforum.org/agenda/2020/05/medical-delivery-drones-coronavirus-africa-us/ [last accessed: 30/6/2020].

[28] https://blog.werobotics.org/2020/04/25/cargo-drones-covid-19/ [last accessed: 30/6/2020].

[29] https://www.usatoday.com/story/travel/hotels/2020/05/01/coronavirus-hotel-robots-japan-debuts-tech-overflow-patients/3065881001/ [last accessed: 30/6/2020].

[30] https://finfeed.com/opinion/ctrl-alt-del/drone-defence-against-covid-19/ [last accessed: 30/6/2020].

[31] https://www.azosensors.com/article.aspx?ArticleID=1957, http://theleadsouthaustralia.com.au/industries/technology/pandemic-drone-could-detect-virus-symptoms-in-crowds/ [last accessed: 30/6/2020].

[32] See https://9now.nine.com.au/a-current-affair/coronavirus-robots-trialled-to-assist-during-covid19-outbreak/db5305ab-d46e-4287-86e9-21fe3f382d20 [last accessed: 12/9/2020].

measures [41],[33] and drones equipped with cameras and algorithms can be developed to detect pedestrians [66], drones can be used for lockdown and social distance monitoring in an efficient and flexible way.[34] Note that even if not necessarily equipped with such algorithmic vision capabilities, videos captured by drones can be streamed to other devices (e.g., mobile devices) for human observation—indeed, "police drones" have been deployed to monitor if people are following lockdown rules, albeit with concerns about surveillance technologies.[35]

In May 2020, Singapore trialled a four-legged robot called SPOT made by Boston Dynamics to broadcast (via a loudspeaker) social-distancing messages in a park—the robot is equipped with a camera to detect multiple persons.[36]

It is noted that the use of robots for different aspects of fighting COVID-19 has been reported in over twenty countries as of April 2020.[37]

Taiwan has used geo-fencing technologies based on smartphone location data, to help monitor people in quarantine.[38] It was reported that when a person's phone was out of battery for just fifteen minutes, the person received text messages and four missed calls from administrative units.

Although robots can be used for remote patient monitoring, there are other methods to reduce physical human contact when monitoring. A MIT project uses changes in wireless signals to detect patient movements, out-of-routine behaviour, sleep patterns, breathing, including monitoring breathing rates, and has been trialled at the Heritage Assisted Living facility just outside of Boston, USA.[39] Patients do not have to wear any device and requires no contact with carers, useful in COVID-19 situations where physical proximity and contact need to be reduced—not just to monitor COVID-19 patients but for any patient in general given the COVID-19 social distancing needs. The device looks similar to a home Wi-Fi device.[40]

---

[33] See https://www.analyticsinsight.net/tracking-social-distancing-through-machine-learning/, https://github.com/Ank-Cha/Social-Distancing-Analyser-COVID-19, https://pjreddie.com/darknet/yolo/ [last accessed: 30/6/2020].

[34] https://www.abc.net.au/news/2020-05-01/new-surveillance-technology-could-beat-coronavirus-but-at-a-cost/12201552 [last accessed: 30/6/2020].

[35] https://theconversation.com/coronavirus-drones-used-to-enforce-lockdown-pose-a-real-threat-to-our-civil-liberties-138058 [last accessed: 30/6/2020].

[36] See https://www.channelnewsasia.com/news/singapore/covid-19-robot-dog-bishan-ang-mo-kio-park-safe-distance-nparks-12716124?cid=youtube_cna_social_29012018_cna, https://www.bbc.com/news/av/technology-52619568/coronavirus-robot-dog-enforces-social-distancing-in-singapore-park [last accessed: 30/6/2020].

[37] See https://theconversation.com/robots-are-playing-many-roles-in-the-coronavirus-crisis-and-offering-lessons-for-future-disasters-135527 [last accessed: 12/9/2020].

[38] https://qz.com/1825997/taiwan-phone-tracking-system-monitors-55000-under-coronavirus-quarantine/ [last accessed: 25/7/2020].

[39] https://techcrunch.com/2020/04/14/mit-developed-a-wireless-box-that-can-detect-covid-19-patients-movement-and-breathing-at-home/ [last accessed: 18/7/2020].

[40] Emerald Innovation, see https://www.emeraldinno.com/ [last accessed: 18/7/2020].

1.3.5   Mobile App for Social Contact Tracing and Location-Based Visualizations

In Australia, the government released the COVIDSafe mobile app[41] which could be downloaded and used to track near-by encounters for use in contact tracing if new cases are found. In general, the more people downloaded the app, the better the data for contact tracing and at the time of writing, there have been almost six million downloads—of course, not every download means the app will be active, and so, notifications are sent as reminders to have the app turned on when leaving the home. The app is based on proximity sensing using Bluetooth Low Energy which is equipped in most smartphones on the market—the protocol is called BlueTrace[42] and is based on Singapore's TraceTogether app.[43]

There is also MIT's SafePaths contact tracing app which uses GPS and Bluetooth[44]—in this app, the location log data collected on the smartphone is stored on the phone, and leaves the device only when the user sends the information to a public health authority—this is a similar design principle to BlueTrace which aims to defer sending of the data from the phone to the authority until there has been a diagnosis of a COVID-19 case.[45]

Apple and Google partnered to provide a privacy-preserving contact tracing solution which is also based on Bluetooth[46] proximity sensing using broadcasted identifiers (i.e., beacon messages), but uses device identifiers that change every 15 minutes on average to avoid device tracking, and different from COVIDSafe, it is noted that the app provides exposure notifications to users in a decentralised manner: "At least once per day, the system will download a list of the keys for the beacons that have been verified as belonging to people confirmed as positive for COVID-19. Each device will check the list of beacons it has recorded against the list downloaded from the server. If there is a match between the beacons stored on the device and the positive diagnosis list, the user may be notified and advised on steps to take next."[47] Note, however, that permission is required by the persons diagnosed with COVID-19 for their devices' beacons to be included in the positive diagnosis list. India has its own contact tracing app called Aarogya Setu also based on Bluetooth

---

[41] https://www.health.gov.au/resources/apps-and-tools/covidsafe-app [last accessed: 30/6/2020].

[42] BlueTrace is an open source application protocol; https://bluetrace.io/ [last accessed: 30/6/2020].

[43] https://www.tracetogether.gov.sg/, https://www.abc.net.au/news/science/2020-04-17/5-questions-the-governments-coronavirus-contact-tracing-app/12151264 [last accessed: 30/6/2020].

[44] https://safepaths.mit.edu/ [last accessed: 30/6/2020].

[45] See https://support.tracetogether.gov.sg/hc/en-sg/articles/360043735693-What-data-is-collected-Are-you-able-to-see-my-personal-data [last accessed: 23/7/2020].

[46] https://www.apple.com/covid19/contacttracing [last accessed: 30/6/2020].

[47] From the specification: https://covid19-static.cdn-apple.com/applications/covid19/current/static/contact-tracing/pdf/ExposureNotification-FAQv1.1.pdf [last accessed: 30/6/2020].

which is open source.[48] There are also other apps such as the We-Care Web app for checking-in and checking-out of locations.[49]

Contact tracing apps around the world have been surveyed in [2, 28], and there have been at least twenty-five contact tracing efforts using such technology.[50] Legal and social issues, e.g., in relation to privacy implications, of contract tracing apps are discussed in [27]. A list of contact-tracing apps around the world has been maintained by the MIT Technology Review,[51] which also has a site discussing pandemic technologies.[52]

1.3.6 Government Health Notifications and Advice via Smartphones

In Victoria, Australia, there is the VicEmergency app via which government notifications concerning emergencies, from bushfires to pandemic advice, are sent to people; an Australian Government Whatsapp group was also set up for people to send queries and to receive updates of the local pandemic situation. Other countries, e.g., Singapore,[53] and even the WHO[54] have used Whatapp to bring health alerts to billions of people in different languages.[55]

1.3.7 Data Analytics for the City

COVID-19 has impacted the economies of the world in a drastic way, causing tremendous reductions, e.g., in both human and vehicle traffic, with consequent impact on businesses. A question is how drastic such reductions were and whether signs of recovery can be observed; in Australia, and other countries, road traffic

---

[48]https://www.mygov.in/aarogya-setu-app/ [last accessed: 30/6/2020].

[49]https://we-care.world/ [last accessed: 30/6/2020].

[50]https://www.technologyreview.com/2020/05/07/1000961/launching-mittr-covid-tracing-tracker/ [last accessed: 27/8/2020].

[51]https://www.technologyreview.com/2020/12/16/1014878/covid-tracing-tracker/ [last accessed: 28/1/2021].

[52]See https://www.technologyreview.com/2020/12/16/1014876/about-the-pandemic-technology-project/ [last accessed: 28/1/2021].

[53]https://govinsider.asia/innovation/singapore-coronavirus-whatsapp-covid19-open-government-products-govtech/ [last accessed: 30/6/2020].

[54]https://www.wired.com/story/whatsapp-coronavirus-who-information-app/ [last accessed: 30/6/2020].

[55]https://www.who.int/news-room/feature-stories/detail/who-health-alert-brings-covid-19-facts-to-billions-via-whatsapp [last accessed: 30/6/2020].

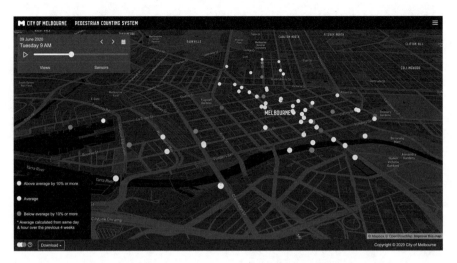

Fig. 1.1 Visualisation of the pedestrian count in the Melbourne CBD [http://www.pedestrian. melbourne.vic.gov.au/#date=09-06-2020&time=9] (used with permission from the City of Melbourne)

sensors (e.g., traffic signal sensors[56] and pedestrian and bicycle counters in Melbourne[57]) have been in place for a while in certain regions, and such traffic data provides a means to measure the extent of such reductions and to monitor changes over time, and mobile phone data gathered via app GPS "pings" can be sourced to detect the aggregate reduced movements of citizens.[58] The City of Melbourne pedestrian counter data for the CBD at 9am on 9th June 2020 is visualised as shown in Fig. 1.1.

Even sewage can be analysed to sense and detect COVID-19. For example, Australia's research organisation CSIRO detected the virus, which leads to the disease COVID-19, in Australian untreated sewage.[59] This also suggests ways of sensing for and detecting virus spread and movement through analysis of a city's waste (not just wastewater) [37]. Although not existing yet, one can imagine robots being put into sewage systems to report on and detect different kinds of virus. The analytics of city waste could be telling.

---

[56]https://www.vicroads.vic.gov.au/traffic-and-road-use/traffic-management/traffic-signals/how-traffic-signals-work [last accessed: 30/6/2020].

[57]https://chartingtransport.com/ [last accessed: 30/6/2020].

[58]See the "UNSW rCITI public webinar on the impact of COVID-19 on mobility patterns in Australia" at https://www.youtube.com/watch?v=fWJxX5ISfGo&feature=youtu.be [last accessed: 30/6/2020].

[59]https://www.csiro.au/en/News/News-releases/2020/Australian-researchers-trace-sewage-for-early-warning-COVID-19-spread [last accessed: 14/7/2020].

Institutions through which citizens conduct business and commerce could provide data for city behaviour tracking. For example, banks can also track the locations and numbers of shopping transactions to determine the health of the economy within a city, and also detect where people are shopping.

There is also a dashboard on the impact of COVID-19 on the Australian Property Market.[60] London has its own dashboard of mobility data in relation to COVID-19 impacts[61] and there are dashboards to help the public track the economic impacts of COVID-19.[62] Facebook also has provided a movement dashboard illustrating movements and staying-put trends since the COVID-19 situation.[63] The reduced economic activity has also resulted in changes in pollution levels as can be observed via data from deployed air quality monitors.[64] Many of the dashboards are based on sensor data collated and processed automatically, but some will involve a degree of manual human input and analysis.

1.3.8   Smart Public Transport Stations

In Seoul, South Korea, at least ten bus shelters have been installed with thermal-imaging cameras, where the door will only open to someone whose temperature is below 37.5 degrees Celsius. The bus shelter also has ultraviolet lamps installed that can kill viruses and cool the air.[65] Temperature screening kiosks have also been developed by Samsung.[66] Singapore has also deployed public temperature screening kiosks at public transit locations.[67]

---

[60] See https://blogs.unsw.edu.au/cityfutures/blog/2020/04/city-dashboards-in-a-time-of-covid-19/ and https://covid19dashboard.be.unsw.edu.au/ [last accessed: 30/6/2020].

[61] https://data.london.gov.uk/dataset/coronavirus-covid-19-mobility-report   [last   accessed: 30/6/2020].

[62] For example, see https://tracktherecovery.org/ [last accessed: 30/6/2020].

[63] https://dataforgood.fb.com/tools/movement-range-maps/ [last accessed: 30/6/2020].

[64] For example, see https://airquality.gsfc.nasa.gov/ and https://www.eea.europa.eu/themes/air/air-quality-and-covid19/monitoring-covid-19-impacts-on [last accessed: 30/6/2020].

[65] See https://www.theguardian.com/world/2020/aug/13/south-korea-installs-anti-virus-bus-shelters-with-temperature-sensors-and-uv-lamps [last accessed: 15/8/2020].

[66] See https://www.samsung.com/us/business/solutions/digital-signage-solutions/back-to-business/ [last accessed: 15/8/2020].

[67] See   https://www.mccy.gov.sg/about-us/news-and-resources/press-statements/2020/jun/ temperature-self-check-kiosks-public-transport-locations-islandwide [last accessed: 15/8/2020].

Application for Covid-19	Key Technology Categories
Robots for infectious disease management and cleaning	Robotics, AI
Delivery (ground) robots	Robotics, AI
Delivery drones	Drones, Robotics, AI
Drones/robots for monitoring/enforcement, wireless device for health monitoring	Drones, Robotics, AI (Computer Vision), Smartphone Tracking, Wireless Signal Processing
Social contact tracing	Mobile Apps, Mobile Sensing, Data Analytics
Health notifications and advice	Mobile Apps, Mobile Communications
Quantifying impact - city analytics of traffic and aggregated citizen behavior, economic and air quality tracking	Sensors (fixed and mobile), Data Analytics
Smart Public Transport Stations	Thermal-imaging (temperature screening, contactless)

Fig. 1.2 A sampling of technological applications in COVID-19 and their broad categorisation

1.3.9 Discussion

Figure 1.2 summarises the applications mentioned above and the general category of technologies involved.[68]

There are many other innovative applications of IT involved in dealing with the COVID-19 situation not mentioned above, including computer simulations to understand the impact of social distancing (e.g., see [7, 33] for the Australian perspective)[69] and possible virus spread indoors such as a grocery store,[70] and IT in medicine to help treat and detect COVID-19 such as a tool to automate temperature screening,[71] a tool to detect COVID-19 progress via cough sounds,[72] an app to collect sounds of breathing and coughing to help develop a system to diagnose

---

[68]This article in IEEE Spectrum summarises a range of robotic applications, some mentioned above, for COVID-19: https://spectrum.ieee.org/robotics/medical-robots/how-robots-became-essential-workers-in-the-covid19-response [last accessed: 2/10/2020].

[69]See also https://www.nature.com/articles/d41586-020-01003-6 [last accessed: 30/6/2020].

[70]https://blogs.unity3d.com/2020/05/08/exploring-new-ways-to-simulate-the-coronavirus-spread/ [last accessed: 30/6/2020].

[71]https://govinsider.asia/innovation/covid-coronavirus-singapore-ihis-kronikare-temperature-ai/ [last accessed: 30/6/2020].

[72]https://thenextweb.com/neural/2020/03/20/this-ai-system-listens-to-coughs-to-learn-where-the-coronavirus-is-spreading/ [last accessed: 30/6/2020].

COVID-19,[73] AI to help find a COVID-19 vaccine[74] and 3-D printing for creating masks and devices such as respirators.[75] More could be said of the role robots can play here as well. For example, robots could be making drinks and pizza reducing human contact in food preparation,[76] or as active proxies for family members and carers in aged care homes and hospitals where visitations are prohibited [10], or telepresence robots to enable those unable to physically visit other physical places (e.g., museums) to do so virtually by remotely controlling robots [55], beyond visiting virtual versions of such places via virtual reality. Virtual retail stores could play a role in providing shopping experiences during lockdowns, especially with high-quality graphics.[77] Reviews of the use of digital technology for COVID-19 are given in [61]. The use of smartphone for health and telemedicine in COVID-19 are discussed in [24]. Applications of virtual reality (VR) technologies for COVID-19 are reviewed in [52].[78]

It is also interesting to note that as more of the world's activities moved online, due to lockdowns, or due to people's own decisions to stay in, from working-from-home to social relationships, many online platforms such as Zoom and Amazon benefited (e.g., in 2020, Amazon stock price increased by 56% from Mid-March to mid-June), while other companies involving human mobility were drastically impacted, e.g., in tourism and travel. Some local shops which have never been online moved online and started taking orders online, and supporting deliveries. As Stefan Hawjkowicz, Senior Principal Scientist (Strategy & Foresight), at Australia's reasearch organisation CSIRO noted,[79] there have been signs of expansions to online grocery shopping and delivery operations by both of Australia's supermarket giants Coles and Woolworths, the software technology company Atlassian went on a recruitment drive during the pandemic, online education and telehealth boomed, and so has online retail (with growth from local orders, rather than international orders as one typically expects of the use of online shopping). We will discuss further the role of these large-scale platforms in the city later in this chapter.

---

[73] https://www.cam.ac.uk/research/news/new-app-collects-the-sounds-of-covid-19 [last accessed: 30/6/2020].

[74] https://www.wired.com/story/opinion-ai-can-help-find-scientists-find-a-covid-19-vaccine/ [last accessed: 30/6/2020].

[75] For example, see https://www.abc.net.au/news/2020-04-03/callout-for-3d-printers-to-help-create-medical-supplies/12115074,https://www.abc.net.au/news/2020-04-05/start-up-company-makes-3d-face-shields-for-coronavirus-treatment/12121978 [last accessed: 30/6/2020].

[76] See https://www.dezeen.com/2018/06/07/nino-robotic-bartender-can-make-any-drink-in-seconds/, and https://spectrum.ieee.org/view-from-the-valley/robotics/industrial-robots/zume-the-robotic-pizza-company-makes-a-pizza-only-a-robot-could-love [last accessed: 18/7/2020].

[77] For example, see Obsess, https://obsessar.com [last accessed: 18/7/2020].

[78] For example, a 3D VR model of a COVID-19 infected lung was developed using HoloLens 2, from https://news.microsoft.com/en-au/features/la-trobe-university-models-coronavirus-infected-lung-in-3d/.

[79] https://aprintern.org.au/2020/06/17/webinar-innovating-in-time-of-crisis/, Webinar on INNO-VATING IN A TIME OF CRISIS [last accessed, 25 June 2020].

Also interesting are ideas about how companies could digitally transform their operations such as sales and delivery to take the human out of the loop (for safety reasons), yet done in a humane way and customer-centric way. For example, a car retailer could think about how it could sell cars to people, perhaps supported by a mobile app to access cars for test-drives (with appropriate controls) and then to eventually buy and complete the purchase transaction online. Car insurance can already be purchased online or over the phone. Similarly, there could be robots to make, sell and deliver drinks and food to people—though perhaps with limitations in dish varieties. If this is integrated with supply chain automation, there could be robots to harvest and deliver ingredients to food factories which could then make and sell this food to people.

The pandemic might have been an opportunity to showcase, or bring to the fore, discussions about automation for many companies, but it nevertheless, conveyed a sense of benefits that could be obtained while also raising societal issues, e.g., surveillance technologies and privacy, and reactions to robots in public. A detailed discussion is given in [18], of a range of COVID-19 technologies, including contract-tracing apps, geo-fencing for quarantine compliance monitoring, tools for tracking and modelling movements of people, and symptom checkers, and their ethical considerations in terms of privacy, solidarity, preserving personal autonomy, justice, beneficence (i.e., public benefit), and non-maleficence (e.g., scientifically validated that the tool or approach will not cause harm)—we will come back to ethical considerations of automation later in the book.

Automation and sensing, as well as conducting life online, seem to play an important role in providing resilience, place-understanding and adaptability in cities, especially in situations of severe pressures and difficulties interrupting normal physical functioning of a city. City services must continue to run, from garbage collection to delivery of mail and medicine, as well as policing. Supply chains for food and goods must continue to run, manned or unmanned. Vulnerable people afraid to leave home or lockdown restrictions increases the need for deliveries ordered via online platforms. Also, citizens and government need to continue to understand the local environment in which they live and the impacts of the pandemic, as well as make evidenced-based decisions. Sensing in its various forms, from mobile phone data, to road sensors to satellite images, provide situation-awareness or context-awareness required to understand in real-time or over time what is happening in the physical world, and automation enables actions to be taken efficiently and with reduced human effort.

The illustrations also showed limitations of current technology and the fact that deployment is actually not as widespread as one might gather from popular press. Only a few cities adopted or trialled some of the above technology, and some solutions might require further instrumentation of the environment and local regulations to work effectively and safely. Some of the robots operated only in a certain part of the city with pre-programmed routes, not in all cities and not everywhere in the city. A hotel of n floors might use n robots because it was difficult to program wheeled robots to use lifts or climb up and down steps, but the SPOT robots deployed in a park in Singapore are all-terrain and copes better with rugged terrain, but has been said to be "creepy",[80] perhaps an issue easily solved via suitable exterior designs or simply with greater public familiarity with robots. Many of the operations might involve humans in the loop to control aspects of the robots or drones. In any case, the above applications are mere glimpses of possibilities afforded by technology.

Also, the impact of COVID-19 is also not equal across society, e.g., with lower income jobs appear to be most at risk in the United Kingdom due to the economic slowdown.[81] And public transport safety and restrictions affect people who most depend on it the most, with some more affected by it than others, e.g., it is noted that "remote working is not an option for most low-income workers in the services sector."[82] There are questions of whether new technological solutions (e.g., a transport subsystem comprising a fleet of Automated Vehicles) could help address inequality in cities, rather than entrench inequality, or at least be built with equitable access in mind, and not just in pandemic times, a topic which we will come back to later in the book.

Will these technologies remain post-COVID-19? Many of the technologies were already being developed pre-COVID-19 and so would be expected to be developed further beyond the COVID-19 situation, some perhaps in preparation for future pandemics (if ever again), and others perhaps repurposed. The opportunity for repurposing and adapting to other application contexts are in fact vast. For example, a robot cleaning plane cabins might be adapted for cleaning train cabins and drones for pedestrian monitoring might be used in emergencies or riot control or helping the elderly transport groceries. We will see more examples of robots and possibilities with automation in cities throughout this book.

Technology acceptance has also been somewhat affected by the pandemic, as robots or online platforms provided a means for business continuity and in fact, life continuity at reduced risks.

Video conferencing software such as Zoom, Skype or Microsoft Teams and social media software (e.g., Facebook Messenger) have unequivocally helped to alleviate the social isolation brought about by confinements and lockdowns. Despite such virtual contact, it has been widely documented that COVID-19 had significant negative impacts on the mental health of the community. The elderly residing in aged care homes were significantly affected mentally as they could not have physical visits of loved ones for months. Their families were, in return, constantly anxious about the well-being of their parents or grandparents. In Australia, millions of

---

[80] https://nypost.com/2020/05/09/robot-dogs-patrol-singapore-park-to-encourage-social-distancing/ [last accessed: 30/6/2020].

[81] https://www.mckinsey.com/industries/public-sector/our-insights/covid-19-in-the-united-kingdom-assessing-jobs-at-risk-and-the-impact-on-people-and-places   [last   accessed: 30/6/2020].

[82] https://theconversation.com/whos-most-affected-on-public-transport-in-the-time-of-coronavirus-133429 [last accessed: 30/6/2020].

dollars were provided by the government to deal with mental health issues in the community due to the pandemic.[83]

Human-like and animal-like robots have been used to help elderly people in aged care [57]. However, it is too early to speculate that such robots could replace warm family interactions in the near future.

COVID-19 was a new disease that no one had encountered before. Policy-makers had the extremely difficult decision in choosing between prioritising the economy or health of the community.

The transmission patterns, survival rate per demographic group, best treatments, duration of disease immunity and so on, were all unknown at the beginning of the pandemic and are still uncertain to this day. In the absence of complete knowledge, health authorities could be forced to make decisions under a great deal of uncertainty.

Data from IoT, transport, e-health records, and individual mobility locations have helped to uncover certain aspects of the transmission pattern of the disease. There is still potentially untapped knowledge that one can discover by fusing data from transport and health sectors. However, citizens are increasingly weary about confidentiality. For example, the COVIDSafe app and similar apps, were in some cases, wrongly portrayed as "big brother" and contributed to slowing up-take. The reactions and perceptions of people to COVID-19 apps could also change over time.[84]

As background, we will next provide an overview of technology areas which will be the focus of our discussions in this book. This is not a complete review of computing today, but highlights areas most closely related to the theme of this book.

1.4   An Overview of Trends in Technology

1.4.1   Internet of Things (IoT), Ubiquitous Computing

According to Norman,[85] the term "Internet of Things" was coined by Kevin Ashton as early as 1999—Kevin was the co-founder of MIT's Auto-ID lab which pioneered the use of RFID (Radio-Frequency Identification) [58] for supply-chain management. In a way, by tagging objects with electronic tags that can be read or written using RF waves, such objects can be tracked and given an identity in

---

[83]For example, see https://www.health.gov.au/ministers/the-hon-greg-hunt-mp/media/covid-19-481-million-for-national-mental-health-and-wellbeing-pandemic-response-plan [last accessed: 14/7/2020].

[84]For example, it was noted that, in April 2020, more than 70% of people in Switzerland were willing to install a COVID-19 app when available, but by the end of June 2020, over half of the people say they would not, from https://ethz.ch/en/news-and-events/eth-news/news/2020/07/blueprint-for-the-perfect-coronavirus-app.html.

[85]https://www.historyofinformation.com/detail.php?id=3411 [last accessed: 17/4/2021].

cyberspace, functioning as a bridge between the physical world existence of the object and the identity or virtual counterpart of the object in the cyber world. This also means that the object is, in this way, connected to the Internet, in the sense that it can be tracked from across the Internet and has a cyberspace presence.

If we were to then apply this same idea to connecting not just objects, but people, places, animals, and things, to the Internet, we can then track, monitor, and even to some extent control or manage, such places, animals, people and things. This can be related to the idea of sensors, and the thriving area of sensor networks where such sensors are networked together in various topologies to allow particular environments to be sensed and tracked, and managed. Connecting actuators or robots to the Internet then allows manipulation of the physical world via the Internet, leading to the notion of Internet-connected robotics or sometimes called the Internet of Robotic Things (IoRT) [29, 49]. A definition of the Internet of Things is as follows:[86]

> The Internet of Things is the interconnection of endpoints (devices and things) which can be uniquely addressed and identified with an IP (Internet Protocol) address. With the Internet of Things, devices can be connected to the Internet, sense, gather, receive and send data and communicate with each other and applications via IP technologies, platforms and connectivity solutions.

But wide-area Internet is not the only way to connect things, various types of shorter range wireless networking technologies have enabled things to connect with other things (and eventually to the Internet), even within shorter ranges, allowing not only wide-area but local machine-to-machine communications and cooperation. There is also a range of protocols developed for the Internet of Things, with a focus on machine-to-machine communications, not just for human communications, e.g., LoRaWAN, NB-IoT, LTE-M, MQTT, LwM2M,[87] and so on [3, 13].[88] Web protocols and standards have also been integrated with the Internet of Things, forming the so-called Web of Things [19].

From the late 1990s, ubiquitous computing [59], or pervasive computing [47], envisions the ubiquity of computing, and the pervasiveness of its usage in a wide range of applications. The momentum provided by ubiquitous computing together with IoT is leading to a proliferation of devices and things embedded with computational ability, sensing capabilities, wireless networking capabilities, and actuators to affect the physical environment—that is, such devices can become cyber-physical, located in both cyber space and physical space, and can be assembled to form cyber-physical systems (CPS).

As pointed out in [30], there could be an estimated ten billion processors produced per year leading towards possibly into an era of trillions of computer

---

[86]https://www.i-scoop.eu/internet-of-things-guide/ [last accessed: 30/6/2020].

[87]https://www.openmobilealliance.org/release/LightweightM2M/Lightweight_Machine_to_ Machine-v1_1-OMASpecworks.pdf [last accessed: 30/6/2020].

[88]See also https://www.rs-online.com/designspark/eleven-internet-of-things-iot-protocols-you-need-to-know-about [last accessed: 30/6/2020].

devices deployed, many in places and applications where one may not normally think of as computers. Recent reports suggest that IoT deployed devices are already in the billions.[89] As such devices begin to proliferate [25, 45], we begin to see many more things, such as devices in the household, commercial, and industrial settings, and even everyday objects, which were traditionally not Internet-connected (e.g., waste bins, cups, pens, desks, luggages, mailboxes, lights, wardrobes, soft-toys, and so on), get connected to the Internet, yielding tremendous growth in the Internet of Things. There is an ever increasing range of devices connected to the Internet, yielding new forms of devices and new possibilities for layers of services above Internet-connected products.

Today, when one thinks of the Internet of Things, one thinks of a collection of technologies, and a whole range of research areas.[90] Some of the areas include (i) engineering the future Internet, involving 5G/6G where there is greater support for machine-to-machine communications and reliability, (ii) IoT infrastructure (comprising sensors, sensor networks and actuators), (iii) Big Data related to Internet of Things data, and the associated data processing and management, (iv) hardware technologies for the IoT, (v) positioning technologies (for people, robots and things for both indoor and outdoor navigation including satellite based methods), (vi) middleware and platforms for IoT applications, (vii) IoT standards and semantic technologies to enable interoperability among devices and systems, (viii) context-awareness so that IoT devices are smarter and can make proactive decisions, and (ix) socio-technical issues of security and privacy in relation to the use of IoT devices as well as models of reputation and trust. We will come back to many of the socio-technical issues in later parts of the book.

Recent work has also begin to look at autonomous systems and their connection with IoT, not just IoRT as mentioned, but also (i) how multiagent systems can be used to facilitate cooperation in the IoT [50], (ii) how IoT, by nature distributed, can connect with other decentralised distributed technologies, such as distributed ledger technologies for the IoT [51, 68], and (iii) Space IoT which is receiving more attention as costs of deployment and operation of satellite-supported machine-to-machine communications (e.g., SAT42M[91]) drops, in comparison to terrestrial deployments using technologies such as LoRaWAN, NB-IoT, LTE-M or Sigfox.[92] Also, there have been use cases of satellites for urban planning and health

---

[89]See https://www.zdnet.com/article/what-is-the-internet-of-things-everything-you-need-to-know-about-the-iot-right-now/ and https://iot-analytics.com/state-of-the-iot-update-q1-q2-2018-number-of-iot-devices-now-7b/ [last accessed: 30/6/2020].

[90]For example, see the topics in three well known journals in the area: ACM Transactions on the Internet of Things, IEEE IoT Journal, and Elsevier's journal on the Internet of Things.

[91]https://sat4m2m.com/wordpress/ [last accessed: 30/6/2020].

[92]https://cordis.europa.eu/article/id/232842-space-iot-takes-off [last accessed: 30/6/2020].

monitoring, e.g., air quality monitoring, geo-hazard monitoring, and monitoring solar radiation to inform solar energy systems deployments.[93]

Not just for consumer products, IoT has tremendous potential in many industries. For example, a PwC report (2018),[94] argued that IoT is a key driver to improve productivity in areas such as construction, manufacturing, healthcare, mining and agriculture (including fishing and forestry).

IoT applications for smart cities are myriad, some of which we mentioned at the beginning of the book, ranging from smart bins and smart trash collection, sensors for infrastructure maintenance (e.g., enabling predictive maintenance), asset tracking for company or local government, smarter services and law enforcement, city monitoring (e.g., traffic and pedestrian movements, air quality, noise, surface temperature, Internet-connected safety cameras and so on) and planning, IoT in transport (including v2x connectivity), IoT in energy infrastructure, water level monitoring to IoT integration into data-centric governance processes [14, 23].[95]

In Australia, smart street LED lights, environmental and water quality sensors, safety cameras, flood sensors on roads, CCTV cameras, smart parking sensors, sensors on public barbeques and bins, smart water meters, and smart urban irrigation, are among recent projects under the smart city banner.[96] In particular, though not in busy urban areas, the La Trobe Valley sensor network shown in Fig. 1.3 provides real-time detection of bushfire and flood detection, thermal and visual imaging, air quality monitoring, and microclimate weather reporting.[97]

Another interesting urban sensor network, in the United States, is the experimental Array of Things sensor network located in Chicago and other partner cities, which incorporates in-network sensor data processing, e.g., sensors detect and count vehicles at an intersection, and can delete raw image data, but report the count. Sensor nodes can measure "temperature, barometric pressure, light, vibration, carbon monoxide, nitrogen dioxide, sulfur dioxide, ozone, ambient sound pressure, and pedestrian and vehicle traffic" with plans to use analytics to detect "other urban factors of interest such as solar light intensity (visible, UV, and IR) and cloud cover

---

[93] See the online workshop on "Space for cities: from innovation to operation. A talk about concrete uses of satellite data and services to support cities' resilience and sustainability" (held in October 2020) https://www.eurisy.eu/event/from-innovation-to-operation/about/ [last accessed: 9/4/2021].

[94] https://www.pwc.com.au/consulting/assets/publications/acs-pwc-iot-report-web.pdf   [last accessed: 30/6/2020].

[95] https://www.visualcapitalist.com/iot-building-smarter-cities/; see also https://www.mckinsey.com/featured-insights/internet-of-things/our-insights/the-future-of-connectivity-enabling-the-internet-of-things [last accessed: 30/6/2020].

[96] For   example,   see   https://www.computerworld.com/article/3535369/meet-the-top-nine-australian-smart-city-projects.html   and   https://infrastructuremagazine.com.au/2020/05/15/smart-technology-solutions-for-cities-and-suburbs/ [last accessed: 20/7/2020].

[97] https://lvin.org/ [last accessed: 20/7/2020].

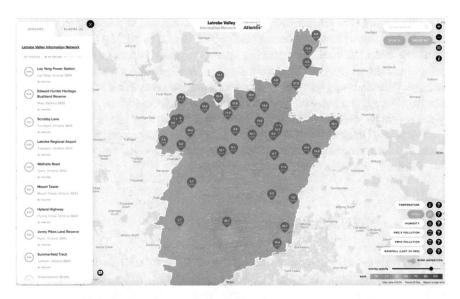

Fig. 1.3 La Trobe Valley Sensor Network, located in the state of Victoria, Australia (Web interface screenshot taken on 20/7/2020 from https://lvin.org/#/)

(important to building energy management), and flooding and standing water."[98] Data collected via the sensor network are publicly available via an open portal.[99]

IoT is not only about sensor networks city-scale or over vast geographical areas, but also very much sensing and analytics in personal spaces. The quantified self movement[100] encourages self-tracking and analytics of the self [36], e.g., via wearable IoT devices, and one can even apply such ideas to understand the human driver [42].

It is not only the functionality within individual things which are increasingly sophisticated, but connectivity technologies are also evolving. As some countries continue to roll out 5G, and 5G subscribers increase, 6G networking technology is beginning to be considered. Samsung Research released a vision for 6G in a whitepaper [101] and highlighted connectivity to support services such as immersive extended reality (or XR) (building on today's augmented and virtual reality technologies), high-fidelity holograms and digital replica (similar to the notion of *digital twins* which are virtual counterparts of physical world objects and places)—indeed, high bandwidth and stable connectivity are required to support such applications.

---

[98] https://arrayofthings.github.io [last accessed: 20/7/2020].

[99] https://data.cityofchicago.org/Environment-Sustainable-Development/Array-of-Things-Locations-Map/2dng-xkng [last accessed: 20/7/2020].

[100] https://quantifiedself.com/ [last accessed: 14/7/2020].

[101] https://cdn.codeground.org/nsr/downloads/researchareas/20201201_6G_Vision_web.pdf [last accessed: 11/1/2021].

For 6G, a peak data rate of 1000 gigabits per second and wireless latency of less than 100 microseconds have been noted, which is said to be fifty times 5G's peak data rate and a tenth of 5G's network latency.[102] Such networks will be used by people and things (machines). Such data rates could provide a means to transfer, if needed, thousands of gigabytes of data that autonomous systems might generate or use in a day, e.g., an automated vehicle that generates thousands of gigabytes of data per day (via its sensors).[103] Research challenges in 6G are noted in [8].

The idea of things, places and people (with devices) connected to each other via short and long range networking technologies will be an enabling technology that we will see many more examples of in this book.

1.4.2   Artificial Intelligence (AI) and Robotics

AI, a term first coined by John McCarthy in 1956 to refer to the science and engineering challenges of making intelligent machines, has a history in a range of novel techniques based on mathematical logic and statistics. The history of AI has a range of ups and downs, including failures to meet hyped expectations, but also tremendous mind-boggling successes. Recent years have seen what is perhaps a resurgence in the excitement of AI due to highly popularised successes such as AlphaGo that defeated a world champion in the game of Go,[104] self-driving vehicles (which we will delve deeper into in later chapters), and as well as Deep Learning and Reinforcement Learning.

There has also been worries that AI will be able to replace human labour in certain areas, and so, take jobs away from people (e.g., see the paper [17] which enjoyed tremendous publicity). However, it seems that it is not so much jobs (that might comprise a set of inter-related tasks) that will be replaced by AI, but that a range of tasks will be automated using AI technologies—and the idea is not only to automate tasks that are considered manual but also tasks requiring human intelligence [46]:

> AI automates tasks normally requiring human intelligence, a definition that distinguishes itself from automation of manual tasks.

AI technologies, being data-driven, can automate transactions, make predictions, perform repetitive tasks and perform adaptations automatically. As noted in [11], AI can help to augment human capabilities in three ways:

---

[102]https://news.samsung.com/global/samsungs-6g-white-paper-lays-out-the-companys-vision-for-the-next-generation-of-communications-technology [last accessed: 12/1/2021].

[103]https://www.networkworld.com/article/3147892/one-autonomous-car-will-use-4000-gb-of-dataday.html [12/1/2021].

[104]https://deepmind.com/research/case-studies/alphago-the-story-so-far   [last   accessed: 30/6/2020].

- *amplify*: AI technologies, or data analytics, can find new insights from a large amount of data that may be hard for humans to discover, or expand the range of considered designs or options for a given problem;
- *interact*: AI can help facilitate interactions with people, or acts as agents to interact on behalf of people;
- *embody*: AI algorithms when combined with sensors and actuators and embedded in the physical world can assist humans with physical world tasks that are beyond ordinary human capabilities.

Applying the above to cities, we see advances in data-driven insights for cities, in up-scaling interactions among people and interactive city services, and automation for tasks relating to the maintenance and development of cities. In the future, humans, complementing such AI, might then play the role of *trainers*—train AI systems to perform tasks or to improve task performance by feeding in appropriately cleaned and tagged data, and refine AI algorithms and fix errors, *explainers*—observe and explain AI algorithmic behaviours and output to stakeholders, and *sustainers*—oversee output quality and raise issues, limit or override AI decisions, and manage AI systems. Workers with AI systems in the cities would then help train, explain and sustain such AI systems.

Slowly but surely, the range of tasks computers can automate is slowly increasing, and so is the level at which a task can be performed. Oxford University's Wooldridge considers AI research in this way [63]:

> The mainstream of AI research today is focused around getting machines to do specific tasks which currently require human brains (and also potentially, human bodies), and for which conventional computing techniques provide no solution.

Wooldridge talks about the increasing range of tasks that has been automated till today and points out tasks that are still difficult to automate. Recent progress in driverless cars and automatic captioning for pictures are two noted milestones achieved by current AI algorithms, even if they both can be further improved.

A useful way to understand the range of tasks AI might automate as technology improves is given in Floridi's two-dimensional characterisation of what is required to perform a task [16]: computational resources and skills. Computational resources involve the hardware requirements and computing power needed to automate a given task, and the skills involve the motor skills required for a physical task, associated with physical dexterity. For example, tying one's shoe laces requires fine motor skills which is hard to build a robot to do while computationally feasible, and dish washing (at least using a dish-washing machine) or playing chess (with digital representations) do not require fine motor skills but requires adequate computational resources. Highly (computationally) complex, but lower skilled tasks can already be done well by computers, given the advances in computational resources and the increasing availability of data.

Floridi further argues that realistic future advancements in AI require *envelopes*, and gives an example of *enveloping* for industrial robotics:

> In industrial robotics, the three-dimensional space that defines the boundaries within which a robot can work successfully is defined as the robot's envelope.

Dish-washing is successfully automated by transforming the problem of dish-washing into actions within the constrained environment of a "box" (into which dishes and cutlery are placed), rather than designing a two-arm dexterous robot to clean dishes like humans do, thereby reducing the skill level required. Another example given is Amazon's robots working in warehouses[105] which are facilitated to work by redesigning the warehouse to be robot-friendly.

Another example is automated vehicles, which according to Floridi, "will become a commodity the day we can successfully envelop the environment around them" [16]. Current thoughts about the introduction of automated vehicles (AVs) in cities involve restricted uses with constraints, e.g., at slow speeds in certain flat areas and dedicated lanes, which could be considered attempts at enveloping for AVs. Such enveloping for AVs and robots could impact on how cities are designed and instrumented.

Yet another (the authors' own) example is the lift in buildings—it would be difficult to build a machine to move people up or down flights of stairs (though there are machines for the disabled that can do that, albeit one person at a time, and more recently, robots with that ability), and to do so quickly and efficiently. Instead, the problem can be transformed into one which moves "containers" up and down a building within vertical shafts, a much easier and more feasible alternative. The invention of the lift has impacted how buildings are designed and constructed, but also enabled much taller buildings, and the transportation of massive weights across long vertical distances, with consequent impact on how people live and work.

One more example (the authors' own) is the bread-maker. Kneading bread is part of the process of making bread, and one way to automate this is to build a robot with two hands and imitate the complex movement of the human hands when kneading. An easier way to automate kneading is to create a bread-maker with a container having a small paddle in the middle that rotates and this rotation essentially throws the dough around, and as the dough is flung around the paddle, it is stretched, and kneading takes place.[106]

A few observations from these examples. One is that the same task can often be done in a different way, in a way that is more easily automated or easier to build machines for. Secondly, the new way of doing something might affect how humans think of the task, and influences how humans use or interact with the machines doing that task. Thirdly, to perform multiple tasks, it is easier often to build multiple machines, each being able to do a specific task well, than it is to build one machine that can do multiple tasks—the human hands can be used for dish-washing and bread kneading (with appropriate positioning and the addition of the necessary

---

[105]https://www.aboutamazon.co.uk/amazon-fulfilment/what-robots-do-and-dont-do-at-amazon-fulfilment-centres [last accessed: 28/1/2021].
[106]See https://www.explainthatstuff.com/breadmaker.html [last accessed: 13/8/2020] for a description of how a bread-maker works.

"ingredients" such as detergent or dough) and many other tasks, but it seems easier to build two (or many more) machines, one for each task, than to build a machine with robotic human-like hands with the full dexterity of the human hands (though perhaps in the future this will be possible).

It can be said that the envelope limits the usage of a particular technology in other contexts. A dishwasher, or a washing machine, will not wash beyond its "box" but adaptations of a concept for different purposes can help perhaps help transfer capabilities across contexts.

Indeed, how to transform, design, or instrument cities so that beneficial automation of different sorts can be feasibly realised is an open question, though we have already seen movements in that direction, e.g., with IoT sensing. IoT sensing of road traffic and water infrastructure, for example, enables data to be collected, so that discovery of patterns and insights or detection of anomalies can be automated. With sensing and data, the ability to make predictions would be possible, from predicting when best to deliver a parcel to when to shop at certain stores to avoid crowds, or providing proactive safety advice and organising transport for the most vulnerable. As AI predictions in cities become increasingly feasible, there will be impact on the behaviour of urbanites, and hence, their careful use is required.

Developments in robotics are myriad, with an exhaustive list of applications detailed in [39], some aiming to work in constrained environments such as a factory, a home such as the disk-like vacuum cleaning robots, and others in more open environments, e.g., public spaces. Among the ten grand challenges in robotics identified in [65], there are some crucial to their use in cities such as human-robot social interactions, ethical usage of robots and the ability of robots to navigate in complex environments (e.g., think of crowded cities in Europe and Asia).

Urban robotics focuses specifically on the design and use of robots in cities. An interesting review of urban robotic experimentation in three cities is detailed in [54]. AI ideas of intelligent algorithmic decision-making, reasoning, learning and planning can be applied in the context of robotics. We return to discussions about urban robots in cities at several points later in the book.

Robotic Process Automation (RPA) refers to automating tasks that typically require human labour such as software robots to help address the information overload or to carry out certain repetitive tasks,[107] including helpdesk management, customer relationship management, workflow management and sales order processing. Software robots used in RPAs might be a program to perform a specific information task, or an enterprise software package. While Automation is not AI, and Automation tends to refer to systems that do monotonous repetitive tasks, based on pre-programmed rules, with the purpose of increasing efficiency, the connection with AI is clear, as AI advances, RPA can draw on these advances not only to automate tasks better but to automate a wider range of tasks, that normally might

---

[107] See   https://www.ibm.com/au-en/products/robotic-process-automation   [last   accessed: 30/6/2020].

require human intelligence to do. The scope of automation in the city would be much broader than that typically considered in RPA.

Chatbots to handle queries and provide city services is an interesting application area. Chatbots can range from simple question-answering systems that provide pre-programmed fixed answers in response to keywords detected in questions, to more sophisticated natural language processing and dialogue. From states in the US[108] to councils in Melbourne, Australia,[109] chatbots are being deployed and experimented with to provide city services.

How AI algorithms can be deployed today and in the future is another important factor that will affect the uptake and the range of applications of AI in the city. With cloud computing well established, many companies provide AI algorithms and AI services (e.g., from chatbots to computer vision capabilities) as cloud services, over the Internet. Machine learning models can be deployed on devices near to the user, the edge devices, leading to smart cameras and smart devices powered by cloud-hosted computations. To reduce data transmissions over long distances and for efficient AI computations entirely on local resource-scarce devices (e.g., appliances, small computers, IoT devices and sensors, cameras, and drones) and wearable devices, even without Internet connectivity or cloud service fees, there have been tremendous efforts to develop AI algorithms to work effectively in resource-efficient ways, e.g., with much less energy and costs, on resource-constrained devices, i.e., AI with edge computing [35, 64, 67]. For example, the work in [53] explains software and hardware co-design for running deep learning efficiently, even on small drones. Cloud-based AI combined with edge AI approaches will enable AI usage to be potentially ubiquitous (in the sense of ubiquitous computing) in the years to come, i.e., towards *ubiquitous AI*.

The use of AI and IoT for algorithmic decision-making and city governance are not without their ethical and societal implications—a topic which we will come back to later in the book.

1.4.3 Platforms, Sharing Economy, Urban Apptivism, and City Operating Systems

The *multi-sided platform* (MSP) has been identified as a key business model upon which some of the largest companies in the world have been built. MSPs [1, 15]:

connect two or more interdependent user groups, by playing an intermediation or a matchmaking role.

---

[108]https://www.govtechreview.com.au/content/gov-digital/news/3-in-4-us-states-plan-to-implement-chatbots-662599812 [last accessed: 23/7/2020].

[109]For example, see the City of Casey where the chatbot Amelia is used, https://www.ipsoft.com/2019/08/21/the-city-of-casey-creating-the-most-liveable-city-with-ai-and-amelia/ [last accessed: 23/7/2020].

Some companies and their platforms are Uber, eBay, Facebook, Airbnb, Alibaba, Amazon, OpenTable, Apple (e.g., Apple Store), and Google (Google PlayStore, Waze, and Youtube), which bring sellers and buyers together, or content producers and content consumers (or prosumers) together.

While they are world-scale platforms, they can help improve local knowledge tremendously, and in fact, enables local businesses in cities and facilitate local communications and networking, as well as local navigation and movements—they are global, yet local. People might interact with friends in the same city or neighbourhood (or even house!) via Facebook and Whatsapp, in the same way they might interact with people across the world, or buy from their neighbourhoods in a similar way as they do from other countries.

Such platforms also become tools for government to connect with citizens and is a key way of engagement via social media. While cities might develop their own smartphone apps and Websites, having a social media presence is part of being external-facing.

As articulated in [5], there is what has been called *platform urbanism*, which

speaks to a set of burgeoning ideas about how the increasing ubiquity of platform ecosystems is reshaping urban conditions, institutions and actors. ...Platform urbanism is also increasingly understood as the manifestation of digital or platform governance for cities.

Network effects are observed, but in fact, with MSPs, there are indirect network effects [15]:

A network effect is indirect when the value of a matchmaker to one group of customers depends on how many members of a different group participate.

While strategies are needed to bring in initial users, network effects enable rapid growth in the number of users—more users attract even more users.

Apart from network effects, with greater usage of these platforms, more data is captured, so that there are also *learning effects* [22]:

Learning effects capture the value added by increasing the amount of data flowing through the same networks—for example, data that may be used to power AI to learn about and improve the user experience or to better target advertisers.

Both network and learning effects help the development and growth of these platforms as the the user base increases.

In a way, a *city is a physical platform* that can pull both providers and consumers, with incentives for both sides, providing a central place for participants to meet, trade, exchange and transact, and does so at scale. But these MSPs are digital software platforms that provide algorithmic solutions to facilitate content and relationship management and discovery of participants and the contributions they bring, and employs the Web to reach users world-wide.

Have such platforms made cities smarter? Many people do use these platforms on a daily basis. A new arrival at a city could resort to these platforms as a means of navigating and moving around in the city, getting recommendations and reviews, or connecting to locals and city services. Although not all platforms are available at all cities, these platforms have become almost an essential part of city living for many. Typically, people do use multiple platforms on a daily basis, or are multi-homed. In the case of transport, a driver may drive for both Uber and Lyft, or be a member of Facebook and LinkedIn, and have a Youtube channel. People can be prosumers on multiple platforms at the same time.

Use of these platforms are not without concerns. The ownership and control of a platform (and its data) can be an important consideration. Fairbnb[110] is an interesting initiative that is similar in function to Airbnb but 50% of the platform fees are used to fund community projects. Data ownership is another key consideration— as platforms gather tremendous data from their usage, will prosumers be able to manage their own data and control how their data will be used? The European GDPR (the General Data Protection Regulation) is a step towards ensuring greater user control of their data, but can have limitations when implemented [56]. Another concern is fairness, e.g., where platforms deliver recommendations and targeted ads, discrimination by buyers and sellers in online marketplaces, or arbitrariness or bias of decisions made by a platform.[111]

The concept of the *city or urban operating system (UrbanOS)* refers to viewing the city using the metaphor of a computer operating system (like Windows or MacOS, or Android).[112] Marvin and Luque-Ayala [31] highlighted how the notion of the urban OS has been framed by large corporations who create software and tools for urban services, and that an urban OS relates to applying IT solutions for city management and governance (*italics ours*):

> A third conception of a city-scale operating system focuses on the linkages between infrastructural development and wider questions of urban control. Easterling ...examines how a combination of infrastructure space, sensors and software are specifically designed to use the medium of information in 'invisible, powerful activities that determine how objects and content are organized and circulated [in] an operating system for shaping the city'. Here an operating system as a *platform*—both updated over time and unfolding in time to handle new circumstances and situations—uses software 'protocols, routines, schedules and choices' to encode relationships between buildings or managing logistics of infrastructures.
>
> We argue that this latter conceptualization of the operating system as a *platform* for urban control–an emerging 'platform urbanism'—is exemplified through specific Urban OS products and processes developed by corporates and urban technologists, representing a distinctive regime of urban governance.

While many cities have constructed their own city dashboards,[113] a number of large companies are providing platform solutions for monitoring multiple aspects of a city, with a focus on city governance. For example, Cisco provides a range of

---

[110]https://fairbnb.coop/ [last accessed: 30/6/2020].

[111]See the chapter on "Testing Discrimination in Practice" in the online book on Fairness and Machine Learning at https://fairmlbook.org/testing.html [last accessed: 13/8/2020].

[112]For example, see https://cityos.io/ [last accessed: 30/6/2020].

[113]There are many city dashboards—just a few examples, see https://citydashboard.com.au/, http://citydashboard.org/london/, http://citydashboard.be.unsw.edu.au/, and urban data platforms: https://urban.jrc.ec.europa.eu/#/en, https://opendata.cityofnewyork.us/data/, https://carto.com/blog/forty-brilliant-open-data-projects-preparing-smart-cities-2018/ [last accessed: 30/6/2020].

IoT technologies for monitoring parking, safety, waste management, urban mobility, lighting, and urban environments, via its Cisco Kinetic smart city framework,[114] IBM offers the IBM Intelligent Operation Center for Smarter Cities[115] [69], and Amazon Web services provides its cloud-based solution for managing smart city data.[116]

There are also platform apps providing local neighbourhood knowledge, such as local roadworks or finding a local plumber, and enabling local community conversations, e.g., NextDoor.[117]

While we typically think of platforms as software applications, cloud-hosted, and used for engaging prosumers, there are also hardware (and associated software) platforms, with distinct physical infrastructure, and devices. Of course, there are the telecommunications base stations and WiFi access point devices, but there could be other types of hardware/software platforms. One interesting example is the street lamp and the idea of Street Lamps as a Platform (SLaaP) [34], using augmented street lamps that are embedded with sensors, networking and computational capabilities. As noted in [34], street lamps are electrically connected and powered, are densely deployed (e.g., over ten thousand or in tens of thousands within the boundaries of a city), and are publicly owned, and can be platforms to host WiFi (and other network) access points, to host edge and fog computing nodes or cloudlets (computational resources) [48], to host sensors for the city (e.g., to monitor air quality, noise, and temperature, or even sensors to detect gunshots and emergency situations, and use holographic projections as first responders), to be charging stations for automated drones and vehicles, and to host a variety of applications and services for civil protection and business (e.g., supporting Augmented Reality applications)—that is, such smart street lamps become effectively hubs. One example of a smart street lamp is the ENE-HUB[118] which has been deployed in several cities In Australia and the United States, e.g. in the City of Geelong.[119]

In the future, one can imagine that such platforms might also become stations for robots in the city to recharge and to undergo upgrades and maintenance. The costs and the effort in deploying such smart street lamps, perhaps replacing traditional existing street lights, however, can be relatively higher.

---

[114]See https://developer.cisco.com/smartcities/ and https://www.cisco.com/c/en/us/solutions/internet-of-things/iot-kinetic.html [last accessed: 30/6/2020].

[115]http://www.redbooks.ibm.com/abstracts/tips0930.html [last accessed: 30/6/2020].

[116]https://aws.amazon.com/government-education/city-transformation/ [last accessed: 30/6/2020].

[117]https://www.nextdoor.com/ [last accessed: 30/6/2020].

[118]http://ene-hub.com [last accessed: 20/7/2020].

[119]http://ene-hub.com/site/greater-city-of-geelong/ [last accessed: 20/7/2020].

One can think of a similar concept not just for street lights, but also street furniture, such as park benches, bus stops and bins. In fact, there are varieties of such smart city benches,[120] smart bus stops[121] and smart bins.[122]

Platforms will have an important role to play in automated cities—we will discuss other platforms for automated cities later in the book.

1.4.4 Digital Tools for Participation, Human Coordination, and Hackable Smart Cities

Social media platforms can be used for civic participation, as discussed in [43], e.g., in democratic processes and political discussions. Other types of technologies have been used to help foster civic participation in urban issues, even public displays [9]. In the FindingPlaces project [38], during workshops held with Hamburg citizens to obtain feedback about where to accommodate refugees in the city, a tangible 3D model, with colour-tagged bricks and a projected map,[123] was used to help participants visualise and discuss this issue, and proved to help obtain high-quality feedback and interaction.

Recent visions of the smart city considers wider scale human coordination and collaboration in the smart city. A notable idea is the vision of *cyber-human smart cities*, where properly incentivized *social orchestration* is an important concept as articulated in [14], involving ICT-aided interactions in complex collaborations among urban citizens:

> ...Social Orchestration is the coordination and composition of activities collectively performed by the human participants

and

> ...the future vision of cyber-human smart cities involving a rich and active interplay of different stakeholders (primarily citizens, local businesses and authorities), effectively transforming the currently passive stakeholders into active ecosystem actors. Realizing such complex interplay requires a paradigm shift in how the physical infrastructure and people will be integrated and how they will interact.

The complex coordinated activities in a city, from [14], can

---

[120]See https://cityos.io/ [last accessed: 28/1/2021].

[121]For example, see https://citygreen.com/case-studies/jurong-smart-bus-station-singapore/, https://www.sageautomation.com/matilda, and https://europa.eu/investeu/projects/smart-bus-stop_en [last accessed: 20/7/2020].

[122]For example, see https://www.smartbin.com and Melbourne's https://www.ecubelabs.com/melbourne-combats-littering-with-ecubes-smart-bins/ [last accessed: 20/7/2020].

[123]This is the CityScope tool developed at MIT, https://www.media.mit.edu/projects/cityscope/overview/ [last accessed: 9/7/2020].

range from collectively organized transportation, private infrastructure sharing, collective learning and game-based learning to gainful activities, such as collaborative software development...

Beyond platforms that just enable urban citizens to report problems with public infrastructure, there could be tools to help organise local participants to work on local issues in the city. Participatory cities[124] is an initiative to promote greater cooperation and collaboration within cities.

ICT-aided collaborative city-making aims to shift urban citizens away from passive consumers towards active co-creators and actors that shape their urban environment, towards the *hackable city* [12]:

a hackable city that combines bottom-up (albeit often professionally initiated) civic organisation with the opening up of top-down government structures and procurement processes.

Many examples are given in [12], concerning digitally-mediated civic participation, collectives organised around communal concerns and models for citizens participating to improve the city or build aspects of the city.

Such participatory city-making goes beyond simply collecting data and making data available to be used, and includes motivating and enabling active participation to solve community problems, or to design and shape the local community, using smart city data or not.

A related idea is *social mobilization*, which refers to getting a large number of people to participate in an activity with social benefits [44]. An interesting Defense Advanced Research Projects Agency (DARPA) challenge to find the coordinates of ten weather balloons placed at different places in the United States involved time-critical social mobilization and was won by an MIT team with a suitable incentive mechanism, and use of social networking [40].

There could be possible explorations of how ad hoc human collaborations, perhaps mediated by human-machine interfaces, could be employed to initiate, to influence, or to remain in the loop of, partially automated processes in the city. Humans and machines can collaboratively shape some aspect of the city, involving human-to-human collaborations, machine-to-machine collaborations and human-machine collaborations. One could also think of futuristic scenarios of humans and a collection of automated vehicles and delivery robots helping to vacate part of a city in the case of an emergency or impending disaster, or organising neighbourhoods to find and meet the needs of the homeless in a sudden cold spell. Some of these ideas involving massive cooperation will be discussed further later in the book.

---

[124]For example, see http://www.participatorycity.org/ [last accessed: 1/7/2020].

1.4.5 Intelligent Transport Systems (ITS) and Automated Vehicles (AVs)

ITS is defined as the applications of information and communications technology (ICT) to all modes of transport. However, it is commonly applied to road transport. ITS is used in vehicles, on the road, on the infrastructure, on the road users or on the interfaces between them.

Historically, the first ITS device was a three colored traffic light signal installed in Ohio back in 1914. Nowadays, cooperative automated vehicles or MaaS are among the most complex types of ITS ever created.

ITS priority areas in Australia[125] include:

- delivering government priorities in transport, e.g. smart/liveable cities with reduced taffic congestion, reduced fuel use (CO2 and pollutants);
- delivering innovative mobility services—an emerging concept is MaaS (Mobility-as-a-Service [21]) whereby different modes of transport (e.g. train, tram, bus, taxis, Uber, rented cars, and micro-mobility vehicles such as Lime,[126]) are integrated for delivering door-to-door transportation solutions, and unified via a common interface for useres, e.g., mobile apps are used to allow travellers to discover, select, book and pay across diverse transport services;[127]
- enhancing future freight productivity, not only trucks but all kinds of freight vehicles involved in logistics requiring computational support; and
- road safety, which investigates how technology can be used to enhance the safety of vehicles and travel in general.

The use of computers and communication systems in transportation systems are myriad. Below are a few examples:

- algorithms for scheduling and control used in the running of public transport systems and freight;
- electronic systems to control traffic lights;
- embedded computers and systems in modern vehicles;
- real-time traffic information collection and visualisation;
- navigation and mapping systems used for vehicles on roads, in the sea and the air, as well as pedestrians;
- devices for road safety; and
- automated and cooperative vehicles.

---

[125]http://itsasia-pacific.com/wp-content/themes/its/images/CountryReport_Australia.pdf   [last accessed: 30/6/2020].

[126]https://www.li.me [last accessed: 30/6/2020].

[127]An interesting company in this area is Trafi (https://www.trafi.com [last accessed: 28/1/2021]) which has provided MaaS for several major cities, including Lithuania, Rio, Jakarta and Berlin.

ITS is key to sustainable development, towards safer, more efficient traffic, greener and smarter cities, including travelling in greater comfort.[128]

Historically, roboticists were the first to seriously investigate the use of Automated Vehicles. Until 15 years ago, vehicle manufacturers were continuously and successfully focusing on new Advanced Driving Assistance Systems (ADAS) which have a limited form of automation. But, early major R&D initiatives in AVs have been driven by IT companies such as Waymo[129] as it required significant IT skills (e.g., AI), as opposed to traditional mechanical engineering characterising traditional auto-makers. Typical new vehicles are heavily software based, featuring about 100 million lines of code, which facilitates rapid design and release of new vehicle advanced functionalities.

The IT innovators such as Waymo and Tesla shook the business foundation and practices of the vehicle industry which started back in 1860. New AV manufacturers such as Navya[130] and Easymile[131] continue to flourish at high pace worldwide. They provide a large range of AV characteristics and services for future transport.

It is important to note that a fully Automated Vehicle (SAE Level 5) is not a culmination of added ADAS functions. The engineering design, legislative and liability implications of a fully Automated Vehicle is fundamentally different from say an adaptive cruise control system due to the absence of a driver.

Many countries have endorsed the 1949 Geneva Convention on Road Traffic; Chapter II, Article 8, Section 1 says:

> Every vehicle or combination of vehicles proceeding as a unit shall have a driver.

An AV does not have a driver, which have profound ramifications on the technology and legislation.

Automated Vehicles are being developed not only by traditional car companies but also by IT companies, notably some of the platform companies mentioned earlier. The recent developments in AI and computer vision, together with more extensive datasets and increased hardware, have enabled the rise of AVs and made them much more realizable than say 50 years ago.

AVs have been classified according to different levels of automation,[132] ranging from providing assistance to human drivers to partial, high, and finally, full automation. AVs have triggered tremendous excitement due in part by their promise for reducing road fatalities, making driving more efficient, and freeing human drivers. But they have also raised many issues that require research and development, from legal frameworks to technical infrastructure and city planning. Just as cars impacted

---

[128]For example, for Asia and the Pacific, see https://www.unescap.org/sites/default/files/ITS.pdf, for the USA, see https://itsa.org/, for Africa, see http://www.its-africa.org/, and for Europe, see https://ec.europa.eu/transport/themes/its_en [last accessed: 30/6/2020].

[129]https://waymo.com [last accessed: 25/7/2020].

[130]https://navya.tech/en/ [last accessed: 25/7/2020].

[131]https://easymile.com [last accessed: 25/7/2020].

[132]See https://advi.org.au/driverless-technology/ [last accessed: 30/6/2020].

the design of cities and urban life when they were first introduced, AVs could have a disruptive impact on cities.

Their deployment in cities and the impact they will have on cities have been discussed extensively in the literature, and we will return to this topic in much greater depth later in the book.

1.5   Conceptualisations of the Smart City

The notion of the Smart City has taken many different forms in the recent decade, contextualised to the character and environment of each city and its population. We first take a brief look at the notion of the smart city from the point of view of standards and then consider three areas of focus for smart cities.

1.5.1   Smart City Standards

In what situation could a city be considered "smart"? A range of smart city standards have been developed, from efforts to identify measurable indicators for what constitutes a smart city, to guides on how one can use technology to enable smarter cities. From the International Organization for Standardization (ISO), there is a collection of standards for sustainable cities:[133]

> ISO standards represent the international consensus on best practice in a wide range of areas that contribute to making a city function better and fulfil the United Nations Sustainable Development Goals to end poverty, protect the planet and ensure prosperity for all. These include overarching frameworks that city leaders and planners can use to define objectives and priorities for making their cities more sustainable, as well as specific guidelines for things like energy management systems, road safety, intelligent transport, responsible water consumption, health and well-being, cybersecurity, connectivity and more.

In particular, looking specifically at ISO 37120:2018 "Sustainable cities and communities—Indicators for city services and quality of life",[134] there are proposed indicators for the different aspects mentioned above, e.g., unemployment rate and number of businesses per 100,000 population for the economy, percentage of primary school student completions for education, total end-user energy consumption per capita for energy, measures of air pollutants, average life expectancy for health, number of firefighters and police officers per 100,000 population, transportation deaths, percentage of water loss, number of Internet connections per 100,000 population and so on. Many of the indicators relate to general socio-economic progress.

---

[133]https://www.iso.org/publication/PUB100423.html [last accessed: 30/6/2020].

[134]https://www.iso.org/standard/68498.html [last accessed: 30/6/2020].

Now, looking at ISO 37122:2019 "Sustainable cities and communities—Indicators for smart cities",[135] there are indicators that relate more specifically to the use of technology, such as the following: the percentage of service contracts providing city services using an open data policy, percentage of city services accessible online, percentage of the city's population with health files online, percentage of households with smart energy meters, percentage of city areas that are covered by digital surveillance cameras, percentage of public garbage bins that are sensor-enabled, percentage of city streets covered by online real-time traffic information, percentage of public parking spaces that are supported by real-time availability information, percentage of roads conforming with autonomous driving systems, number of citizens involved in city planning processes, and percentage of wastewater pipeline network or water distribution network monitored by sensors. To measure and keep track of these indicators, a city would require IoT technologies (such as that provided by the Cisco Kinetic smart city framework or similar,[136] with added value when all the data are conveniently aggregated into a dashboard. This enables city authorities to track progress towards achieving smart city goals as measured via such indicators.

Another ISO standard, the ISO/IEC 30146:2019 "Information technology—Smart city ICT indicators"[137] identify smart city ICT indicators "to evaluate the level of smart city development" relating to the extent of digital services for citizens in e-government, transportation, social insurance, medical, education, employment, e-commerce as well as services for the poor and disabled, use of ICT for city management, public safety, environmental protection, energy efficiency, network infrastructure, open data sharing and use, and cybersecurity. Other ISO standards[138] relate to the specifics about the use of technology in transportation and data exchanges.

Hence, the characterisation of a smart city implied by ISO 37122:2019 and ISO/IEC 30146:2019 concerns the uptake and use of technology, and the automation that such use of sensing and data-driven approaches enables. A smart city is, hence, one which is ICT ready and is mature in the the the adoption of ICT. The ISO 37120 indicators have been used in the IESE Cities in Motion Index to rank cities in 2018.[139]

UK's national standards body, BSI, also has smart city standards which has the following purpose:[140]

---

[135] https://www.iso.org/obp/ui/#iso:std:iso:37122:ed-1:v1:en [last accessed: 30/6/2020].

[136] The Smart City Monitor is another such framework: https://smartcity.pharosnavigator.com/static/content/en/626/, and there are solutions for smart city dashboards, and monitoring at the AWS Marketplace for smart city solutions: https://aws.amazon.com/mp/gctc/ [last accessed: 30/6/2020].

[137] https://www.iso.org/standard/70302.html [last accessed: 30/6/2020].

[138] https://www.iso.org/ics/13.020.20/x/ [last accessed: 30/6/2020].

[139] https://media.iese.edu/research/pdfs/ST-0471-E.pdf [last accessed: 30/6/2020].

[140] https://www.bsigroup.com/en-GB/smart-cities/Smart-Cities-Standards-and-Publication/PD-8100-smart-cities-overview/ [last accessed: 30/6/2020].

> The role of smart city standards is to support the widespread adoption of common approaches to the implementation of smart city products and services in order to facilitate the rapid development of an effective smart city market.

The European Commission lists a set of standards relating to smart cities[141] including ISO standards and also guidelines for smart city open data.[142]

The National Institute of Science and Technology (NIST) has been working on a consensus framework for smart city architectures,[143] also called the Internet-of-Things-Enabled Smart City Framework, with a key aim being to address interoperability challenges across different systems used in smart cities, and to provide a tool to enable users (e.g., city administrators) to make decisions:

> A key component of the IES-City Framework is a simple-to-use analytical tool that enables early investigations of potential smart city applications. Stakeholders can make these analyses before they commit substantial time and funds pursuing an actual deployment. This tool enables review of various smart city application categories and subcategories and their representative applications about three criteria:
>
> - The breadth of functional requirements for these applications.
> - The readiness of the municipality infrastructure to mount these applications.
> - The benefits to their citizenry from acquiring them.

A number of IoT frameworks were compared such as OpenIoT,[144] FIWARE,[145] and OneM2M.[146]

The European standards organisation, the European Telecommunications Standards Institute (ETSI),[147] produces standards for ICT; one notable standard for IoT is oneM2M mentioned above, that focuses on machine-to-machine communiations. ETSI is involved with NIST on the Smart City framework.

The IEEE has a range of working group on technical (engineering and computing related) standards relating to IoT and smart city applications.[148] One is the IEEE Smart City Planning and Technology Standard P2784[149] which aims to provide a guide for creating a smart city plan, involving understanding stakeholder needs and translating them into functional requirements.

---

[141] https://ec.europa.eu/eip/ageing/standards/city/smart-cities [last accessed: 30/6/2020].

[142] See   https://ec.europa.eu/eip/ageing/standards/city/smart-cities/une-1783012015_en   [last accessed: 30/6/2020].

[143] https://pages.nist.gov/smartcitiesarchitecture/ [last accessed: 30/6/2020].

[144] http://www.openiot.eu/ [last accessed: 30/6/2020].

[145] https://www.fiware.org/ [last accessed: 30/6/2020].

[146] https://www.onem2m.org/ [last accessed: 30/6/2020].

[147] See https://www.etsi.org/newsroom/news/1129-2016-09-news-etsi-recognized-in-international-smart-city-framework [last accessed: 9/7/2020].

[148] https://smartcities.ieee.org/ [last accessed: 30/6/2020].

[149] https://standards.ieee.org/project/2784.html [last accessed: 30/6/2020]—a draft standard at the time of writing.

In the Australian context, the Smart Cities Council[150] provides information on smart city developments and relevant standards.[151] The IoT Alliance Australia (IoTAA)[152] is an organisation aiming to support IoT adoption in Australia and has a range of codes of practice and guides, including security guidelines for consumer IoT, an IoT reference framework, and an IoT platform selection guideline.

In summary, some of the above standards have a clear focus on technology, so that the concept of the smart city suggested by these standards is one that effectively applies technology to different aspects of the city, from city services, waste management, connectivity, transport to water management. Some of the standards have measures that go beyond just technology, in ways that capture human aspirations for the city in terms of sustainability, livability, safety and reducing social inequality. Indeed, the values governing the use of technology and whether technologies are used to address social needs and uphold beneficial policies, are just as important.[153] We will come back to discussing social and ethical issues of algorithmic governance and automation later in the book.

In [4], there are documented cases of smart cities from around the world, of how technology has been successfully applied to solve problems.

1.5.2 Three Focus Areas of Technology in Smart Cities

We consider three focus areas of the use of technology in a smart city, according to their perspectives and emphases, as illustrated in Fig. 1.4. The "smart city triangle" is by no means an exhaustive view of what a smart city involves, but provides a framework for positioning the Automated City:

- *the Data-Centric City*: with platforms, different means of urban data collection, processing and understanding, the data-centric city has been a dominant focus of smart city initiatives, business applications, and research; and indeed, will continue to be so; getting insight from data is an early step [26] towards a deeper understanding of issues in the city, and to identify problems, after-which interventions can be identified and predictions about the impact of interventions modelled, before deployment of the solution;
- *the Participatory City*: the participatory city has a focus on encouraging and enabling active citizens in city-making and aims to develop approaches, models and tools to enable human collaboration at scale in cities; participation of citizens

---

[150]https://smartcitiescouncil.com/ [last accessed: 30/6/2020].

[151]https://anz.smartcitiescouncil.com/resources/guidance-note-smart-cities-standards   [last accessed: 30/6/2020].

[152]https://iot.org.au [last accessed: 30/6/2020].

[153]https://smartenoughcity.mitpress.mit.edu/ [last accessed: 1/7/2020].

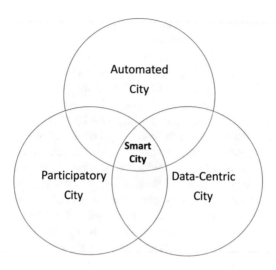

Fig. 1.4 Three focus areas of the smart city

can be considered at different stages, from identifying issues, generating ideas for tackling issues, to getting people on-board on a given intervention;

- *the Automated City*: no less important than the above two, the automated city has a focus on the use of AI, robotics, IoT and automation in the development and improvement of cities, which is the focus of this book; to quote from [60]:

  ... whilst the smart city prioritised issues of data gathering and data knowledge to the existing urban form, the automated robotic city is about the introduction of new physical capabilities that have the potential radically and fundamentally to alter the design, layout and operation of the city.

We see the "smart city" mentioned in the quote as what we have called data-driven smart city, and consider the "smart city" ideally to be at the intersection of all the above three focus areas. While this book focuses on the Automated City, we see the three focus areas above as complementary, and not competing areas.

1.6   Towards Smarter Cities

We have seen how technology has been increasingly used in cities, in a wide range of ways, some of which were highlighted during the COVID-19 pandemic. We have also briefly reviewed major technology trends, including IoT, AI and robotics, platforms, tools for participatory place-making, and Intelligent Transport Systems. We have also looked at contemporary conceptualisations of the smart city, and three focus areas, namely, the Data-Centric city, the Participatory City and the Automated City. In the next chapter, we will further explore the concept of the Automated City.

References

1. Abdelkafi, N., Raasch, C., Roth, A., & Srinivasan, R. (2019). Multi-sided platforms. *Electronic Markets, 29*(4), 553–559.
2. Ahmed, N., Michelin, R. A., Xue, W., Ruj, S., Malaney, R., Kanhere, S. S., Seneviratne, A., Hu, W., Janicke, H., & Jha, S. K. (2020). A survey of covid-19 contact tracing apps. *IEEE Access, 8*, 134577–134601.
3. Al-Sarawi, S., Anbar, M., Alieyan, K., & Alzubaidi, M. (2017). Internet of things (iot) communication protocols: Review. In *2017 8th International Conference on Information Technology (ICIT)* (pp. 685–690).
4. Anthopoulos, L. (Ed.) (2019). *Smart City Emergence: Cases From Around the World.* Elsevier.
5. Barns, S. (2020). *Platform Urbanism: Negotiating Platform Ecosystems in Connected Cities.*
6. Batty, M. (2018). *Inventing Future Cities.* The MIT Press.
7. Chang, S. L., Harding, N., Zachreson, C., Cliff, O. M., & Prokopenko, M. (2020). Modelling transmission and control of the COVID-19 pandemic in Australia. https://arxiv.org/abs/2003.10218.
8. Chowdhury, M. Z., Shahjalal, M., Ahmed, S., & Jang, Y. M. (2020). 6g wireless communication systems: Applications, requirements, technologies, challenges, and research directions. *IEEE Open Journal of the Communications Society, 1*, 957–975.
9. Clarinval, A., Simonofski, A., Vanderose, B., & Dumas, B. (2020). Public displays and citizen participation: a systematic literature review and research agenda. *Transforming Government: People, Process and Policy.*
10. Cortellessa, G., Fracasso, F., Sorrentino, A., Orlandini, A., Bernardi, G., Coraci, L., De Benedictis, R., & Cesta, A. (2018). Robin, a telepresence robot to support older users monitoring and social inclusion: Development and evaluation. *Telemedicine Journal and E-Health: The Official Journal of the American Telemedicine Association, 24*(2), 145–154.
11. Daugherty, P., & Wilson, H. J. R. (2018). *Human + Machine: Reimagining Work in the Age of AI.* Audible Studios on Brilliance Audio.
12. de Lange, M., & de Waal, M. (Eds.), (2019). *The Hackable City - Digital Media and Collaborative City-Making in the Network Society.* Springer.
13. Dizdarević, J., Carpio, F., Jukan, A., & Masip-Bruin, X. (2019). A survey of communication protocols for internet of things and related challenges of fog and cloud computing integration. *ACM Computing Surveys, 51*(6), 1–29.
14. Dustdar, S., Nastic, S., & Scekic, O. (2017). *Smart Cities - The Internet of Things, People and Systems.* Springer.
15. Evans, D. S., & Schmalensee, R. (2016). *Matchmakers: The New Economics of Multisided Platforms.* Harvard Business Review Press.
16. Floridi, L. (2019). What the near future of artificial intelligence could be. *Philosophy & Technology, 32*(1), 1–15.
17. Frey, C. B., & Osborne, M. (2013). The future of employment: How susceptible are jobs to computerisation? Online PDF. http://www.oxfordmartin.ox.ac.uk/publications/view/1314.
18. Gasser, U., Ienca, M., Scheibner, J., Sleigh, J., & Vayena, E. (2020). Digital tools against covid-19: taxonomy, ethical challenges, and navigation aid. *The Lancet Digital Health.*
19. Guinard, D., & Trifa, V. (2016). *Building the Web of Things: With Examples in Node.Js and Raspberry Pi* (1st ed.). USA: Manning Publications Co.
20. Halegoua, G. (2020). *Smart Cities.* Essential Knowledge Series. The MIT Press.
21. Hensher, D. A., Ho, C. Q., Mulley, C., Nelson, J. D., Smith, G., & Wong, Y. Z. (2020). Chapter 2 - what is maas and how it fits into the transport landscape. In D. A. Hensher, C. Q. Ho, C. Mulley, J. D. Nelson, G. Smith, & Y. Z. Wong (Eds.), *Understanding Mobility as a Service (MaaS)* (pp. 13–33). Elsevier.
22. Iansiti, M., & Lakhani, K. R. (2020). *Competing in the Age of AI: Strategy and Leadership When Algorithms and Networks Run the World.* Harvard Business Review Press.

23. Imran, M. (Ed.). (2020). *IoT Technologies in Smart Cities: From sensors to big data, security and trust.* Control, Robotics and Sensors. Institution of Engineering and Technology.
24. Iyengar, K., Upadhyaya, G. K., Vaishya, R., & Jain, V. (2020). Covid-19 and applications of smartphone technology in the current pandemic. *Diabetes and Metabolic Syndrome: Clinical Research and Reviews, 14*(5), 733–737.
25. Kuniavsky, M. (2010). *Smart Things: Ubiquitous Computing User Experience Design: Ubiquitous Computing User Experience Design.* San Francisco, CA, USA: Morgan Kaufmann Publishers Inc.
26. Larson, K. (2018). City science: Toward a new process for creating high performance entrepreneurial communities. In *Mass Customization and Design Democratization.*
27. Leins, K., Culnane, C., & Rubinstein, B. I. P. (2020). Tracking, tracing, trust: contemplating mitigating the impact of covid-19 with technological interventions. *Medical Journal of Australia, 213*(1), 6–8.e1.
28. Li, J., & Guo, X. (2020). Covid-19 contact-tracing apps: a survey on the global deployment and challenges.
29. Loke, S. W. (2018). Are we ready for the internet of robotic things in public spaces? In *Proceedings of the 2018 ACM International Joint Conference and 2018 International Symposium on Pervasive and Ubiquitous Computing and Wearable Computers,* UbiComp '18 (pp. 891–900). New York, NY, USA: ACM.
30. Lucas, P., Ballay, J., & McManus, M. (2012). *Trillions: Thriving in the Emerging Information Ecology.* Wiley.
31. Marvin, S., & Luque-Ayala, A. (2017). Urban operating systems: Diagramming the city. *International Journal of Urban and Regional Research, 41*(1), 84–103.
32. Mayor, A. (2018). *Gods and Robots: Myths, Machines, and Ancient Dreams of Technology.* Princeton University Press.
33. Moss, R., Wood, J., Brown, D., Shearer, F., Black, A. J., Cheng, A., McCaw, J. M., & McVernon, J. (2020). Modelling the impact of covid-19 in australia to inform transmission reducing measures and health system preparedness. *medRxiv.*
34. Mühlhäuser, M., Meurisch, C., Stein, M., Daubert, J., Von Willich, J., Riemann, J., & Wang, L. (2020). Street lamps as a platform. *Communications of the ACM, 63*(6), 75–83.
35. Murshed, M. G. S., Murphy, C., Hou, D., Khan, N., Ananthanarayanan, G., & Hussain, F. (2019). Machine learning at the network edge: A survey.
36. Neff, G., & Nafus, D. (2016). *Self-Tracking* (1st edn.). The MIT Press.
37. Nghiem, L. D., Morgan, B., Donner, E., & Short, M. D. (2020). The covid-19 pandemic: Considerations for the waste and wastewater services sector. *Case Studies in Chemical and Environmental Engineering, 1,* 100006.
38. Noyman, A., Holtz, T., Kröger, J., Noennig, J. R., & Larson, K. (2017). Finding places: Hci platform for public participation in refugees' accommodation process. *Procedia Computer Science, 112,* 2463–2472.
39. Patrick, J. R. (2019). *Robot Attitude: How Robots and Artificial Intelligence Will Make Our Lives Better.* Createspace Independent Publishing Platform.
40. Pickard, G., Pan, W., Rahwan, I., Cebrian, M., Crane, R., Madan, A., & Pentland, A. (2011). Time-critical social mobilization. *Science, 334*(6055), 509–512.
41. Punn, N. S., Sonbhadra, S. K., & Agarwal, S. (2020). Monitoring COVID-19 social distancing with person detection and tracking via fine-tuned YOLO v3 and Deepsort techniques. https://arxiv.org/abs/2005.01385.
42. Rakotonirainy, A., Orfila, O., & Gruyer, D. (2016). Reducing driver's behavioural uncertainties using an interdisciplinary approach: Convergence of quantified self, automated vehicles, internet of things and artificial intelligence. *IFAC-PapersOnLine, 49*(32), 78–82.
43. Robertson, S. P., & Carroll, J. M. (2018). *Social Media and Civic Engagement: History, Theory, and Practice.* Morgan and Claypool Publishers.
44. Rogers, T., Goldstein, N. J., & Fox, C. R. (2018). Social mobilization. *Annual Review of Psychology, 69*(1), 357–381.

45. Rose, D. (2014). *Enchanted Objects: Innovation, Design, and the Future of Technology.* Simon and Schuster.
46. Sako, M. (2020). Artificial intelligence and the future of professional work. *Communications of the ACM, 63*(4), 25–27.
47. Satyanarayanan, M. (2001). Pervasive computing: vision and challenges. *IEEE Personal Communications, 8*(4), 10–17.
48. Satyanarayanan, M., Chen, Z., Ha, K., Hu, W., Richter, W., & Pillai, P. (2014). Cloudlets: At the leading edge of mobile-cloud convergence. In *6th International Conference on Mobile Computing, Applications and Services* (pp. 1–9).
49. Simoens, P., Dragone, M., & Saffiotti, A. (2018). The internet of robotic things: A review of concept, added value and applications. *International Journal of Advanced Robotic Systems, 15*(1), 1729881418759424.
50. Singh, M. P., & Chopra, A. K. (2017). The internet of things and multiagent systems: Decentralized intelligence in distributed computing. In K. Lee, & L. Liu, (Eds.), *37th IEEE International Conference on Distributed Computing Systems, ICDCS 2017, Atlanta, GA, USA, June 5–8, 2017* (pp. 1738–1747). IEEE Computer Society.
51. Singh, M. P., & Chopra, A. K. (2020) Computational governance and violable contracts for blockchain applications. *IEEE Computer, 53*(1), 53–62.
52. Singh, R. P., Javaid, M., Kataria, R., Tyagi, M., Haleem, A., & Suman, R. (2020). Significant applications of virtual reality for covid-19 pandemic. *Diabetes and Metabolic Syndrome: Clinical Research and Reviews, 14*(4), 661–664.
53. Sze, V., Chen, Y.-H., Yang, T.-J., & Emer, J. S. (Eds.) (2020). *Efficient Processing of Deep Neural Networks.* Morgan and Claypool Publishers.
54. Tiddi, I., Bastianelli, E., Daga, E., d'Aquin, M., & Motta, E. (2020). Robot–city interaction: Mapping the research landscape—a survey of the interactions between robots and modern cities. *International Journal of Social Robotics, 12*(2), 299–324.
55. Tsui, K. M., Dalphond, J. M., Brooks, D. J., Medvedev, M. S., McCann, E., Allspaw, J., Kontak, D., & Yanco, H. A. (2015). Accessible human-robot interaction for telepresence robots: A case study. *Paladyn, Journal of Behavioral Robotics, 6*(1), 000010151520150001.
56. van Ooijen, I., & Vrabec, H. U. (2019). Does the gdpr enhance consumers'control over personal data? an analysis from a behavioural perspective. *Journal of Consumer Policy, 42*(1), 91–107.
57. Vandemeulebroucke, T., Dierckx de Casterlé, B., & Gastmans, C. (2017). The use of care robots in aged care: A systematic review of argument-based ethics literature. *Archives of Gerontology and Geriatrics, 74*, 09.
58. Want, R. (2006). *RFID Explained: A Primer on Radio Frequency Identification Technologies.*
59. Weiser, M. (1999). The computer for the 21st century. *SIGMOBILE Mobile Computing and Communications Review, 3*(3), 3–11.
60. While, A. H., Marvin, S., & Kovacic, M. (2020). Urban robotic experimentation: San Francisco, Tokyo and Dubai. *Urban Studies, 58*(4), 769–786. https://doi.org/10.1177/0042098020917790.
61. Whitelaw, S., Mamas, M. A., Topol, E., & Van Spall, H.G. C. (2020). Applications of digital technology in covid-19 pandemic planning and response. *The Lancet Digital Health.*
62. Woetzel, J., Remes, J., Boland, B., Lv, K., Sinha, S., Strube, G., Means, J., Law, J., Cadena, A., & von der Tann, V. (2018). Smart Cities: Digital Solutions for a More Livable Future (McKinsey Global Institute). Technical report, June 2018.
63. Wooldridge, M. (2020). *The Road to Conscious Machines: The Story of AI.* Pelican.
64. Xu, D., Li, T., Li, Y., Su, X., Tarkoma, S., Jiang, T., Crowcroft, J., & Hui, P. (2020). Edge intelligence: Architectures, challenges, and applications.
65. Yang, G.-Z., Bellingham, J., Dupont, P. E., Fischer, P., Floridi, L., Full, R., Jacobstein, N., Kumar, V., McNutt, M., Merrifield, R., Nelson, B. J., Scassellati, B., Taddeo, M., Taylor, R., Veloso, M., Wang, Z. L., & Wood, R. (2018). The grand challenges of science robotics. *Science Robotics, 3*(14), eaar7650.

66. Zhang, D., Sr., Shao, Y., Mei, Y., Chu, H., Zhang, X., Zhan, H., & Rao, Y. (2019). Using YOLO-based pedestrian detection for monitoring UAV. In C. Li, H. Yu, Z. Pan, & Y. Pu, (Eds.), *Tenth International Conference on Graphics and Image Processing (ICGIP 2018)* (vol. 11069, pp. 1141–1145). International Society for Optics and Photonics, SPIE.

67. Zhou, Z., Chen, X., Li, E., Zeng, L., Luo, K., & Zhang, J. (2019). Edge intelligence: Paving the last mile of artificial intelligence with edge computing. *Proceedings of the IEEE, 107*(8), 1738–1762.

68. Zhu, Q., Loke, S. W., Trujillo-Rasua, R., Jiang, F., & Xiang, Y. (2019). Applications of distributed ledger technologies to the internet of things: A survey. *ACM Computing Surveys, 52*(6), 1–34.

69. Zhuhadar, L., Thrasher, E., Marklin, S., & Ordóñez, P. [de Pablos]. (2017). The next wave of innovation—review of smart cities intelligent operation systems. *Computers in Human Behavior, 66*, 273–281.

Chapter 2
The Automated City: Concept and Metaphors

Abstract This chapter reviews the notion (and visions) of the Automated City in popular press, and in research publications, and then attempts to outline a conceptualisation of the Automated City. We first discuss what form the Automated City can take, from a mainly technological perspective. But a city is really constituted by its human inhabitants. We then discuss the Automated City in relation to its inhabitants via metaphors as guiding lenses through which one can view and shape developments towards a vision of the humane Automated City.

2.1 The Automated City in Relation to Current and Emerging Technologies: Concept

What does an Automated City look like in terms of its use and application of technology? We consider this question from a range of perspectives.

2.1.1 Automation of Large Scale City Systems

One way of thinking about the Automated City is to consider large scale systems of a city as becoming increasingly automated. We already have urban trains which are automated (or largely so) in many cities. Another form of popular transport are vehicles. Consider automated vehicles. Central to cities is on-road vehicle-based mobility, where vehicles, cars in particular, and their associated infrastructure have played a key role in shaping today's cities. Along these lines, suppose these cars become increasingly automated, instead of human-driven. Then, how would cities change?

In the conceptualisation of "autonomous cities" in [14], a very interesting analysis and identification of how different urban spaces of a city (e.g., parking lots, sidewalks, building access spaces, underground parking and roadways, dedicated lanes, retail spaces, gas stations as well as spaces related to urban delivery and supply systems) could change with the increasing autonomy of cars is given, with the following three phases:

> The existing city with mixed autonomous and non-autonomous vehicles (Augmented Autonomy); the existing city served only through autonomous mobility (Full Autonomy) and the new city, fully autonomous by design (Future Autonomy).

Apart from cars, there are public transport vehicles, such as buses and deliveries, that are automated—basically, one can imagine the automation of the transport network across different transport modalities.

2.1.2 Predictive and Proactive Cities, and the Availability of Data

The wealth of data available about any aspect of our daily life has never been greater. Terrestrial data from IoT sensing, credit card transactions, and CCTV, or satellite data, provide precise information about locations of things in time and space. Virtually everything can be localised and traced (e.g., transport of goods, people).

Such big data can be stored in large server centers. They are analysed with complex data analytics methods and AI algorithms to yield better smart services for the city, based on patterns of behaviour and predictions. Such predictions can then lead to proactive actions, from preventing crime in parts of the cities, smarter resource (e..g, space, water and energy) provisioning, to city planning.

The phases of data collection, data analysis, decision-making based on the data, and action-taking based on decisions made, can be automated to different extents.

2.1.3 Robots Everywhere

Central to the notion of the Automated City is urban robotics and autonomous systems (or URAS, in short), which considers the use and deployment of robots in cities, not just to automate transport or to automate infrastructure maintenance and repairs, but for other applications including waste management, healthcare, urban policing, security, various city services, and so on [13]. Such deployment of robots might be to serve the individual or the community (urban-wide use) (e.g., be owned by individuals or town council), and be controlled individually or by certain centralised mechanisms.

There have been pilot studies of urban robotics, some of which we mentioned in Chap. 1. The analysis in [27] discussed urban robotics experimentation in three cities: Tokyo, Dubai and San Francisco. Interesting observations include the different cultures and reasons surrounding their deployment, including varying government and commercial impetus. We discuss urban robotics in depth in Chap. 3.

2.1.4   Self-Repairing Cities, Self-Organizing Cities and Self-Regenerating Cities

Beyond the automation of transport systems, there are other related conceptualisa-tions, such as "self-repairing cities". The UK project "Balancing the impact of City Infrastructure Engineering on Natural systems using Robots"[1] on "self-repairing cities" envisions a city with drones and robots to repair public infrastructure, e.g., drones to repair streetlights, and robots to repair potholes and utility pipes. Interesting associated work includes the use of hyperspectral imaging to discover the defects and anomalies in road pavement [1]—consider such imaging done by machines automatically, eventually.

As one can imagine, this idea need not just be about repairs and maintenance, but self-diagnosis as well, where a city could potentially diagnose its own problems, and take action, e.g., from detecting potholes or problems with roads and then repairing them, automatically, and prudently changing the direction of certain roads when it detects much heavier traffic in one direction.

Readers familiar with the notion of autonomic computing [16], typically applied to self-healing computer systems, can see the paradigm applied to cities, yielding self-healing, self-optimizing and self-organizing cities. A self-optimizing or self-organizing city could adjust its overall use and distribution of energy and water resources according to the seasons or inhabitants' needs, reorganise transport for emergency purposes, or physically reorganize, where possible, to adapt to emergency or seasonal changes.

One can extend this idea further to self-regenerating cities, which could self-rebuild in the case of certain fires or floods or damaged buildings (of course, up to a limited extent).

Such self-actioning ideas are still nascent and somewhat fanciful today, but one can imagine gradual developments towards such a direction, starting with automating various subsystems, e.g., sensing and repairing some types of urban infrastructure, and then expanding to transport subsystems and energy subsystems, and thereafter, larger scale developments.

2.1.5   The Automated City as a "Living" Machine

The above ideas are not independent, and each highlights an aspect of automation in cities, each of which has its socio-technical issues of concern. The Automated City is, hence, in a sense "living": the city being proactive, reactive, adaptive, responsive to its inhabitants and their changes of behaviour, and automated, with the ability to self-organise, self-reorganise, self-heal and so on—one could say the

---

[1]https://gtr.ukri.org/projects?ref=EP%2FN010523%2F1 [last accessed: 28/1/2021].

city becomes organic. In particular, the deployment of robots in cities, in different forms, is what we will discuss further in the next section and which we will provide further examples of in the next chapter.

2.2   The Automated City in Relation to its Inhabitants: Metaphors

The Automated City is hence concerned with the automation of many of the cities operations and services, and the provision of new forms of services that automation (as powered by technologies such as AI, robots, IoT, and platforms) yields, in ways that potentially impact its inhabitants in profound ways. We consider a range of metaphors for thinking about this coupling of automation with humans in cities.

In the following sections, we consider three ways of thinking about the Automated City, corresponding to three ways of considering the interplay of automation and humans in cities:

- *machines as partners*: an Automated City formed by adding machines to human environments;
- *machines as hosts*: an Automated City when humans live within machines; and
- *machines as art*: an Automated City as an expression of human living, human activity, and human aspirations.

2.2.1   Machines as Partners: Machines Living in Human Environments

Here, we explore the notion of machines as partners of humans in city life and work. Humans can benefit from machines that do tasks humans cannot do, are unwilling to do, or should not do, and enable machines to amplify and increase what humans can, need, and want to do. Hence, the idea of machines "complementing" humans has broad interpretation. For example, it could mean machines doing certain tasks so that humans (don't have to and so) can do something else, but both working towards an overall goal, or that humans and machines cooperative actively in performing a task.

2.2.1.1   Human-Machine Symbiosis

If autonomous systems (e.g., robots) are to be introduced in cities effectively, one view is that they should complement humans in their daily life and work, or to use a biologically-inspired metaphor, there should be a symbiotic relationship between human inhabitants and the machines that live with them and work autonomously in the city.

One could think of such a symbiotic relationship between humans and machines as mutualistic, where humans would benefit, and machines as well, though what it means to benefit machines might be less clear—for some machine-human partnerships, one could think of machines increasing their ability the more they are used by humans, due to learning effects, and as they are further fine-tuned and improved on usage. For some other machine-human partnerships, the symbiotic relationship can be thought of as commensalistic, where one party benefits but the other may not, but is not harmed, which can be interpreted as the machines not harmed, or should not be harmed, in most part, by its usage, at least not directly (exceptions are wear and tear and so on).

Another dimension of such human-machine partnerships is whether they can be required (obligatory) or optional (facultative), where humans have to use the machine as partner, perhaps as the only way to accomplish a particular task, or as required by regulatory reasons, or machines are used because of the value added, not essential. The reliance on machines in an instance of a human-machine partnership can be an issue, if the dependency becomes essential in daily life and if there is chance that the machine will not operate or co-operate as needed.

Humans and machines might live together symbiotically, yet the nature of interactions might be mostly passive—e.g., humans simply letting the robots do what they need as needed, and interactions are to the extent as needed for the robots to do what they need (e.g., getting out of the way of the robot cleaner). Humans and robots might share physical spaces, i.e., a room, a house, or a building but need not interact, but there could be partnerships where both parties are active and mutually engaged.

We elaborate further on cooperation and partnerships between humans and robots below.

2.2.1.2   Human Cooperation with Robots or Smart Devices

Robots are meant typically to replace humans in performing tedious manual repetitive tasks. Contemporary use of robots evolved from industrial manufacturing chains where they operate in isolation (from humans for the most part) and in very static environments, to more cooperative settings such as human-inhabited environments, and so, now requiring interactions with humans; e.g. in automated vehicles, the human passengers are in cooperation with the vehicle to achieve the goal of getting from A to B safely.

Facilitating the collaboration between humans and robots is a very active area of research and development.

In the area of Automated Vehicles, there are significant research gaps in understanding the users' intentions to operate conditional and fully Automated Vehicles. The authors in [9] have found initial insights into the underlying behavioural and control beliefs that may motivate drivers to use AVs and highlighted the similarities and differences in drivers' perceptions towards SAE Level 2 vehicle automation.

Interactions or collaboration with humans sometimes require robots to behave like humans and perhaps take more human-like, or at least human-sized, forms (e.g., be able to function within homes, fit within doorways and so on), being in typical human-inhabited environments. Unlike earlier versions of robots, the state of the art robots are equipped with various degrees of perception, cognition, and interaction ability to facilitate interactions with humans in very dynamic environments.

As mentioned earlier, endowing robots with human-like behaviour is an ultimate challenge to facilitate collaboration between humans and robots. Machine learning algorithms continue to play a significant role in this endeavour. The term *cobots* [17], short for collaborative robots, was coined as a new research area where robots are assistive-cooperative devices, in co-working spaces.[2] For example, driving assistant systems devices can check the fatigue level of drivers with the view to anticipate and adjust mitigation strategies when it detects dangerous hazards so that it thinks the driver would not be able to manage.

Aside from the considerable work in Human Machine Interface and Computer-Supported Collaborative Work (CSCW), our society needs to determine what types of task, when and how robots can be ethically allowed to assist humans.

2.2.1.3   Intimate Cooperation

Another form of cooperation or partnership between humans and machines is more intimate, and relates to on-body and wearable computers, which can range from smart watches, fitness devices (e.g., Fitbit), wearable glasses, prosthesis to chip implants in humans (e.g., cyborg-style concepts). Consider a smart watch which continually prompts the user when s/he has been sitting down for too long or has not been outdoors for a while, or which helps coach its user in fitness activities, or a device that provides guidance for a tourist within an area or helps people in their work (e.g., a smart assistant to someone in sales or a field engineer), perhaps using augmented reality style interfaces.

Such devices may have software agents capable of autonomously taking action (providing suggestions and recommendations, or guidance) but also monitors the "performance" of the user, and adapts to the user's behaviour and actions, literally forming a partnership towards certain preset goals (e.g., keeping physical fitness to certain levels or keeping to certain health regimes, or work-related targets). While such on-body devices are typically taken up by individual choice, rather than at city-level, certain societal level priorities might facilitate their adoption at scale. For example, the LumiHealth initiative is a collaboration between Apple and the

---

[2]https://www.inria.fr/en/fundamentals-fluidifying-interactions-between-humans-and-cobots [last accessed: 17/7/2020].

Singapore government to effectively pay citizens for keeping healthy using smart watches.[3]

One might also envision tourists, or inhabitants of a city, needing to wear particular devices while they play, live or work in that city, where such a device becomes a portal to the city's amenities, services and conveniences. Through such a device, city-level constraints or recommendations can be implemented or provided to users, but also, ideally such a device would adapt to and takes into account the preferences of its user, in a partnership where the user ultimately maintains control.

2.2.1.4   Metaphors for Interacting with Autonomous Systems

Horse, butler and elevator are three metaphors mentioned in [23] for thinking about how humans might interact with autonomous systems. Each metaphor can influence design in different ways—and affect how humans think about the way they engage with the robot. Husband and wife [8] is also another metaphor used for automated vehicles (the husband is the automated vehicle), where the wife might help decide where to go, suggest alternative routes to the husband who is driving, and warn about hazards she thinks the husband might miss, but the wife usually does not worry about the husband's capabilities.

The metaphor one might use could depend on what level of autonomy and what kind of human-machine interaction is involved in accomplishing tasks. Next, we discuss in further detail the notion of levels of autonomy.

2.2.1.5   Levels of Autonomy

From [2], *autonomy* is defined as follows:

> The extent to which a robot can sense its environment, plan based on that environment, and act upon that environment with the intent of reaching some task-specific goal (either given to or created by the robot) without external control.

Indeed, levels of autonomy in a particular system is what may affect how humans should or need to intervene or interact with the system. There could be levels of autonomy [2], where for each task and subtask, the level of autonomy given to machines can be varied. Figure 2.1 illustrates a task to be automated by a machine, but to a given degree. The task has three subtasks, each of which corresponds to different levels of autonomy given to the machine. A (sub)task may have part of it done manually and the other part delegated to the machine which makes it own decisions and takes its own actions.

While the level of autonomy given to a machine performing a task can vary, the degree of unpredictability can also vary, in the sense of whether the machine

---

[3]https://www.bloomberg.com/news/articles/2020-09-16/singapore-to-pay-citizens-for-keeping-healthy-with-apple-watch [last accessed: 17/9/20].

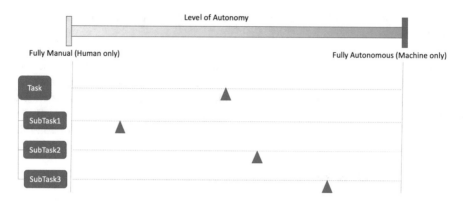

Fig. 2.1 Levels of autonomy for a machine or robot performing tasks—a task with three subtasks is shown against the autonomy scale, where each subtask might be associated with a level of autonomy given to the machine performing the task

is confined to automating a clearly specified task based on a given set of rules and behaves predictably, or whether the machine is allowed the liberty to take "creative" actions to get the task done, perhaps in unexpected ways (e.g., a solution that the human did not expect). These two dimensions of autonomy and unpredictability (also called task entropy) have been proposed as early as 1978 in [21], which also has a third dimension of anthropomorphism of tool used. A humanoid android (that we see in Star Trek) is at the extreme end of machine autonomy, unpredictability and tool anthropomorphism.

We mentioned levels of automation for Automated Vehicles earlier in the book and we will discuss this further later as well. When allowing a machine to have higher levels of autonomy, especially for critical tasks such as driving, one would need to be cautious, as it could lead to death, not only for the passengers in the vehicle but others outside.

2.2.1.6　Scenarios of Integration and Cooperation

A very interesting scenario is provided by Poole in 2014:[4]

> A woman drives to the outskirts of the city and steps directly on to a train; her electric car then drives itself off to park and recharge. A man has a heart attack in the street; the emergency services send a drone equipped with a defibrillator to arrive crucial minutes before an ambulance can. A family of flying maintenance robots lives atop an apartment block—able to autonomously repair cracks or leaks and clear leaves from the gutters.

---

[4]https://www.theguardian.com/cities/2014/dec/17/truth-smart-city-destroy-democracy-urban-thinkers-buzzphrase?page=with:img-8 [last accessed: 28/1/2021].

One can continue this scenario. An elderly person puts rubbish into a small bin in her home and this (robotic) bin, when full, moves outside to transport its contents to a larger bin, and does so, as often as needed, or till the larger bin is full. Other small bins in the house also do the same—when almost full, they move and empty themselves into the larger bin. The larger bin, when full or when the time is right, moves out to the curbside to "wait" for the arriving automated garbage truck. The automated (driverless) garbage truck receives a message from the larger bin that it is ready to be emptied, and schedules itself to visit the larger bin. On arrival, the automated garbage truck has a robot arm to pick up and empty the larger bin. When emptied, the larger bin moves back into its position in the property—the small bin can continue emptying its contents. The automated garbage truck, on returning to its station, will have its garbage automatically sorted via robotic arms and the different types of waste disposed accordingly.

Consider another scenario involving transport. A disabled person pushes his/her wheelchair into an automated vehicle which then transports the person to the destination, and picks the person up when summoned. An elderly parent visiting his/her child in a foreign country might not be able to drive around while the child is busy, but can be taken on a tour via a combination of an automated vehicle and a robot tour-guide in a shopping mall.

The stories could continue, but many of these convey a mix of private and public automation, and the *the idea of automation within the home of an individual connecting to automation at the level of city services*. Urban spaces are private or public, individually owned or shared by a community, and hence, there is an interplay of these spaces in deployment of automated solutions.

In fact, there are different levels of ownership and control—e.g., robots could be individually owned and controlled, or owned by the city and control decentralised— and be used to serve an individual, everyone in an apartment block, a neighbourhood or a community [13].

Robots owned by and serving individuals might also be pooled together for the community on certain occasions, or be made available for rent (in the sense of Airbnb, where idle spaces can be rented out temporarily), supported by some platform.

2.2.1.7   Embedding Automation in Cities: The Internet of Robotic Things

Together with automated transport systems, there could be smart bins, smart streetlights, chatbots for city services and a range of computerisation of city services, as popular media have considered, under the banner of the Automated City.[5]

---

[5]For example, see https://www.theguardian.com/cities/2016/sep/20/automated-city-robots-run-public-services-councils [last accessed: 9/7/2020].

The Internet of Things integrated with robotics has been discussed comprehensively by [22] and [18], leading to the notion of the Internet of Robotic Things.

Rather than just speaking of robots, we can use a more generalised phrase *robotic things* [18, 25], when we want to refer to both robots and smart things, i.e., "everyday objects with autonomous sensing, reasoning and acting capabilities that form part of the Internet of Things—which may not take the typical form of a robot" [11], as in [6, 10, 12, 20]. Robotic things can be robotic vehicles and drones, or fixed items such as smart park benches, smart bookshelves, smart furniture, smart street signs, or smart sculptures.

For example, a connected smart sculpture can be remotely programmable to take action and move its parts, e.g., to be proactive in providing shade for those nearby, or move to provide more light for the plants placed on top of it. One might think of the sculpture as a robot, though it might not take on the form of a typical (anthropomorphized or humanoid) robot. A smart bookshelf could automatically take action to rearrange the books on it or can be asked to highlight particular books being sought, or even be queried by a friend online to see if contains a certain book.

The concept of robotic functions incorporated into everyday street furniture could provide another dimension to the Automated City.

2.2.1.8 Discussion

We have explored the notion of machines as partners, including adding machines to urban environments to help with the day-to-day running and activities of daily living in the city, and touched on the complex issues involved.

To summarise some of the key points discussed:

- machines can partner with humans at different scales, from one-to-one partnerships of individuals co-working with one or more robots, to robots servicing an entire community;
- machines can partner with humans to different extents, and be involved in tasks to different degrees, performing tasks with different levels of autonomy, where metaphors can help define or clarify the nature of such partnerships;
- in cities, there are private and public spaces, so that machines functioning in both such spaces might need to interact, providing integration, and the potential need for cooperation, even among robots in both these spaces;
- machines embedded in cities with robotic capabilities of sensing, reasoning and actuation might take forms beyond what might have been stereotyped in popular media, and perhaps somewhat unrecognizable to humans, without closer scrutiny—a spectrum of robotic capabilities might be expected from different artifacts;
- machines in cities, e.g., urban robots, will also need to fit socially into human environments, be socially relevant, be accepted and protected, and yet useful (we discuss this further in Chap. 3);

Fig. 2.2 Three dimensions of
development for
human-machine
partnerships—the dashed
arrow illustrates a possible
trajectory of development

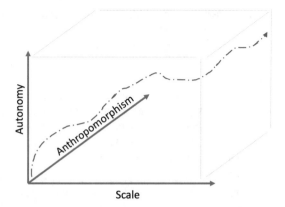

- cyber-physical infrastructure and physical adjustments are required to support and accommodate machines in cities, with their subsequent need to be maintained, from possibly robot stations to knowledge-based environments for robots, in order to access real-time and geographical knowledge of cities, necessary for their functioning.

Inspired by and adapting the classification from [21], Fig. 2.2 illustrates three dimensions of development in human-machine partnerships, as technology improves and new technologies are developed:

- the scale that this happens (e.g., number (and size) of robots or robotic things and people involved),
- the level of autonomy given to the machine(s) in the partnership,
- and the degree of anthropomorphism (relating to the forms, characteristics or behaviour of these robots), in particular if they need to fit, physically, cognitively, or socially, within environments designed for humans.

Perhaps science fiction, but if one imagines the robot in humanoid form (e.g., in the movie *I,Robot* or the android *Data* in *Star Trek*), and considers a large number of them, helping to service a large population of humans, we would be at the high end of all three dimensions. Such an advanced humanoid robot at home helping one person might be at the low end of the scale but at the high end of autonomy and anthropomorphism.

Today's home robot might be near the low/mid-level of autonomy (arguably), at the low end of scale, and somewhat at the low end of anthropomorphism. A future highly automated vehicle and its passenger might be at the low end of scale and low end of anthropomorphism (arguably) but at the high end of autonomy. A large fleet of advanced fully automated robotaxis might then be considered at the high end of the scale, and at the high end of autonomy, but at the low end of anthropomorphism (arguably).

It is also to be noted that the human-like form and size for a robot is not always the ideal depending on what tasks the robot is to do. But one can take a broader view of anthropomorphism, beyond the human-like physical appearances, to consider robots having characteristics of humans and human behaviour (even if not similar to the human physical form and size, e.g., looks like a box), such as being able to respond to emotions and be emotionally engaging, being able to understand and converse in human language, easily controllable using human gestures and commands, and behaving in ways that are comprehensible and socially appropriate, could aid acceptance and ease use of technology, i.e., in short, anthropomorphism can aid human engagement or partnership with the machine. Advances in natural language processing, affective computing and related fields will help in this direction. As noted in [28]:

> The practical advantage of building anthropomorphic robots is that it facilitates human-machine interaction…It also creates familiarity with a robotic system and builds on established human skills, developed in social human-human interactions…A human-like machine enables an untrained human user to understand and predict the machine's behaviour-animatronic toys and entertainment robots are an obvious example but anthropomorphizing is valuable too in the case of industrial robots…

From the origin in Fig. 2.2, we imagine possible developments along a trajectory towards the opposite "corner", as far along each axis as technology and society would allow.

Developments along these dimensions (and others) are not without socio-technical challenges. For example, even with anthropomorphism, we encounter the *Turing Red Flag law* [26]: "An autonomous system should be designed so that it is unlikely to be mistaken for anything besides an autonomous system, and should identify itself at the start of any interaction with another agent." Scaling up the use of robots and AI in a city has its issues such as social acceptability, accountability and machine protection, and autonomous cyber-physical systems still might often require humans to remain in-the-loop, depending on the application.

In the next chapter, we will look in detail into further application-specific considerations in a range of domains, and a range of considerations specific to the type of robots and autonomous systems being deployed in cities.

But first, in the next section, we consider a different perspective of machines and cities.

2.2.2 Machines as Hosts: Humans Living Inside Machines

We have discussed a perspective of the automated city in terms of how machines are added to human environments, and briefly discussed the nature of this human-machine partnership. This section considers a different perspective of the Automated City, that is, of machines acting as hosts.

2.2.2.1   Smart Cities from Scratch

Halegoua [7] considered *smart-from-the-start* cities which are:

> entire cities built from scratch with digital infrastructure and data analytics as integral aspects of their master plan

Among the examples mentioned are Songdo in Korea and other developments in Asia and the Middle East. There are indeed hundreds of new cities being built around the world.[6]

Building a new city from the start, one can plan for and build smart city capabilities from the beginning, and once ready, people can then be added to the city. There could be advantages in thinking about smart technologies from the start rather than trying to fit new technologies into old structures. However, the long history and architectural development of a city is often what gives the city character—the impact from a city's organic evolution over centuries together with the people and culture developed over generations in the city can be missing from a new city freshly built from scratch.

Based on the idea of a smart city built from the start, without any people in it before it is ready, one can imagine an interesting perspective on how the city stands in relation to its inhabitants which are later added. The city, if smart enough, can be viewed as basically a complex machine, i.e., the Automated City as a robot (albeit an enormous and complex one!), which hosts humans.

2.2.2.2   City-Sized Robots

Bruce Schneier suggested that the Internet of Things will be a world-sized robot.[7] Quoting Schneier in the *Intelligencer*:[8]

> We are building an internet that senses, thinks, and acts. This is the classic definition of a robot. We're building a world-size robot, and we don't even realize it.

However, in the article, Schneier also notes:

> The world-size robot is less designed than created. It's coming without any forethought or architecting or planning; most of us are completely unaware of what we're building.

and goes on to highlight security issues and the need for governance. Indeed, it is difficult to imagine planning and building a world-sized robot in a systematic way, but instead, different parts of it are built separately, in a decentralised way,

---

[6]https://www.forbes.com/sites/wadeshepard/2017/12/12/why-hundreds-of-completely-new-cities-are-being-built-around-the-world/#775a7e2214bf [last accessed: 28/1/2021].

[7]https://www.forbes.com/sites/bruceschneier/2016/02/02/the-internet-of-things-will-be-the-worlds-biggest-robot/#10515f897b07 [last accessed: 28/1/2021].

[8]https://nymag.com/intelligencer/2017/01/the-internet-of-things-dangerous-future-bruce-schneier.html [last accessed: 28/1/2021].

perhaps independently, though based on guidelines (including perhaps standards to facilitate inter-operability of parts) and appropriate governance, even if without an overall master-plan, and then eventually, parts constituting the overall robot coming together, and the whole emerging from the parts.

A city-sized robot is, hence, not out of the question and much more modest than a world-sized robot. Even more feasible are smart buildings and smart homes, to further consider different levels of spatial granularity and size.

2.2.2.3 Buildings as Machines

Alibaba opened FlyZoo, a hotel located in Hangzhou, China, that is effectively completely automated, from a robot-operated restaurant to automated check-in and robot butlers.[9] A completely automated hotel can be considered a machine, but actually comprises a collection of components, from robotic receptionists to robots to handle luggages and room service. One can consider the boundaries around a "smart thing" and what its constituents are and how smart things could compose to form smart things at larger granularity. One could think of such a hotel as *one machine* comprising a collection of components (its robots and systems). It must be noted, though, that people would also be involved in the continued maintenance and management of such hotels, even when the extent of automation and the performance of tasks improves as AI and robotics technologies advance.

One could also imagine humans staying in hotels in space, for the purposes of space tourism. In such hotels, manpower or human labour is likely extremely limited and automation is needed. In fact, human tourists could be mostly taken care of by robots, and a computer manages the entire station,[10] even if accompanied by some human staff. Interestingly, Orion Span is a company building the Aurora Space Station, with space tourism as a possible application;[11] in the near future, human space tourists would still need to be trained and certified.

Living in a large structure, which is a machine, is hence, not inconceivable.

The Swiss-French architect and urban planner, Le Corbusier, has the popular maxim "a house is a machine to live in" [3]. While this maxim was stated in the 1920s, long before the extensive computerization, AI and the Internet of Things of today, one can consider a contemporary version of this statement (different from the context of the original): "a house is a robot to live in".

In a typical house in many cities, the sewage system is built in, and so are power and water supply, though one may still need to take out the garbage.

---

[9]https://www.businessinsider.com.au/alibaba-hotel-of-the-future-robots-ai-2019-10?r=US&IR= T [last accessed: 28/1/2021].

[10]Just for illustration, one might remember HAL (Heuristically Programmed ALgorithmic Computer) in the 1968 move *2001: A Space Odyssey*, which controls the spacecraft and interacts with the ship's inhabitants—though keeping in mind this is science fiction.

[11]See https://www.orionspan.com/tourism [last accessed: 28/1/2021].

Smart home concepts have lighting and temperature control automated, as well as allowing remote control of different aspects of the house, from blinds to alarm systems. Imagine an "automated house concept" where garbage collection and waste management have been automated as well as the cleaning and care of the entire house, perhaps with the use of a collection of (cooperating) robots, including robots to clean the toilets,[12] a robot to vacuum and clean the floor, a robot to clean the windows, a robot to clean the gutter,[13] robots to manage waste and clean the walls, a robot to take care of the laundry, a robot to do the dishes (and to cook if required), a robot to mow the lawn,[14] and a robot to trim hedges and deweed.[15] There could be a robot to farm vegetables in the backyard.[16] Also, all associated utilities bills, once set up, are automatically managed and paid. Such a collection of robots will, however, need to be coordinated, even if they are working within the one house, to be managed (e.g., need charging infrastructure, and a way to keep themselves cleaned) and to have their faults addressed.

Many scenarios for ownership, deployment and setup of such home robots could be imagined, including separate ownership and management, or part co-ownership and sharing models, e.g., a collection of gardening robots that serve a given neighbourhood (perhaps cooperatively owned and maintained) to neighbourhood-shared robot-operated farms. Robot maintenance and management, i.e. support for the robots, are then part of the contract with robot providers.

Smart building concepts can be imagined with greater automation, from lifts to all the building controls, including security, temperature, lighting, appliances and so on. Similarly, one can imagine the entire building run by robots, similar to the Alibaba hotel concept and the automated house concept mentioned above, which tasks robots with even the cleaning and care of the building.

2.2.2.4 Architectural Robotics

The MIT project CityHome and a related spin-off company Ori Living[17] considered micro-apartments for high-density living that can transform its spaces, e.g., via human gesture recognition, so that the same space can be a bedroom or a living room. This novel idea of what has been called architectural robotics, suggests new

---

[12]See https://www.thisiswhyimbroke.com/worlds-first-toilet-cleaning-robot/ [last accessed: 28/1/2021].

[13]For example, see https://store.irobot.com/default/looj-gutter-cleaning/irobot-looj-330/L330020.html [last accessed: 28/1/2021].

[14]For example, see https://www.husqvarna.com/au/products/robotic-lawn-mowers/ [last accessed: 28/1/2021].

[15]https://tertill.com [last accessed: 28/1/2021].

[16]https://farm.bot [last accessed: 28/1/2021].

[17]https://oriliving.com/ [last accessed: 17/9/2020].

possibilities of living in a "machine" effectively, which can transform physically, at the user's (or inhabitant's) command.

One could imagine scaling this up to the level of buildings that can transform its spaces to accommodate mixed-use scenarios. The notion of groups of buildings transforming in such a way is likely a little far-fetched, but work on modular construction[18] suggests that living blocks comprising modules (viewed as micro-apartments) can be constructed, and arranged and rearranged as needed, even perhaps robotically if there is a reason to do so (e.g., when there are special events in the city, disaster management purposes, urban upgrades and re-planning, or at the collective whim of the inhabitants of the modules who would like a change of environment—one could think of modules taking turns to become the penthouse or modules seasonally moving from one building to another to provide a different window scenery for its inhabitants).

2.2.2.5   Cooperating Machines as Hosts

Now take the concept of buildings-as-machines further and envision a collection of buildings, and then a collection of buildings connected by bridges. Figure 2.3 illustrates the idea of a collection of buildings integrated via their computer systems which can be viewed as "one machine" in which people live, work and play, where maintenance and care (from waste management, cleaning, indoor farming, to cooking) are automated, i.e., taken care of by a collection of robots, sensors and computer systems.

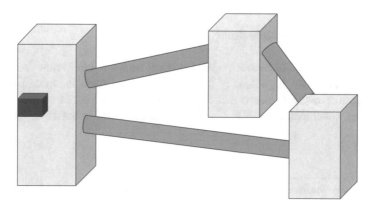

Fig. 2.3   A collection of smart buildings containing smart rooms, linked by smart bridges, forming "one integrated machine" housing its inhabitants

---

[18]For example, see https://www.kasita.com/#factory-built-suites [last accessed: 17/9/2020].

For a more futuristic example, consider a collection of space hotels and other types of stations in space, where people can travel between such stations to live, play and work, where these stations are linked and cooperate as needed, and take action cooperatively (e.g., move collectively to avoid space debris if detected, or recombine in different ways according to function or to self-repair).

One can view the combination of automated hotels, terrestrial or in space, as a machine hosting its inhabitants, playing the role of caretaker for the buildings and associated structures as well as helping to maintain the environment for its human inhabitants.

Consider an automated cafe, where ordering, preparing of food and beverage, serving of the food to customers, and cleaning up and maintenance are all automated, perhaps via a collection of different robots, each robot specialised for its task, but coordinated. In fact, there have been a range of robots developed to make coffee and to cook. There are machines to automatically make coffee (a robo-barista) (e.g., in the form of a robotic arm[19]), automate burger-making (e.g., the robotic arm Flippy works with human cooks[20]), cook an omelette (e.g., a robotic arm at the M Social Hotel in Singapore[21]), automate salad-making (e.g., Sally[22]), and cook a variety of dishes (e.g., the Spyce robot kitchen[23]). One could also imagine meet-and-greet hospitality robots in a cafe.

While the robots mentioned above might not all be working in the same place, imagine that they all do, in the same cafe. Then, one perspective is that such robots can collectively form the coordinated components of *one machine* that works to host customers, from the time they enter a cafe, taking their orders and cooking for them, taking care of them while they eat, till they leave (and even after they leave, e.g., cleaning up and so on).

One can even broaden the perspective to include robots at the farm, and robots harvesting and processing farm produce and then performing the delivery to cafes and restaurants which then have robots to cook and serve food. Humans will be hosted as customers, but humans will also need to be involved in maintenance and overseeing of this entire system (even if such monitoring can be aided by machines). Such automated cafes and supply-chain systems might not replace or displace all human involvement, but perhaps change the role of involved human workers.

Also, one could think of public spaces acting as hosts for its visitors, or even an entire city, that hosts its tourists. Tourists in many cities can already download and use a city app to search for city events and subscribe to related notifications. In a way, such an app is a guide but also a virtual host of the tourist, depending on the extent of services the app provides. Such a city app might also integrate with

---

[19] E.g., see https://www.nanalyze.com/2019/03/robot-baristas/ [last accessed: 20/8/2020].

[20] See https://misorobotics.com/flippy/ [last accessed: 20/8/2020].

[21] See   https://www.youtube.com/watch?time_continue=6&v=CAJJbMs0tos&feature=emb_title [last accessed: 20/8/2020].

[22] Sally, the robot https://www.chowbotics.com/our-solutions/ [last accessed: 20/8/2020].

[23] https://www.spyce.com/ [last accessed: 20/8/2020].

robotaxi services to provide not just information (e.g., find an event) but the ability to act on the information (e.g., go to the event).

An automated vehicle might be viewed as a host of its passengers, adding to other possible metaphors for human-AV interaction discussed earlier. A robotaxi as host might provide a tour guide service if the passengers are tourists, and may provide a music and massage (e.g., via an in-vehicle massage chair) capability for passengers, or even serve drinks, if the vehicle is equipped to do so. Such a robotaxi might integrate with or cooperate with the city app providing a uniform view and feel, as if the robotaxi and the city app are parts of one system. To take this scenario further, upon arrival at the event, a robot host could receive the tourist (signaling to the robotaxi where exactly to stop), greet the tourist as s/he emerges from the robotaxi, and continue guiding the tourist to exactly the venue where the event is held.

2.2.2.6   Discussion

We explored the metaphor of machines as hosts of humans in the smart city, be it machines in which human inhabitants live or machines which host humans at a place for a short time. Previously, we considered the metaphor of machines as partners of humans, and considered how development might proceed in three dimensions: the degree of autonomy in the partnership, the scale of the partnership and the degree of anthropomorphism of the machines in the human-machine partnerships. Where a machine acts as a host to humans, and interacts with humans, anthropomorphism might be useful as well. The degree of autonomy is also a dimension along which development can take place in the context of machine-as-host in terms of what humans need to do and human involvement. In terms of scale, we can consider the size of the machine (or its components), the range of capabilities, and the extent of cooperation of the components (e.g., robots) involved in a machine acting as host.

In both metaphors (see Sects. 2.2.2.5 and 2.2.1.6), as it is difficult to build machines that can do well in multiple tasks, and generally, easier to build a number of machines each specializing in different tasks, cooperation and integration of multiple robots or systems, forming a unified machine, becomes an interesting possibility for expanding the scope and range of cyber-physical automation in the city.

We discussed the issues of accommodating machines in cities, e.g., the need for urban robots to be socially relevant and accepted by humans. In the case of adding humans to machines, the hosting machines must be designed to be habitable, providing not only the basic necessities but providing comfort and conveniences for everyday living for humans, in a way that is acceptable to humans, and in ways that humans remain in control of their environment.

2.2.3   Machines as Art: Machines as Expressions of Human Living

The Oxford dictionary defines *art* as follows:[24]

> The expression or application of human creative skill and imagination, typically in a visual form such as painting or sculpture, producing works to be appreciated primarily for their beauty or emotional power.

Here, we consider the Automated City beyond its functional role, and beyond its typical association with efficiency and convenience. We consider machines that constitute the Automated City, beyond their function as partners or hosts, as art or human expression, constructions of human creativity, and a reflection of society; we explore the notion that aesthetics is important for machines that live and partner with humans.

2.2.3.1   Beauty and Aesthetics of Machines and Cities

Indeed, the benefits drawn from a machine is not simply its function but can also be its aesthetics.

Friedman and Hendry [5] noted Tagore's story that a water vessel is not just a tool from which a human can drink, but also the vessel should be beautiful, i.e., "our tools gives consideration not only to functionality but also to human flourishing"; a work of beauty does not need a function to justify its existence but it is simply "to be".

By analogy with machines we have in daily life, such as cars and computers, we would like such machines to somehow look good to us (at least as good as a car, a smartphone or a computer can look!) in its own way.

Donald Norman noted that aesthetics is important in the design of things, that "pleasing things work better, are easier to learn, and produce a more harmonious result" and that positive affect is important as it encourages creativity and tolerance.[25]

We admire and appreciate beautiful cities, beauty as often observed from images of a city's layout and structures, the way its buildings and environment come together. There are various rankings of the most beautiful cities on earth.[26] Is a beautiful city a better city? Perhaps not necessarily so, but all things being equal, perhaps a beautiful city (in terms of aesthetics and design) is likely much more appreciated than an "ugly" city, though what is beautiful or ugly can be rather subjective.

---

[24] https://www.lexico.com/definition/art.

[25] See https://jnd.org/emotion_design_attractive_things_work_better/ [last accessed: 9/8/2020].

[26] For example, see https://www.readersdigest.com.au/travel/the-worlds-50-most-beautiful-cities-ranked-by-travel-experts [last accessed: 4/6/2021].

2.2.3.2 Cities as Machines That Create Experiences

Edmonds has a different perspective on machines as art [4]: "A machine that is art is a working machine that is doing something. We might argue, taking this point further, that the art in an art machine is in what it does much more than in how it looks. Perhaps how it looks is of little concern at all. One perspective on machines as art is to consider them doing something that creates the aesthetic experience that defines the art. It is this view that informs the kind of machine as art that I am reporting here."

The Automated City may create new and wonderfully aesthetic experiences for its inhabitants, as its inhabitants interact with it (and have their lives and behaviours shape by it while also shaping the city itself), and in so doing, becomes art.

Machines may adapt to its inhabitants so that the experience of the inhabitants could depend on the inhabitants' explicit or implicit "inputs". The experience of a city, from the way mobility happens, to the way it is governed or city services delivered, as facilitated by machines, could draw on the behaviour or preferences of its people. Consider a fully adaptive automated transport system, and having sensed that only particular routes are used by people, might specialise and optimise to facilitate those routes only—a change of inhabitants and preferences, over time, could find those routes changing.

We may want this to go both ways, i.e. the automated transport system adapting to human behaviours but also being able to influence human behaviours for the better—e.g., gradually reducing services on less efficient routes so that humans gradually move to the more efficient route. A negotiated outcome might turn out to be better.

A machine that is a home will adapt to its inhabitants so that visiting someone's home will reflect the person's life and habits—this is already true without considering automation or machines, but perhaps this "imprint" of the inhabitants will be further emphasised from seeing how the machine (i.e., the home) has adapted to its inhabitants.

2.2.3.3 Machines and Cities that are Expressions of Human Culture and Values

The grandeur of some cities could reflect the grandeur of an empire. A technologically advanced city would not just have machines that work well in maximising efficiency and productivity, but such machines might also be beautiful in their own way. Machines used in such a city could be symbols of progress or embody special meanings within a culture.

For example, the ancient architecture of Rome and Egypt with their impressive structures reflect the grandeur and splendor of the civilization at the time. Many more examples of structures may come to the reader's mind, considering civilizations past and present. One could extrapolate from today's cities and consider the cities 20, 50, 100, 200 or 500 years from today, and consider new structures and buildings that perhaps could not be built with today's technology. It is not only that AI can be used to design new structures and forms, in partnerships with humans,[27] but paralleled with current developments in AI and robotics, robots can be used to construct structures or buildings.[28] Moreover, extrapolating from there, it is not only that machines can construct living environments, but that the living environment itself is a complex machine interwoven with architectural form and function, perhaps with the ability to self-regulate (e.g., in terms of temperature and energy use as in smart buildings of today), self-repair, self-restructure, and cooperate with other buildings (e.g., in terms of shared energy generation and consumption via solar), as needed (i.e., as mentioned earlier, the self-actioning properties).

In fact, machines are already integral to architecture as noted by Inaba:[29]

> Architecture relies on machines. They make the structures of our cities livable. In their absence, buildings would lack basic services like water and power. There would be no heating, cooling, lighting, fire safety, and elevators. Repairs and maintenance would be impossible; digital and communication technology also out of the question. The capacity to support life would be severely diminished. Architecture would be reduced to basic shelter.

and:

> Machines are vital to the life of buildings and it would be undesirable to have architecture without them. It would be better in fact if architecture were itself conceived of as a machine whose forms, spaces, and technology collectively condition the interior. Certainly, this technological aspect doesn't have to be seen in the experience of the architecture, just as buildings today and for that matter building machinery, don't look like the technologies housed within them.

The context is mechanical machines with typical functions, but AI and robotics could take things a step further, to living environments (or machines) that self-design and can change by themselves, to "living architecture", or the notion of architectural robotics we mentioned earlier.

The forms and shapes of the Automated City might depend on local preferences and culture, while also allowing human values that we want embodied [24]. Because such machines occupy the physical world and, depending on the application, can be widely visible and public, their form, design and behaviour, could be extensions of individuals and of a society as a whole.

Large buildings already have displays on them for advertising or decoration, but consider even streets as a large display on which road signage and various markings are displayed and can be changed, or modules of one building moving into another. However, not all localities might want such buildings or streets, but preferring a more traditional feel and more subtle non-conspicuous uses of technology.

---

[27]See AI in architecture at https://towardsdatascience.com/ai-architecture-f9d78c6958e0 and the thesis at https://issuu.com/stanislaschaillou/docs/stanislas_chaillou_thesis_ [last accessed: 16/9/2020].

[28]For a review, see https://www.dezeen.com/2016/05/10/10-projects-that-look-future-robotic-construction-robots-architecture/ [last accessed: 17/9/2020].

[29]http://volumeproject.org/machines-for-architecture-to-be-lived-in/ [last accessed: 16/9/2020].

Will the Automated City be one which reflects the culture and values of a locality? Likely so. Will urban robots in one city behave differently from those of another, reflecting the local culture and values? Will large scale automated systems be culturally-aware? These questions might only be answered in time to come, but culturally-aware robotics are already underway, e.g., [15, 19]—for example, conversations of a robot would need to adapt to the culture of the users.

It is expected that Automated Cities in different parts of the world and cultures, whether comprising a myriad of robots partnering with humans, or large scale machines that host humans, will be culturally distinct and locally contextualised.

2.2.4 The Humane Automated City

The Automated City is a concept originating from observations about how technologies are advancing with their possible implications for urban life, but a city is also its people. We have employed the metaphors of the Automated City as *partner* of city inhabitants to empower them and enable their daily life and work, as *host* which welcomes, organises, and helps provide for inhabitants' needs (as required), and as *art*, an expression of its inhabitants, towards a vision of a more humane Automated City, in contrast to an impersonal dystopian technological vision that is a threat to human life and values.

Figure 2.4 illustrates the three metaphors of partner, host and art in relation to people in cities and homes. The metaphors are meant to capture human-friendly behaviours that should be in the future Automated City.

Any vision of an Automated City needs to consider a wide range of considerations in relation to how machines relate to humans, but also how human values can be incorporated or embodied in the technology employed. A machine partner or host has to successfully do what humans want them to do. Current research on value alignment for AI systems are relevant here, i.e., to use this definition from Christiano:[30]

> When I say an AI A is aligned with an operator H, I mean: A is trying to do what H wants it to do. The "alignment problem" is the problem of building powerful AI systems that are aligned with their operators.

It is not just that the AI machine should try to do what the operator wants in a specific context, but more broadly, the machine, i.e., its behaviour and the way it is used, should align with human values. While "human values" is a broad term, to make this discussion concrete, we can use the working definition of "value" in value-sensitive design from Friedman and Hendry [5]:

> what is important to people in their lives, with a focus on ethics and morality

---

[30]https://ai-alignment.com/clarifying-ai-alignment-cec47cd69dd6 [last accessed: 29/9/2020].

Fig. 2.4 An illustration of the metaphors: machine as partner, as host and as art in relation to humans in cities and homes

which refers to human values implicated in the design of systems including human welfare, privacy, universal usability, accountability, environmental sustainability and courtesy, to name a few—e.g., we expect machines to be designed and deployed taking into account human welfare, proper handling of privacy preferences, usability for as many people as possible, traceability of actions, courtesy towards humans and impact on the environment. There are other aspects of human values with ethical and moral considerations which we will discuss in subsequent chapters.

2.3   The Automated City: A Working Definition

Towards conceptualising the Automated City, we started this chapter by talking about technology and how city-scale systems can be largely automated. We then considered the need for the Automated City to be human-centric, and humane, and explored how a conceptualisation of the Automated City should not merely be characterised by the technology but can be *partner* and/or *host* for its inhabitants, and even *art*. Hence, the vision of the Automated City should be one that captures and advances human aspirations for human flourishing, where the technology and automation are to be aligned with societal values.

Gartner has used the word "hyperautomation" to refer to automating tasks once done by humans,[31] referring to automation in a broader context than cities, but implying a larger extent of such automation. Such hyperautomation can be accompanied by a *digital twin*, a replica of a living or non-living object, or, in the case of cities, a detailed geographical model of a city connected to real sensors deployed in the city. Indeed, we imagine an Automated City to be hyperautomated, from policing, waste collection and management, infrastructure maintenance, transportation, care, businesses, citizen engagement, to town services, but not without humans kept in-the-loop.

There are tremendous benefits and reasons for such automation, including convenience for humans, freeing humans from drudgery, robots to improve efficiency/effectiveness (in fact, performing better than humans in numerous tasks), amplifying and complementing human abilities or aiding, not necessarily replacing, humans in numerous tasks, safety where robots take over dangerous tasks from humans, and enhancing the resilience of cities allowing certain operations and functions to continue even when humans cannot, i.e. fire-proofing or flood-proofing or in the midst of virus/diseases.

Coming back to our earlier discussion in Chap. 1 on using AI to augment human capabilities, i.e. to amplify human capabilities, to facilitate interactions, and to assist humans with physical world tasks beyond human capabilities, we might consider the future Automated City as playing such a role for its inhabitants, as a partner or host, which augments the capabilities of its human inhabitants. The inhabitants, as partner and patron, could help train and sustain the Automated City.

With the above background of ideas, we provide a working definition of the Automated City:

> An Automated City is a city where advanced Information and Communication Technologies (ICT) (particularly, AI, robotics, and IoT/CPS technologies) are deployed on a large scale to automate city operations and support its human inhabitants in many aspects of urban life and work, with careful consideration of how such deployments relate to the inhabitants and their values. Such deployments are supported by adequate social (e.g., legal and ethical frameworks) and technical infrastructure (e.g., software platforms and wireless communication networks). Guiding metaphors in terms of technology include the "living" city with self-actioning properties (for systems and subsystems) responsive to its inhabitants, proactive and reactive behaviours, and multiple interacting and cooperating cyber-physical components with possible synergistic effects, and metaphors for the Automated City in relation to its inhabitants include partner, host and art.

We use the term "working" here to suggest that the Automated City is a "concept in progress"; as technology and thinking evolves, how one sees the Automated City could change. Being a place with adequate technical and social infrastructure, an Automated City provides a "platform" for new services to be added for its inhabitants (perhaps operated and delivered by its own inhabitants and companies, i.e., third-party providers, rather than government), allowing innovation to happen.

---

[31] https://www.gartner.com/smarterwithgartner/gartner-top-10-strategic-technology-trends-for-2020/ [last accessed: 1/10/2020].

The next chapter focuses on three types of technology that are emerging and which we envision will form part of the Automated City of the future, and considers specific technological and socio-technical issues surrounding them.

References

1. Abdellatif, M., Peel, H., Cohn, A. G., & Fuentes, R. (2019). Hyperspectral imaging for autonomous inspection of road pavement defects. In M. Al-Hussein (Ed.), *Proceedings of the 36th International Symposium on Automation and Robotics in Construction (ISARC)* (pp. 384–392), Banff, AB, Canada, May 2019. International Association for Automation and Robotics in Construction (IAARC).
2. Beer, J. M., Fisk, A. D., & Rogers, W. A. (July 2014). Toward a framework for levels of robot autonomy in human-robot interaction. *Journal of Human-Robot Interaction, 3*(2), 74–99.
3. Corbusier, L., Cohen, J. L., & Goodman, J. (2007). *Toward an Architecture.* Getty Research Institute.
4. Edmonds, E. (2019). Communication machines as art. *Arts, 8*(1), 22.
5. Friedman, B., & Hendry, D. G. (2019). *Value Sensitive Design: Shaping Technology with Moral Imagination.* The MIT Press.
6. Gershenfeld, N. (1999). *When Things Start to Think.* New York, NY, USA: Henry Holt and Co.
7. Halegoua, G. (2020). *Smart Cities.* Essential Knowledge Series. The MIT Press.
8. Ju, W. (2015). *The Design of Implicit Interactions.* Synthesis Lectures on Human-Centered Informatics. Morgan and Claypool Publishers.
9. Kaye, S.-A., Lewis, I., Buckley, L., & Rakotonirainy, A. (October 2020). Assessing the feasibility of the theory of planned behaviour in predicting drivers' intentions to operate conditional and full automated vehicles. *Transportation Research Part F: Traffic Psychology and Behaviour, 74*, 173–183.
10. Kuniavsky, M. (2010). *Smart Things: Ubiquitous Computing User Experience Design: Ubiquitous Computing User Experience Design.* San Francisco, CA, USA: Morgan Kaufmann Publishers Inc.
11. Loke, S. W. (2017). *Crowd-Powered Mobile Computing and Smart Things* (1st ed.). Springer Publishing Company, Incorporated.
12. Loke, S. W. (2018). Are we ready for the internet of robotic things in public spaces? In *Proceedings of the 2018 ACM International Joint Conference and 2018 International Symposium on Pervasive and Ubiquitous Computing and Wearable Computers*, UbiComp '18 (pp. 891–900). New York, NY, USA: ACM.
13. Macrorie, R., Marvin, S., & While, A. (2019). Robotics and automation in the city: a research agenda. *Urban Geography, 42*(2), 197–217.
14. Noyman, A., Stibe, A., & Larson, K. (2017). Roadmap for autonomous cities: Sustainable transformation of urban spaces. In *AMCIS*.
15. Papadopoulos, C., Hill, T., Battistuzzi, L., Castro, N., Nigath, A., Randhawa, G., Merton, L., Kanoria, S., Kamide, H., Chong, N.-Y., Hewson, D., Davidson, R., & Sgorbissa, A. (2020). The caresses study protocol: testing and evaluating culturally competent socially assistive robots among older adults residing in long term care homes through a controlled experimental trial. *Archives of Public Health, 78*(1), 26.
16. Parashar, M., & Hariri, S. (2005). Autonomic computing: An overview. In J.-P. Banâtre, P. Fradet, J.-L. Giavitto, & O. Michel (Eds.), *Unconventional Programming Paradigms* (pp. 257–269). Berlin, Heidelberg: Springer.

17. Peshkin, M. A., Colgate, J. E., Wannasuphoprasit, W., Moore, C. A., Gillespie, R. B., & Akella, P. (2001). Cobot architecture. *IEEE Transactions on Robotics and Automation, 17*(4), 377–390.
18. Ray, P. P. (2016). Internet of robotic things: Concept, technologies, and challenges. *IEEE Access, 4,* 9489–9500.
19. Recchiuto, C. T., & Sgorbissa, A. (2020). A feasibility study of culture-aware cloud services for conversational robots. *IEEE Robotics and Automation Letters, 5*(4), 6559–6566.
20. Rose, D. (2014). *Enchanted Objects: Innovation, Design, and the Future of Technology.* Simon and Schuster.
21. Sheridan, T., Verplank, W., & Brooks, T. (1978). Human and computer control of undersea teleoperators. NASA Technical Reports Server: https://ntrs.nasa.gov/search.jsp?R=19790007441.
22. Simoens, P., Dragone, M., & Saffiotti, A. (2018). The internet of robotic things: A review of concept, added value and applications. *International Journal of Advanced Robotic Systems, 15*(1), 1729881418759424.
23. Strömberg, H., Pettersson, I., & Ju, W. (2018). Horse, butler or elevator? metaphors and enactment as a catalyst for exploring interaction with autonomous technology. In *DRS2018* (pp. 1193–1207).
24. van de Poel, I. (2020). Embedding values in artificial intelligence (AI) systems. *Minds and Machines.*
25. Vermesan, O., Bröring, A., Tragos, E., Serrano, M., Bacciu, D., Chessa, S., Gallicchio, C., Micheli, A., Dragone, M., Saffiotti, A., Simoens, P., Cavallo, F., & Bahr, R. (2017). Internet of robotic things : converging sensing/actuating, hypoconnectivity, artificial intelligence and iot platforms. In *Cognitive Hyperconnected Digital Transformation: Internet of Things Intelligence Evolution* (pp. 1–35).
26. Walsh, T. (June 2016). Turing's red flag. *Communications of the ACM, 59*(7), 34–37.
27. While, A. H., Marvin, S., & Kovacic, M. (2020). Urban robotic experimentation: San Francisco, Tokyo and Dubai. *Urban Studies, 58*(4), 769–786. https://doi.org/10.1177/0042098020917790.
28. Zlotowski, J., Proudfoot, D., Yogeeswaran, K., & Bartneck, C. (2015). Anthropomorphism: Opportunities and challenges in human–robot interaction. *International Journal of Social Robotics, 7*(3), 347–360.

Chapter 3
Automated Vehicles, Urban Robots and Drones: Three Elements of the Automated City

Abstract As illustrations of what constitutes the Automated City, this chapter high-lights (among many) three types of technologies: (1) automated vehicles, (2) robots in indoor public spaces and outdoors (on city streets, e.g., cleaning robots, delivery robots, and other applications), and (3) drones (Unmanned Aerial Vehicles) in urban environments, discussing their potential and specific issues. Existing advancements and current limitations are highlighted, including technical challenges, human-machine interaction, and socio-technical issues including governance and safety for these three types of technologies.

3.1 Introduction

We have discussed a wide range of technologies in previous chapters. This chapter takes a deep dive into three types of technologies: automated vehicles, urban robots and drones, discussing their potential and specific issues. Of course, an automated city will have many more technology elements, beyond these three, but we focus on three in this chapter.

An automated vehicle can be considered an urban robot on wheels and running on roads, and drones, if they work autonomously over the city sky, might be considered forms of urban robots, or, if they carry passengers (e.g., flying taxis), an automated passenger vehicle. However, we consider them in separate sections in view of their specific use cases and issues.

Our choice of these technologies is influenced by the following considerations. All three types of technologies occupy physical space if deployed in the city, and can be deployed at scale. Also, they will likely interface and interact with humans in some way, especially in public spaces. While these technologies are nascent, there have been real deployments and real interests from industry, academia and government, with an increasing range of use cases. All three also relate to the range of technologies we have been discussing, namely, IoT/CPS, AI, and robotics, and will be largely supported by communication and cyber infrastructure (e.g., cloud computing resources), i.e., they are cyber-physical, and can collectively form large systems of inter-connected components and potentially exhibit swarm-like emergent self-organizing behaviours. They also play important roles in the mobility of goods and people in cities, and has potential to automate many city operations. Discussions of their ethical and socio-technical considerations have also been increasing in recent years in popular media.

3.2 Automated Vehicles (AVs)

The transport sector is changing radically thanks to the revolutionary progress in automation, communication and computing. Automated Vehicles and drones are among the most spectacular and recent technologies which have disrupted research and development in transport. Such technologies have changed the way things (people and goods) move. Disruptive technologies are shaking the very foundations of transport norms.

Over 100 robotaxis have already been rolled out in China, in Shanghai, Shenzhen, Wuhan, and other cities, by the company AutoX.[1]

An automated vehicle can function at different levels of autonomy. The Society of Automotive Engineers six levels of Driving Automation have been popularly cited, referring to increasing levels of automation or decreasing levels of required human involvement, with the final Level (Level 5) referring to cars that can work autonomously without driver involvement.[2]

Figure 3.1 shows an automated vehicle on trial in a project in Queensland called Queensland's Cooperative and Automated Vehicle Initiative (CAVI),[3] which the second author is involved with the Queensland Government and iMOVE CRC. The vehicle is a SAE Level 4 vehicle where automation is enabled for certain geographical areas and the human driver can take back control. How the human driver takes control back safely and the safety implications of the ability of the vehicle to communicate with infrastructure and other users will be investigated in the project.

While the SAE Level 4 automation vehicle can and should be human drivable, fully automated vehicles need not, and so, can take on forms which are different from normal human-driven vehicles. For example, automated vehicles designed by Zoox[4] take the form of vehicles which are symmetrical in the sense that the front and back ends of a vehicle are not differentiated. Figure 3.2 illustrates a symmetrical vehicle, based on the Zoox design. Passengers sit in the car which can move in either direction.

---

[1] https://www.autox.ai/ [last accessed: 22/1/2021].

[2] https://www.sae.org/news/2019/01/sae-updates-j3016-automated-driving-graphic [last accessed: 2/12/2020].

[3] https://www.qld.gov.au/transport/projects/cavi/cavi-project [last accessed: 2/12/2020].

[4] http://www.zoox.com/ [last accessed: 7/1/2021].

Fig. 3.1 The automated and electric Renault Zoe2

Fig. 3.2 A sketch
emphasizing symmetrical
design based on the Zoox
vehicle

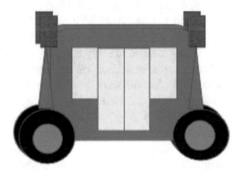

One can envision even vehicles that can spin around (provided the wheels can be designed to allow this kind of movement).

AV (Automated Vehicles) are also called autonomous vehicles, driverless cars, connected automated vehicles, or cooperative automated vehicles. Connectivity and cooperation are not the same as automation, as a connected vehicle (with the Internet and vehicle-to-vehicle communications) can be human-driven. An automated vehicle need not be Internet-connected or be able to communicate with other devices but usefully does so, e.g., to gather more information to be used for its automation.

The correct terminology would be cooperative automated vehicles (though we will simply use AV, for short) for the following reasons:

- *an AV is never completely autonomous*: an AV provides automation function-alities but not in an autonomous manner. It relies on external information such as GNSS or High Definition Map to operate. Furthermore, for safety reasons, an AV has to have redundancy built into its information acquisition mechanisms and algorithms.
- *an AV communicates*: an AV requires external information conveyed via some form of network connectivity. For example, an AV can rely on Cooperative Intelligent Transport Systems (C-ITS) consisting of Vehicle-to-Vehicle communications (V2V) or Vehicle-to-Infrastructure communications (V2I), or V2X in general.
- *an AV cooperates*: C-ITS allows vehicles and the infrastructure to cooperate and achieve a common goal such as improve safety or mobility. The communication is not a mere conduit for exchanging information; they communicate to achieve cooperation. Therefore, the correct appellation of an AV should be Cooperative Automated Vehicles (CAV).

An automated vehicle is equipped with sensors capable of analyzing the road in real time as well as AI algorithms to process camera images. It also has actuators, computing power and algorithms to "drive" the vehicle without human assistance [48].

An AV's operation revolves around three axes: perception, decision and action: perception (sensors), decision-making and path planning, and action (actuators). Sensors such cameras, LIDAR and RADAR can enable AVs to sense over 150 m around it in all directions.[5] Computer vision analysis and then AI planning enable the vehicles to drive in fairly complex environments.

There are a multitude of different possible types of vehicles, for different purposes, not just the stereotypical four wheel car. For example, there are automated vehicles developed for the last-mile delivery such as Kar-go[6] as well as other possible vehicles (e.g., automated motor-cycles, automated bicycles, automated scooters to work on walkways, automated wheelchairs (or their extensions for the disabled), and delivery robots, discussed further in the next section). Also, there are automated trucks for logistics that could form the basis for an automated freight network of locations, served by such vehicles.[7]

There are a large number of AV trials around the world, and an index developed for AV readiness of cities[8]—the top three countries in 2018 are the Netherlands, Singapore and the United States. In particular, the Netherlands has a large number (and high density) of electric vehicle charging points as well as efforts in bringing AVs to the logistics industries. Singapore has been proactive in its policies and

---

[5]For example, see https://zoox.com/autonomy/ [last accessed: 8/1/2021].

[6]https://www.academyofrobotics.co.uk/discover-kar-go.html [last accessed: 4/12/2020].

[7]For example, see https://www.vox.com/recode/2020/7/1/21308539/self-driving-autonomous-trucks-ups-freight-network for such a network in the US.

[8]See https://assets.kpmg/content/dam/kpmg/tw/pdf/2018/03/KPMG-Autonomous-Vehicle-Readiness-Index.pdf [last accessed: 8/1/2021].

technological explorations and trials in AVs, e.g., its Road Traffic Act was amended to allow self-driving vehicles to be tested on public roads in as early as 2017, the Singapore Autonomous Vehicle Initiative in 2014, and the announcement in 2019 of the whole of Western Singapore (1000 km of public roads) as a test-bed for AVs.[9]

3.2.1 The Potential of Automated Vehicles

Technology will drive innovation in transport. Automated vehicles will revolutionise transport for cities. Certainly, the advantages of saving time during travel (by being freed from driving) or the conveniences from being able to delegate driving to someone/something else is clear (even removing the need to be concerned about searching for parking, etc.). Moreover, AVs have often been proposed as a means to improve road safety by reducing human errors [6].[10] Also, AVs can potentially work together to optimise traffic, to reduce traffic jams and to improve traffic flow [21, 49]. AVs can improve road traffic capacity and allow tighter, yet safe, car following [85].

AVs can be a mobility solution for people who are unable to drive due to a disability, people unable to obtain a driver's license, or people no longer able to drive safely.

AVs has the potential to impact the way cities are designed. City transport network systems could be designed to be optimized for people instead of vehicles.[11] For example, parking spaces in main CBD areas can be removed, so that valuable real estate can be re-purposed. For convenience, there could be numerous drop-off and pick-up points in the city. Cars can enter into the lobbies of buildings to drop-off or pick-up passengers, provided the building is designed to allow this. Signage for human drivers can be reduced.

However, designing and planning cities for automated vehicles continues to be a challenge [7, 22, 30, 75], with the impact of AVs (when widely deployed) on a range of aspects including urban sprawl, traffic laws, city services, emergency services, shared mobility services with the removal of the human-driver, and the use of curb space and road space [19]. But the rethinking of cities for AVs offers tremendous opportunities to improve mobility and cities overall, e.g., as a means to address issues such as traffic congestion, transportation safety, environmental impact of vehicles, and transportation related social inequity.[12] And large scale test-beds (e.g.,

---

[9]https://www.straitstimes.com/singapore/transport/western-spore-set-to-become-test-bed-for-self-driving-vehicles [last accessed: 8/1/12021].

[10]For example, see https://www.zdnet.com/article/how-autonomous-vehicles-could-save-over-350k-lives-in-the-us-and-millions-worldwide/ [last accessed: 8/1/2021].

[11]See https://www.wired.com/story/self-driving-cars-cities/ [last accessed: 8/1/2021].

[12]See also https://www.wired.com/story/cities-trying-again-plan-autonomous-vehicles/ [last accessed: 8/1/2021].

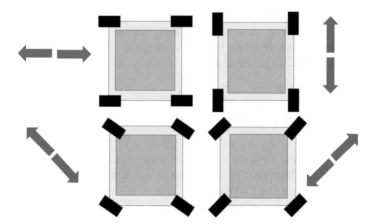

Fig. 3.3 Each view is from above looking down on the top of a square form vehicle with four wheels capable of synchronized movement in any direction—sketches emphasizing symmetrical design, and therefore, movements in any direction, eight directions are illustrated

the Western Singapore area) will be important for their eventual integration into society and uptake.

In general, the range of AV types might proliferate with specialized AVs for different use cases, e.g., for someone on a wheel chair, for the elderly, for children, for delivery, for groups, for last mile travel and so on. However, adaptable AVs might also be developed to be automatically re-purposable on-demand.

Being human-driver-less, one can consider many different forms of AV designs. For example, they can be compositional (multiple cars can combine to form a larger car, without the need to worry about where a human driver should sit, or multiple cars platooned). An AV can move in any direction, without worrying about where a human-driver would be facing—e.g., see Fig. 3.3.

AVs can have cabins swapped in and out of the vehicle body, cabins that can be extracted from one vehicle and inserted into another, or "origami" vehicles that can be folded to be stored when not in use. One could also think of vehicles that do not use ordinary wheels and so, need not be driven the same way as normal human-driven vehicles (and in fact these vehicles are self-driven!)—e.g., multiple terrain legged vehicles.

Combining the ideas of Japanese or Hong Kong "coffin" apartments or cubicles, and caravans, one could imagine people staying in automated vehicles (i.e., automated (self-driving) caravans), in a kind of ultra-modern nomadic life-style, where someone's (mobile) home is, effectively, a collection of vehicles (perhaps a collection of connectable caravans), which can combine in different ways at different times as needed—e.g., a family can own six automated caravans: at a suitable caravan park, the six caravans combine (and are connectable with internal passages between vehicles) to form a large "home", but when on the move, the six separate and travel as six different (automated) vehicles. Of course, there are the issues of comfort and required infrastructure to support this (e.g., public shared facilities, from waste management to vehicle charging, in a park for automated caravans).

Together with connectivity and automation is electric power. Connected automated electric vehicles have been often mentioned as the future of cars. As electric charging stations proliferate, electric vehicles, human driven or not, will become increasingly common. Apart from cars moving to charging stations, there are ideas of charging stations moving to cars. For example, the Volkswagen[13] charger robot concept can move to parked cars and can connect the energy storage device to the car autonomously—in this way, every parking bay can be a charging bay, effectively. The charger robot can also be summoned via a smartphone app.

3.2.2 Issues and Limitations

We might have seen science fiction movies where cars are driverless, summoned to go anywhere and talk to users as would a "chauffeur". In reality, we are years away from such a scenario still [20]. There has been work mentioned on automated valet parking, where after the passengers have alighted (including the driver), the vehicle can go on its own to the parking spot, and could be summoned from the parking spot to come to the passengers.[14] But there are still a number of issues:

- *AVs cannot go anywhere, anytime, under any condition.* AVs can only technically operate in a predefined operational domain. A range of algorithms, including AI based, are used to allow an AV to navigate safely but they can operate only inside a specific and well determined operational domain (e.g., requiring certain sensors and perception system to be functioning and "healthy", certain roads with clear road markings and road infrastructure conditions[15] and within certain levels of busyness and traffic complexity). For example, a number of automated vehicle trials in different parts of Australia are revealing requirements on road infrastructure (e.g., pavement markings, etc.) for automated vehicles.[16] A study by Austroads on the implications of pavement markings for machine vision [56] noted that the contrast ratio (between pavement markings and the surroundings) need to be sufficiently high (e.g., 3-to-1) and pavement marking configurations such as line width and continuity are important for effective functioning of machine vision algorithms.

---

[13]https://www.volkswagenag.com/en/news/stories/2019/12/volkswagen-lets-its-charging-robots-loose.html [18/1/2021].

[14]https://www.bosch.com/stories/automated-valet-parking/ (using the Mercedes S class) [last accessed: 4/12/2020].

[15]https://hbr.org/2018/08/to-make-self-driving-cars-safe-we-also-need-better-roads-and-infrastructure [last accessed: 4/12/2020].

[16]https://austroads.com.au/drivers-and-vehicles/future-vehicles-and-technology/trials [last accessed: 4/12/2020].

One can think of the Operational Design Domain (ODD) of an automated vehicle as the domain in which an automated vehicle can operate safely. In [13], the concept of the Restricted Operational Domain (ROD) is introduced to capture the idea that the current context (e.g., system health) can change what the vehicle can do safely:

> The specific conditions under which a given driving automation system or feature thereof is *currently* able to function, including, but not limited to, driving modes.

The idea is that the vehicle would be considered safe in its ROD and the ROD can be updated in response to changes—e.g., if a subsystem (e.g., a camera) was damaged and so on—under healthy fully functioning normal conditions, the ROD is equivalent to the ODD.

A human can drive a vehicle off the road to go on a rural terrain where there are no clear road markings or even to drive over a curb if needed, or over grass (e.g., to avoid a collision), but for an AV to do all that could be going beyond its anticipated ODD.

- *Similar to any software, AVs are not well suited in reacting to the unexpected.* Vulnerable Road Users (VRU) such as pedestrians, cyclists, and motorcyclists are notoriously unpredictable on the road. Detecting and predicting their trajectories are very difficult, e.g., see [23] and [38].

It should be noted that Machine Learning (ML) algorithms can be notoriously bad in handling unknown or very rare events. Driving consists of millions of events and situations which drivers learn to handle. In Queensland, a learner driver has to spend at least 100 h of supervised driving to be entitled to drive. During such a period, the learner will be exposed to a particular driving situation such as entering a roundabout, learning from it (supervised learning) and then safely navigate through other similar roundabouts with confidence later on.

A human driver can intuitively find the similarities between driving situations. However, even the most powerful machine learning (ML) algorithms might still struggle in determining such similarity with high accuracy. For example, roundabouts have different geometry characteristics and offer different fields of view as assessed by the on-board vehicle's perception devices (e.g., LIDAR, and camera). Different perceptions will affect the associated path planning algorithm. Worldwide, road crashes are the leading cause of death among young people aged 15–29. Driver's inexperience is the main contributing factor to this high-risk crash. Road safety research has showed that the most effective long-term method to reduce a young novice driver's crash risk is to gain more on-road driving experience. During such experience, a learner driver becomes a safe driver by learning what not to do and what to do. For example, s/he learns that s/he should not follow the leading car too closely. This is not necessarily a pattern of behaviour that the learner will learn by doing the action or from experience. In other words, to learn to avoid a crash, the learner doesn't need to have been involved in a crash.

This is where machine learning might show its limitation in safety critical driving situations. A ML algorithm is trained by telling it what to do in a particular situation. Therefore, if we want to train it on how to avoid crashes, it has to learn from crash or pre-crash (called near misses) data. Unfortunately, circumstances in which road crashes or near misses occur are very rare events. Therefore, it might not be always practical to train an algorithm with all possible rare events because they are by definition very rare.[17]

ML algorithms can also be easily fooled. For example, street signs can be tampered with in a way that is not detectable by humans but which could be read very differently by an algorithm. Subtle changes can cause an ML algorithm to "see" a stop sign as a speed limit sign, and a right turn sign as a stop sign.[18] Such signs have been called toxic signs [77] or adversarial traffic signs which have been shown to be able to fool even commercial-grade traffic sign recognition systems of a real car [61]. Of course, an AV need not depend on road signs and have road information electronically transmitted to it, bypassing the need to read road signs, but this would require additional digital infrastructure beyond current physical road signage.

The notion of "naked highways", or highways without roadside signage of any kind, with such information transmitted directly to vehicles, has been proposed with supporting technologies being trialled in the UK.[19] This notion is not restricted to highways, but that would be a start. Other roads can also be "naked", as long as vehicles have a continuous reliable Internet connection. Removal of such physical road signage can save costs and allow greater flexibility and easier changes. One can extrapolate this idea to intersections and road markings where digital vehicle-to-vehicle communications and cooperation [49] could take over the coordination, especially in the case of AVs.

- *Despite the rapid evolution of AI, a natural conversation between a human and computer has not passed the Turing test completely.* The Turing test investigates whether people can detect if they are talking to machines or humans. Humans are not accustomed to talking to machines naturally as they do with other humans. During a conversation, a human might adapt his/her tone, syntax or style. For example, a human would speak louder or utter syntactically incorrect sentences, depending on the situation. This could affect how humans interact with AVs, if natural language conversation is one way.

  Despite some already deployed commercial in-car solutions with limited natural language interaction, natural language interaction with an AV is an area of research, and has been investigated in [66]. Beyond just voice, multimodal approaches have been considered [67, 68] for interaction between an AV and its passengers. Passenger and AV interactions, pedestrian and AV interactions,

---

[17]https://bdtechtalks.com/2020/07/29/self-driving-tesla-car-deep-learning/   [last   accessed: 4/12/2020].

[18]https://spectrum.ieee.org/cars-that-think/transportation/sensors/slight-street-sign-modifications-can-fool-machine-learning-algorithms [last accessed: 4/12/2020].

[19]https://www.intelligenttransport.com/transport-articles/92700/the-naked-highway-digital-signage-and-safety/ [last accessed: 22/1/2021].

AV interaction with human drivers (in other vehicles), and AV to AV interaction remain areas of further investigation. Effective interaction of an AV with other parties is important for its effective use and controllability—including the human–machine partnership models mentioned in Chap. 2.

- *AVs are still relatively high cost.* While there are industry efforts to bring down the cost of vehicles that have SAE Level 4 and above, this will take some time. A study[20] estimated that, given normal market conditions, using a robotaxi can cost consumers almost three times more—on a per mile basis—than if they owned and used an older vehicle.

- *There are also issues of privacy and cybersecurity risks for AVs as noted in [46].* In particular, there are issues on informational and data privacy that relate to how information collected about an AV might be stored and used. For example, such AVs would be connected and will be continuously trackable. Insurance companies might use such information to inform premiums. Marketing companies might use real-time and historical data about AVs to target ads at passengers. Automated vehicles might be tracked by the manufacturers or sellers in order to provide services to these vehicles. There are clear economic opportunities, but who needs to provide consent to such myriad uses of data is an issue. And how would such historical data be stored safely is another issue. The European GDPR[21] rules aim to provide control of data back to people (e.g., the data "producers"), and could apply to AV manufacturers and related services companies.

  Given that such AVs are practically networked computers, the concern of vehicle hackability is valid—even if hacking vehicles is not easy, there are books on the topic (e.g., [78]). Demonstrations of hacked connected vehicles have raised such concerns.[22] The dangers of a hacked vehicle are, of course, tangible, from brakes that stop working to directing vehicles at physical targets. The cybersecurity risks of connected and automated vehicles are explored in [76], including a case study involving GPS spoofing, as GPS is critical for the correct navigation of such vehicles. Hence, it is not only the vehicle itself that can be hacked but the surrounding infrastructure that the vehicles depend on, e.g., for software updates and telematics.

  The cybersecurity concern of such vehicles is compounded by vehicle-to-vehicle communications (and vehicle-to-roadside infrastructure communications) [40], and vehicle-to-vehicle cooperative behaviours, Vehicles could send fake or misleading messages to other vehicles [87], or exploit cooperative behaviours among vehicles (e.g., to gain parking advantages [2]).

---

[20] In the Harvard Business Review, see https://hbr.org/2019/01/the-cost-of-self-driving-cars-will-be-the-biggest-barrier-to-their-adoption?ab=at_articlepage_recommendedarticles_bottom1x1 [last accessed: 4/12/2020].

[21] https://gdpr-info.eu/ [last accessed: 8/1/2021].

[22] For example, see https://www.wired.com/2015/07/hackers-remotely-kill-jeep-highway/ and https://www.cnet.com/roadshow/news/2019-automotive-cyber-hack-security-study-upstream/ [last accessed: 8/1/2021].

- *Issues of algorithmic-decision making are inherent in AVs especially if they make decisions in relation to choices of life and death.* The well-publicised notion of the moral dilemma of the automated vehicle illustrates the philosophical "trolley problem" in a possible reality, e.g., whether a vehicle should swerve to avoid hitting a pedestrian while endangering the passengers or it should hit the pedestrian so as to prioritize the safety of its passengers [5]. Such issues and ethical behaviour for AVs have been discussed elsewhere, including ethical guidelines for AV manufacturers, the use of algorithmic social contracts, legal and frameworks and appropriate regulations, and mechanisms for computing trade-offs [47, 52]. The range of situations in which AVs might find themselves may be hard to anticipate exhaustively.
- *Even if an AV (say fully automated) has been successfully engineered and has been tested and validated to be able to move successfully between any two points in a region, there are still deployment concerns.* For example:
  - What should an AV do when something bad happens? An example is the "The Molly Problem" described as the following:[23]

    A young girl called Molly is crossing the road alone and is hit by an unoccupied self-driving vehicle. There are no eye-witnesses. What should happen next?

    In a survey conducted on this problem,[24] it was observed that over 90% of 296 respondents expected that the AV should be aware of the collision, the AV should stop at the site of the collision, the AV should indicate that there is now a hazard to other road users, and the AV should call emergency services. Over 90% expected that the AV should also be able to recall the time and place of the collision, the time when the AV identified the risk of a collision, whether the AV actually detected Molly (and if so, when), whether the AV detected Molly as human (and if so, when), whether the AV took mitigating action (and if so, when, and what action was taken). Also, the AV should have recall capabilities for near-miss events.

    Hence, together with the development of AVs, there should be related thinking about deployment concerns, on what should happen with AV incidents (though we might think that a well-tested AV should have few incidents).
  - How should an AV fit within the existing transport ecosystem consisting of multiple modes of transport, physical and network infrastructure, software services, users, and regulatory frameworks? This question has been considered in a number of AV trials around the world.[25] Basically, it should complement

---

[23]https://www.itu.int/en/ITU-T/focusgroups/ai4ad/Pages/MollyProblem.aspx [last accessed: 28/1/2021].

[24]https://www.itu.int/en/ITU-T/focusgroups/ai4ad/Documents/Survey-Results.pdf?csf=1&e= wb7tAs [last accessed: 28/1/2021].

[25]For example, see the ITU workshop on "Autonomous Driving safety data and metrics—what do we really need?" (Perspectives from Asian-Pacific stakeholders to foster a global harmonization) at https://www.itu.int/en/ITU-T/Workshops-and-Seminars/20201202/Pages/default.aspx [last accessed: 28/1/2021].

and work with other transport mechanisms, which may vary city from city, and an AV might be contextualised and configured to fit within a certain context of use or ecosystem.

– How does an AV deal with unexpected situations? We already noted that AVs can have difficulty with situations that were not anticipated at design time. This might include floods and fires, as well as various types of animals or bizarre events on the road. One can try to design and test AVs to work with as many situations as possible, but the behaviours that an AV defaults to whenever it encounters an unanticipated situation will need to be considered. There are, however, continuing efforts towards building AVs that can cope with a wide range of situations. For example, by training on recorded data (provided by the BMW Group) of instances where autonomous driving was disengaged, the recent work in [43] was able to predict failures with over 85% accuracy, seven seconds ahead of time, with a false positive rate of 20%. The Safety Pool Initiative[26] aims to build a database of reference scenarios for testing, validating and certifying Automated Driving Systems (ADS). A set of safety performance metrics for ADS is outlined[27] by the Automated Vehicle Safety Consortium, a program of the Society of Automotive Engineers Industry Technologies Consortia—the metrics include crash severity and frequency of the ADS, compliance with traffic regulations, if the ADS maintains a safety envelope, detecting objects and event response times of the ADS, and safe vehicle motion control (e.g., jerk and acceleration). Hence, one might argue, with such efforts, the ability of a large number of connected vehicles to collect and share data, and scenarios generated via simulations (e.g., [29, 41, 89]), a comprehensive (even if not complete) coverage of scenarios is attainable.

Indeed, despite being a promising technological solution for transport, the limitations of AVs for reducing traffic congestion, reducing the environmental impact of road travel, and improving road safety have been noted [14, 24, 65].[28] As AVs become integrated into the transportation infrastructure, there are issues of societal implications to be addressed [34, 60]. Indeed, the impact on jobs and the transportation industries, energy consumption, car ownership, mobility choices and behaviour, required services and regulations associated with AVs, and the structure of cities and life will need to be considered. The impact of large scale deployment of AVs on traffic congestion, energy consumption and safety remains to be seen, but has been discussed [31].

---

[26]https://www.safetypool.ai/ [last accessed: 5/4/2021].

[27]See https://www.sae.org/standards/content/avsc00006202103/ [last accessed: 5/4/2021].

[28]https://www.washingtonpost.com/outlook/five-myths/five-myths-about-autonomous-vehicles/2019/08/15/245c39bc-bec6-11e9-b873-63ace636af08_story.html [last accessed: 8/1/2021].

3.2.3 Summary on Automated Vehicles

We have outlined the forms and potential of AVs. We have also outlined issues in relation to the deployment and use of AVs. How cities will be transformed by AVs is a key question likely to be concretely answered in the coming future, as many companies begin to bring AVs into our cities. Perhaps not every impact of the use and deployment of AVs will be anticipated, but the automated city will feature automated transportation in many forms, with AVs likely to play a central role among the mix of technologies.

3.3 Urban Robots

We noted in earlier chapters various kinds of robots appearing in public to help monitor social distancing compliance, to help deliver items, to help interact with and conduct tests, to help serve customers in a contact-less way, and to help clean areas, in the context of the pandemic.

As noted in [50], robots are appearing in public spaces. Consider the following list of urban robots in public, indoors and outdoors:

- delivery robots, from wheeled robots[29] to bipedal robots[30]
- robots acting as security guards, such as the Knightscope robots[31]
- robots for policing in public, such as the Singapore police robot shown in Fig. 3.4
- self-driving robocarts[32]
- robots to help with luggage in hotels[33] and to automate hotel reception;[34] robots in tourism are reviewed in [35]
- cleaning robots, including robotic vacuum cleaners which are common, and some larger ones are used in shopping malls, such as in Chadstone Shopping Centre, Melbourne, Australia—see the cleaning robot shown in Fig. 3.5 and the Singaporean cleaning robot to assist human cleaners[35]

---

[29] https://www.fastcompany.com/90291820/8-robots-racing-to-win-the-delivery-wars, https://www.engadget.com/2019-09-09-starship-delivery-robots-at-purdue-university.html [last accessed: 8/10/2020].

[30] For example, see https://spectrum.ieee.org/automaton/robotics/humanoids/ford-self-driving-vans-will-use-legged-robots-to-make-deliveries [last accessed: 14/6/2021].

[31] https://www.knightscope.com/ [last accessed: 14/6/2021].

[32] US Patent 20160260161, at http://appft.uspto.gov/.

[33] https://www.telegraph.co.uk/travel/hotels/articles/hotel-robot-room-service/,https://aethon.com/sheraton-hotel-to-use-tug-robots/ [last accessed: 14/6/2021].

[34] See Japan's robot receptionists at https://asia.nikkei.com/Business/Robot-staff-make-Japan-s-Henn-na-Hotels-quirky-and-efficient and Alibaba's automated hotel at https://kohler.design/flyzoo-hotel/ [last accessed: 14/6/2021].

[35] https://www.lionsbot.com [last accessed: 5/10/2020].

Fig. 3.4 Police robot in Singapore

- robots waiting, cooking and making coffee at cafes and restaurants, such as the Shelley robot in a cafe in Ringwood, Melbourne, Australia[36] and robots making pizza and helping to cook, e.g., in the form of robotic arms[37]
- healthcare robots [69], which could be hospitals as already mentioned and even in aged care homes, e.g., [18, 88]
- service robots in retail,[38] public spaces and office buildings for meet and greet and as mobile information kiosks, which have appeared in many places, such as Pepper[39] in Japanese retail shops as shown in Fig. 3.6 and in exhibitions as early

---

[36] See https://www.facebook.com/spacewalkcafe52/posts/shelley-the-robot-waitress-brings-food-to-your-table-at-ringwoods-spacewalk-cafe/2288916167834535/.

[37] See https://www.theguardian.com/food/2019/mar/07/food-tech-the-march-of-the-robots-reaches-the-kitchen, the robot burger flipping arm at https://misorobotics.com, https://www.moley.com, and more on coffee making robots at https://www.roboticstomorrow.com/story/2020/05/five-best-robot-coffee-baristas/15296/, and https://rozum.com/coffee-robot-barista/ [last accessed: 5/10/2020].

[38] https://hbr.org/2020/10/what-robots-can-do-for-retail [last accessed: 5/10/2020].

[39] https://www.softbankrobotics.com/emea/en/pepper [last accessed: 28/1/2021].

Fig. 3.5 Cleaning robot in Chadstone, Melbourne, Australia

as 2005 [36], Robovie which was tested for 3 years in a mall [71], KeJia robot in a shopping mall [11], Keylo robot in the US,[40] robots in libraries [62, 80],[41] and a PAL REEM robot trialled in an Australian airport [84].[42]

- robots in city canals, e.g., in Amsterdam's canals[43]
- robots for waste collection and management, such as Urban Swarms [1],[44] the Bluephin robot to collect floating waste from urban water bodies,[45] Clean-

---

[40] https://www.generationrobots.com/en/402797-robot-keylo.html [last accessed: 5/10/2020].

[41] See also the robot in Oodi, a Helsinki library, at https://towardsdatascience.com/the-little-robot-that-lived-at-the-library-90431f34ae2c [last accessed: 5/10/2020].

[42] See also the project http://being-there.org.uk/ [last accessed: 5/10/2020].

[43] http://roboat.org [last accessed: 5/10/2020].

[44] The MIT project is at https://www.media.mit.edu/projects/urban-swarms/overview/ [last accessed: 5/10/2020].

[45] https://bluephin.io [last accessed: 5/10/2020].

Fig. 3.6 Pepper robot in a store in Osaka, Japan in 2015

Robotics's TrashBot which can sort wastes,[46] and DustCart which was experimented in Italy as a concept robot to collect garbage from houses and deposit them in a designated area [27].

- small robotic vehicles for people; an example is Persuasive Electric Vehicles (PEVs) which can run on bicycle lanes and can be summoned to where the client is via a mobile app (but the passenger can then ride it like a bicycle)[47]
- automated vehicles as discussed earlier

Another form of robots that could be used in cities increasingly are farm robots, located within urban farms, say. The COVID-19 pandemic has adversely impacted global supply chains. Singapore, for instance, has pushed towards vertical farming as an approach towards being self-sufficient.[48]

Such high-tech vertical farms are situated within warehouses and employ robots. For example, Ironox[49] is said to have created the world's first fully autonomous vertical farm in California. There are various robo-farm solutions such as Farmbot[50]

---

[46] https://cleanrobotics.com [last accessed: 21/1/2021].

[47] https://www.media.mit.edu/projects/pev/overview/ [last accessed: 28/1/2021].

[48] https://www.technologyreview.com/2020/10/13/1009497/singapore-vertical-farming-food-security [last accessed: 19/10/2020].

[49] https://ironox.com/ [last accessed: 28/1/2021].

[50] https://farm.bot/ [last accessed: 19/10/2020].

in the market. An advantage of such vertical farms for the increasingly high density urban areas is that they are situated near to people, within high-density housing areas, and local production of food avoids having to transport food over long distances.

There is little doubt that the range of use cases and applications will continue to increase. Robots might not need Internet connectivity to function, but often, many commercial service robots connect to a cloud platform and can be easily Internet-enabled, and robots may need to connect to other robots.

3.3.1 The Potential of Urban Robots

Still nascent and many are prototypes, from the above review, urban robots can be used to fulfill a range of functions in the city, including

- goods delivery and logistics (e.g., last-mile),
- aids for people shopping,
- aids for helping with luggage in hotels and reception,
- cleaning including canals and monitoring,
- waste collection and disposal,
- food beverage preparation and serving,
- security guarding,
- policing,
- health care and aged care and related monitoring,
- meet and greet, and information kiosks at airports, libraries, shopping centres,
- robot operated autonomous urban farms, and
- moving people over short distances, including people with disabilities or people requiring help in moving around.

While it might seem to replace many jobs, the above robots would often work together with humans to make their jobs more efficient and convenient, amplifying their abilities, and complementing humans, at least in the ways considered today. And so, rather than replacing jobs, it seems to displace workers, shifting the role of workers to focus on certain tasks in their jobs that robots still cannot do, and possibly elevating them to be *trainers*, i.e. train AI/robotic systems to perform tasks and refining AI algorithms and fixing errors, *explainers*, i.e. explaining AI/robotic algorithmic behaviours and *sustainers*, i.e. overseeing output quality and raise issues, as mentioned in Sect. 1.4.2.

New industries could emerge as cloud-enabled robotics take shape and allow scalable computational resources to be employed for robots. Also, new business models surrounding such deployment of urban robotics can be envisioned, including services for managing and maintaining the robots, and for upgrading the software on the robots.

Ownership and control models have been noted in [55], including private control/ownership versus distributed or community ownership models. Other modes of usage and access apart from own-and-use would be rent-and-use and *robot-sharing* akin to car-sharing economies. Corresponding to ownership/control of the robots is the ownership/control of the data collected by the robots. New data and service management and infrastructure will be needed, with potential for new business models.

3.3.2 Issues and Limitations

This subsection considers a range of socio-technical issues and limitations regarding urban robotics, specifically.

3.3.2.1 Public Acceptance

Consider a city with some of the robots mentioned above.

> As you walk down a street, you see delivery robots on wheels and some on legs walking pass you and some robots are walking next to their human users carrying goods for them. On the other side of the street, several robots are cleaning the walkway and the side street (including removing broken bottles from the previous night and stains), while being careful not to obstruct human passersby too much. Further up the road, a robot goes around from bin to bin collecting waste—you noticed the robots making some effort to ensure all the bags of rubbish are removed from the bin.
>
> As you turn the street corner, you feel hungry and decided to visit a nearby "fast food" shop. A robot takes your order and prepares your food and beverage—you noticed how the robot arm expertly flipped the burger, while another robot arm makes your cafe latte with machine precision. Within six minutes exactly, your order is served to you, with a thank you. After the quick meal, you walk into an alley taking a shortcut, and a robot on wheels in the shape of a cone on wheels slowly approaches you—you noticed what looks like a beam of blue light aimed at your direction for a second as you pass by it. You look again at it and noticed the words "auxiliary police" clearly printed on it. On your right, as you look into a restaurant, you noticed a frail elderly gentleman helped by a bipedal four-armed robot to stand and speak to someone over the counter, while robots serve food and take orders from customers sitting at a table nearby.
>
> You arrive at the shopping mall. As you go in, you noticed several robots accompanying different groups of shoppers carrying their shopping for the day, and see someone talk to what looks like a robot kiosk for directions. You walk through the mall and arrive at the lobby of the hotel connected to the mall—a robot takes your small luggage and offers you a sit while you are being checked in. The robot then takes you to your room, together with your luggage, and tells you how to operate the room controls.

The above scenario involves many of the robots mentioned in the previous section. While this is not yet a reality, the direction of the technologies is such that the different types of robots are a possible reality. Of course, not all of these robots would be deployed in the same locality as depicted here, at least not yet.

Such robots occupy human spaces and interact with humans. An obvious question is whether the public will accept this—technology acceptance is a key issue for machines in public spaces. Will people want to talk to robots in retail? Will people accommodate or make way for robots on walkways? For example, it was mentioned that a survey showed 95% of respondents (comprising 1200 consumers and 400 retail executives located in the US, UK and Australian) didn't want robots in shops.[51]

Wheeled food delivery robots were sometimes kicked,[52] and in fact, they were banned in most of San Francisco.[53] A security robot was knocked over in San Francisco[54] suggesting that some people were unhappy with their presence. The story of a similar robot knocking over a toddler was also reported, which didn't help public acceptance of their presence.[55]

The Henn na hotel in Japan removed half of its 243 robots, because they ended up creating more work as customers sought human help regarding the robots.[56]

For some, such robots might be considered an "intrusion" into human spaces and possibly the creation of a new type of burden on humans, that of dealing with robot issues.

When humans and machines do interact, the engagement may be physical, cognitive or both. Robots occupy physical space and hence will affect the physical environment of a city if and when they are deployed. We have seen that the need to accommodate the use of vehicles shaped the way cities and buildings are designed—will there be a corresponding reshaping of cities for urban robotics? This is still an open question.

Nagenborg [63] raises the question of "whether we should build cities for robots or robots for cities" and noted a mixed approach is most likely the way to go. Indeed, one perspective is that robots should be built around people, i.e., a human-centred design, and not the opposite, and machines should not just be designed for humans but also adapt to humans as needed once deployed. The shapes and sizes of robots that fit within a home should fall within the constraints imposed by humans, e.g., in terms of the size of doorways and so on, or robots that use public walkways should not be too wide or be too noisy, and perhaps be programmed to be "polite", not take photos of persons without permission, and not scare, harm or injure humans in trying to accomplish their tasks.

However, if we want to deploy robots in these ways, there is a need for humans to get use to such technology or be comfortable with them, as Salvini [72] noted, "the social acceptability of autonomous systems is still uncertain." There is also the need to adapt the built environment to the use of robots, e.g., the notion of "enveloping"

---

[51] https://www.ns-businesshub.com/science/future-of-retail-robots/ [last accessed: 8/10/2020].

[52] https://www.businessinsider.com.au/people-are-kicking-starship-technologies-food-delivery-robots-2018-6?r=US&IR=T [last accessed: 8/10/2020].

[53] https://www.zdnet.com/article/san-francisco-bans-delivery-robots-in-most-of-the-city/ [last accessed: 8/10/2020].

[54] https://www.dezeen.com/2017/12/13/k5-knightscope-security-robot-sfspca-san-francisco-bullied-off-street/ [8/10/2020].

[55] https://www.bbc.com/news/technology-36793790 [last accessed: 8/10/2020].

[56] https://www.wsj.com/articles/robot-hotel-loses-love-for-robots-11547484628 [last accessed: 8/10/2020].

for AI and robots mentioned in Chap. 1. There is also the question of what kinds of new infrastructure are required to support urban robots at large, e.g., analogous to charging stations for electric vehicles, special road signage and traffic lights for vehicles, we might have stopping stations for urban robots, special road signage to warn pedestrians, or special crossings and traffic systems to take such urban robot traffic into account. However, such changes are likely difficult to make on a large scale, unless there are sufficient economic and social incentives.

There are also robots that interact with humans directly and those that don't (e.g., maintenance), so that, appropriate behaviours and social norms for robots would need to fit their mode of usage and level of interaction with users. Also, ideally, robots in cities also should not cause inconvenience to humans and not accentuate social inequality—e.g., only those who can afford it enjoy the benefits of robot services at the cost of public interests (we discuss this further later). The types of robots and their roles are myriad, and hence, a one-size-fits-all approach is not likely to work.

The dynamics of human-robot interaction in cities goes beyond just how a person might work together with a robot to accomplish a specific task. In social contexts, as noted in [54], there are factors such as human vandalism of robots and to what extent robots should be allowed to protect against this, humans helping robots when they get stuck, and expected socially relevant behaviours for robots (beyond being "polite" as mentioned earlier) such as being kind and available in the following sense, to quote from [54]:

> ...robots ...provided services that can be seen as forms of care towards humans. For example, participants envisioned situations where a delivery robot carried a first aid kit and contacted police in case of an emergency, or offered to throw trash in the dumpster after making a delivery. Similarly, other participants thought of surveillance robots could help tourists to find a place to stay or help homeless people to charge their phones or provide heat. In these perspectives, the robot becomes a social actor.

Humans may help robots in public but robots might be expected to help humans as well.

In general, quoting Nagenborg [63]:

> To say that 'X is an urban robot' should therefore be read as 'X is considered to be an urban technology in the sense that it shapes or is shaped by city life.'

The design of urban robots still needs much consideration, as much as the design of cities that accommodate urban robots also does.

3.3.2.2 Enhancing and Entrenching Social Inequality

Will robots increase social inequality? According to the OECD, the digital divide refers to:[57]

> the gaps in access to information and communication technology (ICT)—threatens the ICT "have-nots", whether individuals, groups or entire countries. Education and learning lie at the heart of these issues and their solutions

Will the rich employ multiple urban robot assistants while the poorer will need to make way for such robots.

Consider an extreme example first highlighted in [53], where instead of an entourage of people normally accompanying a V.I.P. in public, there is an entourage of robots accompanying this person. The idea of robots being able to follow humans is useful. For example, Temi telepresence robots[58] have the ability to follow and track humans. We imagine individuals could take their own robots to shopping and have them follow them around with limitations on the type of ground wheeled robots can keep up. (Two legged robots[59] and four-legged robots that work on non-flat terrains such as Laikago,[60] Spot,[61] and Anymal,[62] can potentially follow its user through all kinds of areas.) Figure 1 (left and middle) illustrates a Temi robot carrying a bag, and a Temi robot can also be a launchpad for mini-drones ("flying cameras").

But what if some individuals take this too far and employ an entourage of robots? Fig. 3.7 (right) illustrates such an entourage. Then, from [53]:

> Let us consider a shopping spree scenario. One could imagine an entourage of one or more such robots (and drones), following the user, and carrying bags of shopping during a shopping spree in the city, or many individuals each with his/her own entourage. A personal drone also follows the shopper to record the experience. One could only drive one car, but multiple robots could follow autonomously. A question is then whether this would be socially or publicly acceptable and whether one needs to register such robots (and drones) and purchase permits from the city council in order to legally take such robots around—similar to how one pays registration and road tax for being able to legally have a vehicle use public roads. This could also be a deterrent for individuals taking a dozen of such robots in an entourage that could perhaps cause congestion on walkways, or laws might prohibit the size of such an entourage.
> :
> One could imagine an entourage not only with robocarts but also robotic prams that automatically fold and unfold and could follow parents around—or auto-wheelchairs for elderly shoppers or elderly parents accompanying shoppers. Again, shared public spaces

---

[57]https://www.oecd.org/site/schoolingfortomorrowknowledgebase/themes/ict/bridgingthedigitaldivide.htm [last accessed: 8/10/2020].

[58]https://www.robotemi.com/ [last accessed: 28/1/2021].

[59]https://www.wkbw.com/news/national/ford-is-developing-a-robot-that-would-carry-deliveries-to-your-front-door [last accessed: 28/1/2021].

[60]http://www.unitree.cc/ [last accessed: 28/1/2021].

[61]https://www.bostondynamics.com/spot [last accessed: 28/1/2021].

[62]https://www.anybotics.com/anymal-legged-robot/ [last accessed: 28/1/2021].

Fig. 3.7 Temi robot with a bag and as a launchpad for a drone (Hover—https://gethover.com—in the picture). An illustration of an entourage comprising Temi-like shopping robots to help carry goods and a drone (represented by the hovering oval)

can become busy with such robotic things, and would require careful design to comfortably and safely accommodate such robots.

Would those people with robots "occupy" much more public space than those without? Permits, akin to certificates allowing a car on the road, might be required for someone to use an urban robot in public spaces.[63] Likely, rules and regulations of robot usage can rule out certain scenarios. While an extreme perhaps stylized example, it serves to epitomize a potential divide where even physical public space is unequally occupied by those with robots and those without.

According to Thomasen [82]:

The regulation of robots is interesting especially because they are expected to become prolific. A prime example of another, similarly transformative technology that reconfigured cities and prompted a range of laws restricting or reorganizing what were once common public activities was the automobile. It is not uncommon for developers and some regulators to compare the dramatic change that robotic systems will bring to public space to that of the car.

and noted that

According to this second view, for a space to serve its communal public purpose, it requires careful regulation to ensure that it is a desireable destination for members of the public.

Indeed, Thomasen concludes as follows with two principles regarding regulating robotic systems in public spaces:

First, the entry of a robotic system into a public space should never be prioritized over human access to and use of that space. And second, where a robotic system serves to make a space more accessible, lawmakers should be cautious to avoid providing differential access to that space through the regulation of that robotic system. Foundationally, lawmakers

---

[63] See also https://techcrunch.com/2019/08/07/postmates-lands-first-ever-permit-to-test-sidewalk-delivery-robots-in-san-francisco/ [last accessed: 21/10/2020].

should resist any arguments by users or manufacturers of robotic systems that public space, by virtue of its public nature, should be freely available for the use of robotics.

On another perspective on enhancing social inequality, automation with AI and robotics could take jobs from humans, especially low-skilled jobs from lower income workers, as suggested in a report;[64] this could further increase income inequality. We saw in the earlier "walking down the street" scenario that many tasks that would be done by human workers, from cooking to waste collection, were done by robots, though we think that it will be a while before robots could replace humans completely in those tasks—the idea of machines as partners with humans is a more likely scenario, at least in the near future.

3.3.2.3 Enveloping and Autonomous Urban Navigation

In Chap. 1, we have already mentioned the idea of enveloping for AI, where providing constraints within which AI can work effectively is key. It is indeed easier to build machines that work within certain environments to perform the same tasks that humans do in other environments, e.g., the dishwasher or the washing machine for laundry.

The parallel here for urban robotics is the enveloping and perhaps initially, the scaffolding, required for the urban robots to operate in the physical world, particularly in busy cities. How will the curbside need to be designed to allow delivery robots and walkway cleaning robots? How will shopping centres and arcades be designed to accommodate robots? How will the robot need to be designed to not get in the way of people or to get out of someone's way when needed? How will a robot be designed to make its way through a crowd while conforming to societal norms?

Current research attempts to build robots to work in existing real-world environments, avoiding the need to redesign or change the environment at high cost, with a combination of AI, computer vision, autonomous navigation and obstacle avoidance methods.

This continues to be a challenge, including the mapping and navigation systems required for robots, which would combine GPS based solutions with other wireless signal based positioning, LIDAR based navigation, and computer vision based navigation approaches.

Another aspect relating to the data needs of urban robots is noted in the extensive review of robots in cities in [83], which is the need for data about the city to empower robots, linking the data-centric city with the automated city. Data is then not only useful for human consumption but as a basis for providing knowledge to robots in order that they make better sense of the city and perform tasks within the city—what is called *knowledge-based environments for the city*, from [83]:

---

[64] https://www.weforum.org/agenda/2020/05/automation-robot-employment-inequality/ [last accessed: 8/10/2020].

…the need of empowering robots with the ability of reasoning with the knowledge from the city, addressing problems such as:

- leveraging semantic technologies to increase interoperability between robots and city ecosystems;
- exploiting the large amounts of machine-accessible external (and open) knowledge to improve robot tasks;
- enlarging, extending and refining the representations of domain knowledge that can be relevant to robots (and robotics in general);
- encouraging and exploiting open data initiatives.

The ability of robots to navigate in urban environments which are crowded with people is an active area of research [10, 15, 26, 33, 39, 42, 44, 45, 57, 81]—for example, the ability to understand human poses and guess the possible human trajectories, and successfully signaling to humans when proposing a cooperative navigation solution within social rules, in a way comfortable to humans, are among the complexities addressed.

What may seem easy or obvious to humans need to be programmed into robots. For example, delivery robots need to be able to find entrances (e.g., front door) to houses using AI and computer vision techniques, e.g., using semantic SLAM (Simultaneous Localization and Mapping) proposed in [25].[65] In addition, for delivery robots, there are issues such as being visible to people (so that people won't accidentally knock into or kick one), needing to go into the street when its path on the walkway is blocked, waiting around when someone is not home, and handing over the package.[66] These challenges relate to delivery robots, but there could be specific challenges for other domains.

For more complex navigation, to go where humans do go (including up and down flights of stairs and shortcuts across terrains, jumping over obstacles, etc.) in the way humans do (e.g., with politeness, varying speeds as required, and signaling or gesturing to make way and avoid collision, etc.), a question is what combination of enveloping (with possible changes to the environment) and equipping of robots to navigate the real-world will be needed. The above are research challenges that are needed to be tackled in order to make urban robot applications robust and viable in the real-world.

On enveloping for urban robots, simplifying or engineering the city to make it easier for urban robots to operate might be hard for the general public to accept, and as insightfully noted by Sumartojo et al.,[67] creating "robot-centric spaces" can "come at a cost of the loss of the very things that make public space vibrant and valuable" and "could reinforce the spatial injustices that already plague many cities".

---

[65] https://www.sciencedaily.com/releases/2019/11/191104141700.htm.

[66] https://techcrunch.com/2019/06/06/how-amazons-delivery-robots-will-navigate-your-sidewalk/.

[67] https://www.mediapolisjournal.com/2020/08/robotic-logics-of-public-space/ [last accessed: 9/6/2021].

3.3.2.4 Compositionality

One can envision a future city where the number and range of robots at a place increases over time. It would be useful if the new robots could work with the existing robots, or different deployments of robots can work together.

McCullough's vision of piling technologies in a place [58] is relevant here. One can imagine adding robots to a particular place over time (while decommissioning some), so that over time, the system of robots can grow in capability.

One can also consider how adding new robots could enhance the capabilities of existing ones, i.e., the notion of devices blending with each other and enhancing each other [74].

This is the ideas of *compositionality*, where one can compose different teams of robots from a collection for a certain purpose or function, and *complementarity*, e.g., where Apple devices (smartwatch, smartphone and laptop) might be able to complement each other in some way (e.g., the watch getting notifications from the smartphone and replaying notifications on the watch, or using the Apple watch to log into the laptop). There are questions of how robots owned and operated by different providers could inter-operate or complement each other in society.

Another aspect of compositionality is where the robots in a community, perhaps separately owned and maintained, can be pooled together in an ad hoc manner in order to meet the needs of the community at the time, e.g., the robot lawn mowers of different households are pooled together to cut the grass on sidewalks and a nearby park. Also, multiple autonomous vehicles of a neighbourhood can be pooled together voluntarily in case of an emergency situation, e.g., emergency vacuation during a bush fire.

3.3.2.5 Challenges in Organizing Urban Robots

How could the different urban robots be organized? We mentioned urban robots that the public interacts with regularly, but there could be urban robots that perform key functions without the general public noticing them. We mentioned in earlier chapters some examples of robots cooperating.

An analogy we consider here is with insect societies (e.g., bees, termites, ants), with different roles for different specialised insect forms within the same species or society, but they work together in amazing ways.

Such insect societies are said to self-organize, as it seems they are able to fulfill their respective roles without central command-and-control [9]. Each members of the insect society has a role and each performing its role yields emergent swarm behaviours.

Analogously, we can consider the notion of *robot societies*, each society comprising a collection of robots with different roles and complementary functions which swarm together to perform larger system functions.

Examples noted in [53] include organized collections, or societies, of robots for particular tasks and places. In each society of robots, each member robot has its own specialised role according to its type. Consider the following examples:

- *a collection of robots for cleaning a building*: this could include robots that vacuum, mop floors, clean windows, clean walls and clean ceilings, and robots that search and clean dirty areas continually; other smart devices in the building can aid the operation of the robots, including sensors and smart cameras (e.g., a camera detects a dirty area or a spillage on the carpet which then calls robots into the area to clean);
- *a collection of robots for garbage/waste management*: this can include robots that collect garbage from smart bins or robotic bins with wheels/legs that can move into larger bins to transfer the garbage, or robots that can collect garbage from street bins; the large bins can then move into autonomous vehicles to be transported to garbage processing sites, where other robots filter and sort the garbage and process the waste; this robot society might cooperate with the robot society for cleaning;
- *a collection of robots for managing urban food supply*: robots for growing food, robots for transporting food to places where other robots prepare and cook the food; robots/systems might take orders from customers and also deliver the food to them; a robot society around the food supply chain can be envisioned;
- *a collection of robots for transportation needs of certain sectors of society*: one can imagine a robot society comprising autonomous micro-mobility vehicles, automated taxis, autonomous trains, and autonomous wheelchairs, to provide transportation needs of a population in an area;
- *a collection of robots to help in an aged care facility*: the idea is not to take humans out of caring for the aged here but for a robot society that can perform routine tasks and allow human carers to do what only humans could do; there could be a society of robots to clean the facility, to help carers take care of the special needs of certain individuals and robots to facilitate communication between people outside the aged care home (family members) and the people living in the home (e.g., telepresence robots); and
- *a collection of robots for the library*: this can consist of robots specialised for cleaning the entire library building, robots for sorting out books, retrieving books, orientating users, helping users carry books or use the library system, facilitating interaction among visitors to the library, and handling particular queries; a robot society in the library can aid librarians in such tasks.

One can consider many other examples of such robot societies, many of which could work in the "background" without much interaction with the general public or with customers, but some might interact with users. How such societies organize themselves, and interfacing between collections of robots, will continue to be challenges and issues.

3.3.2.6   Layers of Requirements and Expectations

Robots that need to function in people-intensive applications, e.g., a robot that interacts with customers in retail, a robot that is helping to carry goods for someone, or a robot that cleans busy public streets, will need to work in ways that satisfy social norms contextualised to where they work.

Noted in [51], one can consider *layers of behaviour*:

1. *correct functional behaviour*: the robot performs its primary function it was designed for—e.g., a walking path cleaning robot should indeed clean the path properly;
2. *correct regulations-governed behaviour*: the robot, while performing its primary functions (layer (1)), does so according to the local rules and regulations—e.g., the path cleaning robot does not enter into privately own properties, or go on to the road, and must stay within public paths; and
3. *good social behaviour*: the robot performs its primary function (layer (1)) and does so abiding by the local rules and regulations (layer (2)), but also fulfills societal expectations of proper behaviour and social norms—e.g., the path cleaning robot "politely" pauses to give way to another robot or human walking past, and uses polite persuasion (e..g, "excuse me") when wanting humans (or other robots) to shift or to move out of the way (just as a human cleaner might). Related to the idea of robots needing to coordinate with each other is the interesting incident of standoffs at the Changi General Hospital in Singapore (which utilises a number of mobile robots from different manufacturers), which we will call the *robot standoff problem*—e.g., where two delivery robots are stuck in an impasse as they detect each other and unable to work out how to get around each other.[68] Hence, such good social behaviour is not only about how robots should act towards humans, but also how robots should act towards other robots (especially if they are from different manufacturers or owned by different parties)—a coordination platform or protocols among communicating robots would be required for this purpose (as we outline in Chap. 4).

Context is relevant here. There could be geo-centric rules: rules that robots need to follow while working in that particular street and rules that the robots need to follow being in that city, and rules relating to being in that country, that is, there are *geographical layers of rules* to follow.

Figure 3.8 illustrates the layers of behaviour for urban robots. This is not detailed enough to be an implementable architecture, but the idea of the layering is that layer (1) is normally the *raison d'être* for the robot, but given that they work within the urban context, layers (2) and (3) are needed above what would be required for layer (1). Moreover, often the functionalities across the layers are related—e.g., the need to fulfill layer (2) requirements at a certain time could mean that layer (1) functions

---

[68] See https://www.wired.com/story/robots-fill-workplace-must-learn-get-along/ [last accessed: 17/2/2021].

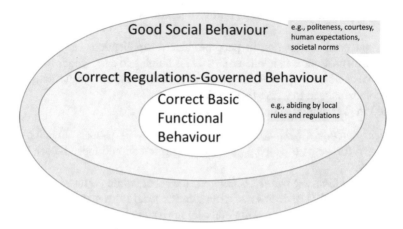

Fig. 3.8 Layers of behaviour for urban robots

cannot be fulfilled at that time, and fulfilling layer (3) requirements could ensure the long term acceptance of the technology.

3.3.3 Summary on Urban Robots

We have reviewed a range of urban robotics technologies and identified issues and challenges specific to this type of technology, including public acceptance, social inequality, autonomous urban navigation in public spaces, compositionality and complementarity of deployed robots, organization of robots into robot societies for specific functions, and layers of social and functional requirements. There are, of course, other concerns such as the ethical behaviour of these robots and the ethical behaviour of people towards these robots, and relevant laws that would apply or possibly new laws developed, as discussed in detail in [86] and in [82].

3.4 Urban Drones

Drones, sometimes called Unmanned Aerial Vehicles (UAVs), come in different shapes and sizes and have been used by military and hobbyists. Different sizes of drones can carry different weights over varying distances. There have been interesting developments in not just the technology of drones, but in their deployment. For example, the FAA issued Amazon Prime Air[69] a certificate on August 29, 2020 allowing Amazon to use Unmanned Aircraft Systems (UAS) to operate commercially, towards a vision of 30 min delivery time.[70]

Back in 2017, Amazon has patented an idea for a bee-hive like drone station[71] as well as a flying warehouse.[72] Figure 3.9a and b show the drone station and flying warehouse concepts.

There have been trials for using drones for delivery in over 20 countries around the world,[73] from deliver medical supplies to parcels and pizzas.[74]

Beside the delivery of goods, the idea of beating traffic jams in busy cities and reducing travel times between destinations using air-taxis for people has been widely publicised—also called *urban air mobility* systems. There are a number of companies working on urban air mobility solutions. One example is Uber's Elevate intiative[75] which includes Uber Air and Uber Copter programs taking ride-sharing to the air. The Volocopter[76] air taxi service is being trialled and soon to be a service in particular cities. The company also looks into building ports for its drones, called Voloports. Many of such air taxis would be expected to work autonomously, without a trained pilot on-board, and be electric/battery powered—often called eVTOL (Electric Vertical Take Off and Landing) vehicles. A recent project aims to build an urban air port for such eVTOL vehicles in the United Kingdom.[77] Instead of air-taxis, these eVTOL vehicles can also be ambulances.[78] An extensive review of market opportunities, the regulatory environment, vehicle design, operational challenges for eVTOL vehicles in Australia is given in [16].

---

[69] https://www.amazon.com/Amazon-Prime-Air/b?ie=UTF8&node=8037720011 [last accessed: 26/10/2020].

[70] https://www.businessinsider.com.au/amazon-prime-air-delivery-drones-faa-ruling-2020-8?r= US&IR=T.

[71] See https://www.theguardian.com/technology/2017/jun/26/amazon-drones-delivery-beehive-patent; original US patent: http://appft.uspto.gov/netacgi/nph-Parser?Sect1=PTO1&Sect2= HITOFF&d=PG01&p=1&u=/netahtml/PTO/srchnum.html&r=1&f=G&l=50&s1=20170175413. PGNR.&OS=&RS= (MULTI-LEVEL FULFILLMENT CENTER FOR UNMANNED AERIAL VEHICLES).

[72] See US patent: http://patft1.uspto.gov/netacgi/nph-Parser?Sect1=PTO1&Sect2=HITOFF&d= PALL&p=1&u=%2Fnetahtml%2FPTO%2Fsrchnum.htm&r=1&f=G&l=50&s1=9305280.PN.& OS=PN/9305280&RS=PN/9305280 (Airborne fulfillment center utilizing unmanned aerial vehicles for item delivery).

[73] https://www.unmannedairspace.info/latest-news-and-information/drone-delivery-operations-underway-in-26-countries/ [last accessed: 26/10/2020].

[74] See https://www.chargedretail.co.uk/2020/01/29/top-5-upcoming-retail-drone-delivery-services/ [last accessed: 2/11/2020].

[75] https://www.uber.com/in/en/elevate/ [last accessed: 26/10/2020].

[76] https://www.volocopter.com/en/ [last accessed: 26/10/2020].

[77] See https://www.coventry.gov.uk/news/article/3691/world-first_electric_urban_air_port_secures_uk_government_backing [last accessed: 3/4/2021].

[78] See the design concept at https://www.argodesign.com/work/drone-ambulance-argodesign.html [last accessed: 16/3/2021].

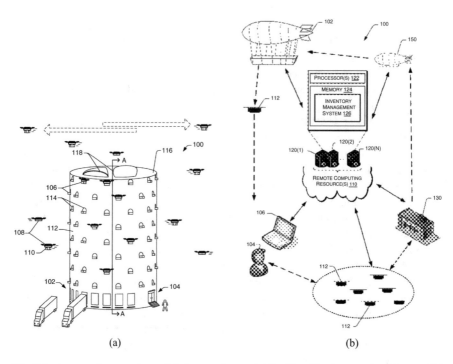

Fig. 3.9 Amazon drone station and flying warehouse. (**a**) Beehive-like drone station (Source: US patent pub. no.: 2017/0175413 A1, 2017). (**b**) Flying warehouse (airship) concept (Source: US patent No. 9,305,280 B1, 2016)

The degree of automation of drones and what aspect of a drone is automated can vary. Drones can be viewed to have different levels of autonomy (similar to automated vehicles).[79] Similar to the SAE levels for automated vehicles on the road, a scale for drone autonomy proposes the following five levels:[80]

- Level 0: no automation, the drone is manually controlled
- Level 1: low automation, the drone autonomously controls one key function but the rest is human controlled
- Level 2: partial automation, the drone takes over more functions but the human pilot retains full responsibility for operations
- Level 3: conditional automation, the drone can perform all functions without human control but the human pilot acts as a fall-back
- Level 4: high automation, the drone is fully autonomous, and has backup systems and is failure-safe, and the human pilot is out of the loop
- Level 5: full automation, the drone uses AI tools to plan their own flights

---

[79] https://www.ansys.com/blog/challenges-developing-fully-autonomous-drone-technology [last accessed: 26/10/2020].

[80] https://dronelife.com/2019/03/11/droneii-tech-talk-unraveling-5-levels-of-drone-autonomy/ [last accessed: 26/10/2020].

Such scales might vary depending on the type of drone and how the drone is used. As AI technologies improve and with the ability to run AI algorithms on resource-constrained devices, drones can become increasingly autonomous.

Note that the technology required is not only the drones involved, but the relevant infrastructure that needs to go with the drones, including places to land drones, ways for drones to drop goods and people off (and pick them up), stations for drones to refuel and to be serviced, and mechanisms needed to monitor these drones and to regulate and manage their flights and urban air traffic.

The above are some key developments from sizeable companies but many other companies are exploring the notion of drones for goods and people delivery.[81]

Indeed, beyond moving goods and people, drones, whether manually piloted or autonomous, have myriad uses, from various types of monitoring, movie-filming, fun-making, to wildlife monitoring. We discuss further applications in the next section.

3.4.1 The Potential of Urban Drones

Recent reviews of urban drone applications suggest the many promising ways in which drones can be used; applications include:

- *delivery of goods and supplies*: drones can deliver goods faster beating land transport and traffic jams, and in some cases, can be greener and more energy efficient, especially with smaller sized drones [79]; it is also ideal for places with poor roads, hard to reach via land or sea transport, and remote or rural areas in countries such as the UK, Korea, Malawi, China, Canada, Australia, and elsewhere[82]
- *transportation of people*: there has been recent excitement about air taxis or eVTOL vehicles that can beat traffic jams and shorten travel times, especially, connecting remote communities to cities as mentioned; but eVTOL vehicles can also be greener provided the batteries are charged via renewable supplies; the idea of direct building-to-building transportation via drones can also be considered, as illustrated in Fig. 3.10, which can be more efficient than moving small goods up and down through buildings and across the busy city in a land vehicle.

---

[81]For example, see a recent review at https://www.digitaltrends.com/cars/all-the-flying-cars-and-taxis-currently-in-development/.

[82]For example, see https://www.unicefusa.org/stories/long-range-drones-deliver-medical-supplies-remote-areas-malawi/36084, https://360.here.com/drone-delivery-healthcare, https://www.suasnews.com/2020/06/drone-delivery-to-be-available-for-remote-areas-in-korea/, https://www.aljazeera.com/videos/2020/06/28/uk-tests-drone-to-deliver-medical-supplies-to-remote-areas/,https://www.unicef.org/wca/press-releases/drones-good-corridor-launched-drones-take-flight-deliver-medicine-remote-areas, https://www.abc.net.au/triplej/programs/hack/lifesaving-drones-delivering-blood/10107932 [26/10/2020].

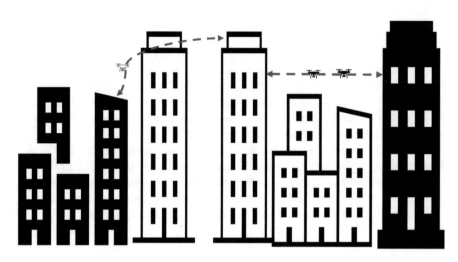

Fig. 3.10 An illustration of building-to-building transportation via drones. Dotted red lines indicate flight paths for drones transferring items between buildings with stations within buildings themselves

- *urban environment monitoring*: drones can provide an efficient way to monitor air pollution in a city—there are already commercial deployments[83] as more automated solutions continue to be researched [8, 32, 70, 90]; drones can also monitor buildings, bridges and city infrastructure.
- *health and emergency*: drones can be used in a number of health and emergency settings; one example is the use of drones to deliver Automated External Defibrillators (AEDs);[84] research has shown that drones for AED delivery is safe, feasible and can shorten response times [12, 73] but further research with real-life studies is still required [59]; a range of applications for health care include using drones to deliver blood and medical supplies, and even helping the elderly[85]— Professor Hovakimyan "believes that drones could ultimately be used to perform all manner of household chores, like reaching under a table to grab an object, cleaning chandeliers and weeding the lawn"[86]
- *security*: drones can be used for surveillance and security monitoring, not only of buildings but also in homes; an interesting application of the idea of sensors

---

[83] For example, see companies with drones for air monitoring: https://www.aeroqual.com/outdoor-air-quality-monitors/urban-air-monitoring, https://www.libelium.com/libeliumworld/success-stories/3d-air-quality-modeling-with-sensor-drones-in-greece/, and https://botlink.com/air-quality-drone [last accessed: 2/11/2020].

[84] https://www.heart.org/en/news/2019/11/15/drone-delivered-aeds-fly-a-step-closer-to-saving-lives [last accessed: 28/1/2021].

[85] https://www.dronesinhealthcare.com [last accessed: 1/11/2020].

[86] https://healthmanagement.org/c/it/news/the-future-is-coming-drones-and-healthcare   [last accessed: 1/11/2020].

and autonomous drones working together for security monitoring is a solution by the company Sunflower labs[87] which has a developed a system that can sense a disturbance at a property (via a network of motion and vibration sensors called "Sunflowers") and send a message to the property owner—the owner can then launch an autonomous drone (called the "Bee") to obtain real-time footage of the property;[88]

- *repairs and assembly*: the recently funded project on drones for repairing potholes and streetlights[89] has provided a vision of drones not just as passive observers but as actuators, able to do things in cities; indeed there have been demonstrations of drones for assembling structures though very much at a nascent stage[90]

Many other applications of *drones as a service* in the urban context are discussed in [4, 28, 64]. The impact of drones on urban design has been extensively discussed in [17].

3.4.2 Issues and Limitations

In [3], a range of issues with urban drones have been identified. We review some of these issues below as well as further considerations.

- *City aesthetics.* The impacts of drones on the environment as well as noise have been considered in a recent Australian National Aviation Policy Issues Paper on Emerging Aviation Technologies.[91] However, another aspect to highlight is the notion of city aesthetics. There have been various demonstrations of drone swarms as a light show mainly as events,[92] but light shows aside, more broadly speaking, if drones were to be used, say for deliveries, on a much larger scale, the city skyline could be affected (hence, the aesthetics concern) with drones appearing in mass haphazardly in the sky (even if silent) unless the drones are routed along particular pathways (e.g., "air highways") for most of their journeys (imagining streams of drones moving orderly through the sky, as part of the city skyline, which can perhaps even contribute to aesthetics positively); a question

---

[87] https://www.sunflower-labs.com [last accessed: 2/11/2020].

[88] https://www.unmannedsystemstechnology.com/2020/01/fully-autonomous-residential-security-drone-announced/ [last accessed: 28/1/2021].

[89] The project is a 4.2 million pounds project in the UK, though futuristic, has met with some skepticism: https://spectrum.ieee.org/automaton/robotics/industrial-robots/you-probably-shouldnt-expect-city-repairing-drones-any-time-soon [last accessed: 2/11/2020].

[90] https://raffaello.name/projects/flight-assembled-architecture/ [last accessed: 28/1/2021].

[91] https://www.infrastructure.gov.au/aviation/drones/ [last accessed: 19/11/2020].

[92] For example, see https://skymagic.show/ [last accessed: 19/11/2020].

is how we will allow drones to shape the city skyline if they would be used on a large scale, in the longer term.

- *Regulatory framework around new infrastructure, ground and in the air.* eVTOL vehicles and drones would require recharging stations, ports (for pick up and drop off) and drone stations. There could be a need for policy/rules regarding where such drone ground stations could be sited and their impact on the locality, as well as a policy on what types of in-air stations should be allowed and where they can be located. Also, regulations to ensure fair use of air spaces and balancing interests of multiple stakeholders, from city inhabitants to drone service operators, will be needed.
- *Identification of drones and their purpose/intention of flight from afar via wireless electronic means.* A question is whether such a wireless electronic identification system can and should be developed, and who would be able to interrogate such drones to extract this information, and whether the public should be permitted to extract some of these information if the drones are going over public/private air-spaces.
- *Drones flying over private property.* If drones are permitted to fly over private property, there are issues of access—above a certain altitude is likely less obtrusive (not only in terms of noise but also visual aesthetics)—a question is whether there will be mechanisms to buy/rent-out access to low-attitude airspace over private property.
- *Drones for actuation.* Several key uses of drones/eVTOLs were mentioned earlier include transport and passive forms of surveillance, but also mentioned is the category of applications of drones for actuation, with the ability to repair hard-to-reach objects or certain actions (e.g., via a robotic arm) or using drones in construction – to consider more futuristic applications; there would be a need for further consideration of this category of drones, including what they are permitted to do.
- *Mandating certain safety features on drones.* There would be a need to mandate certain safety features on drones, e.g., akin to parachutes and airbags (analogous to the Australian ANCAP safety rating for road vehicles). Also, there could be a need for resilient blackbox recorders for drones to record flight events in case of incidents (though how secure they can be is a question) and companies operating drone services might need to keep a record of all flights of their drones which are presumably tracked (for improved traceability and accountability, in case of the need for any future investigations into incidents).
- *Security of drones and drone protection rules.* There could be a need for certification of drones, not only that they are mechanically "air-worthy" but also that they have basic cyber-security features embedded (or "cyber-worthy" to coin a term). For example, their communications need to be encrypted and protected, so that they cannot be easily hacked and hijacked or their communications easily intercepted. Also, the use of geo-fencing is needed for example to detect drones in no-fly zones or to exclude the drones, but geo-fencing devices are potentially hackable via GPS spoofing—laws/rules for property protection would need to be adapted for drone protection.

3.4.3 Summary on Urban Drones

We have reviewed a range of possible drone applications in cities, covering autonomous drones as well as piloted drones, but it is hard to be comprehensive given that what they can be used for depends on the imagination of many. However, technical and societal issues to ensure safety and best use of such drones (and eVTOL vehicles) and services deployed via drones will need to be addressed—these issues will evolve as the technology evolves and would require a gradual acceptance from the general public. Indeed, drones can bring economic and environmental benefits, but a broader societal engagement in the discussion of drones in public spaces, and further studies on demonstrating drone benefits will still be needed—see also [37].

3.5 Summary of Chapter

This chapter has reviewed three different types of advanced ICT technologies that are fast emerging in cities. All three involve not only AI and IoT but also communications and networking infrastructure to support their effective operations. They are inter-related and could work together, e.g., as part of a full scale city wide transportation infrastructure.

Their introduction to cities will be gradual. For example, initially, automated vehicles might only be allowed in certain areas, restricted to certain lanes, or be used for certain specific purposes (e.g., transportation of passengers between airport terminals and hotels, robotaxis in certain areas, particular freight routes, or within a large park). Urban robots might only be employed for delivery and other purposes in certain areas at first and at certain times of the day. And autonomous drones, of certain forms and sizes, and with specific supporting sensors and infrastructure, may only be allowed to fly over certain zones along certain routes. And then, as the technologies and accompanying regulations mature, the scope of their use and activity can increase.

There are many questions still to be answered. To what extent will a city's real estate be devoted to such machines? How will humans share life and city spaces with autonomous machines? How will humans cohabitate with such machines and work effectively with them? Will such machines be inter-connected so that any machine can "talk" to any other machine, if and when needed (of course, likely, not every machine will need to talk to every other machine)? Will cities thrive or strive with such machines?

Perhaps the automated city of the future will have AVs, robots and drones as commonplace, as a new norm, without its inhabitants even worrying about their presence. While they may exist in preliminary forms in the near future, and through a gradual process, such technologies could mature so that they become more advanced and can automate an increasing number of tasks, while maintaining safety and social acceptance.

References

1. Alfeo, A. L., Ferrer, E. C., Carrillo, Y. L., Grignard, A., Pastor, L. A., Sleeper, D. T., Cimino, M. G. C. A., Lepri, B., Vaglini, G., Larson, K., Dorigo, M., & Pentland, A. (2019). Urban swarms: A new approach for autonomous waste management. In *2019 International Conference on Robotics and Automation (ICRA)* (pp. 4233–4240).
2. Aliedani, A., Loke, S. W., & Glaser, S. (2020). Robust cooperative car-parking: Implications and solutions for selfish inter-vehicular social behaviour. *Human-Centric Computing and Information Sciences, 10*(1), 37.
3. Alwateer, M., & Loke, S. W. (2020). Emerging drone services: Challenges and societal issues. *IEEE Technology and Society Magazine, 39*(3), 47–51.
4. Alwateer, M., Loke, S. W., & Zuchowicz, A. M. (2019). Drone services: Issues in drones for location-based services from human-drone interaction to information processing. *Journal of Location Based Services, 13*(2), 94–127.
5. Awad, E., Dsouza, S., Kim, R., Schulz, J., Henrich, J., Shariff, A., Bonnefon, J.-F., & Rahwan, I. (2018). The moral machine experiment. *Nature, 563*(7729), 59–64.
6. Bensrhair, A., Morando, M. M., Tian, Q., Truong, L. T., & Vu, H. L. (2018). Studying the safety impact of autonomous vehicles using simulation-based surrogate safety measures. *Journal of Advanced Transportation, 2018*, 6135183.
7. Bezai, N. E., Medjdoub, B., Al-Habaibeh, A., Chalal, M. L., & Fadli, F. (2021). Future cities and autonomous vehicles: Analysis of the barriers to full adoption. *Energy and Built Environment, 2*(1), 65–81.
8. Bolla, G. M., Casagrande, M., Comazzetto, A., Dal Moro, R., Destro, M., Fantin, E., Colombatti, G., Aboudan, A., & Lorenzini, E. C. (2018). ARIA: air pollutants monitoring using UAVs. In *2018 5th IEEE International Workshop on Metrology for AeroSpace (MetroAeroSpace)* (pp. 225–229).
9. Camazine, S., Franks, N. R., Sneyd, J., Bonabeau, E., Deneubourg, J.-L., & Theraula, G. (2001). *Self-organization in biological systems*. Princeton, NJ: Princeton University Press.
10. Chen, X., Milioto, A., Palazzolo, E., Giguère, P., Behley, J., & Stachniss, C. (2019). Suma++: Efficient lidar-based semantic slam. In *2019 IEEE/RSJ International Conference on Intelligent Robots and Systems (IROS)* (pp. 4530–4537).
11. Chen, Y., Wu, F., Shuai, W., & Chen, X. (2017). Robots serve humans in public places—KeJia robot as a shopping assistant. *International Journal of Advanced Robotic Systems, 14*(3), 1729881417703569.
12. Cheskes, S., McLeod, S. L., Nolan, M., Snobelen, P., Vaillancourt, C., Brooks, S. C., Dainty, K. N., Chan, T. C. Y., & Drennan, I. R. (2020). Improving access to automated external defibrillators in rural and remote settings: A drone delivery feasibility study. *Journal of the American Heart Association, 9*(14), e016687.
13. Colwell, I., Phan, B., Saleem, S., Salay, R., & Czarnecki, K. (2018). An automated vehicle safety concept based on runtime restriction of the operational design domain. In *2018 IEEE Intelligent Vehicles Symposium (IV)* (pp. 1910–1917).
14. Combs, T. S., Sandt, L. S., Clamann, M. P., & McDonald, N. C. (2019). Automated vehicles and pedestrian safety: Exploring the promise and limits of pedestrian detection. *American Journal of Preventive Medicine, 56*(1), 1–7.
15. Corominas Murtra, A., Trulls, E., Torres, O. S., Pérez-Ibarz, J., Vasquez, D., Mirats-Tur, J., Ferrer, M., & Sanfeliu, A. (2010). Autonomous navigation for urban service mobile robots (pp. 4141–4146).
16. Creighton, D., Parsons, H., Alvarez, L. M. U., Gunn, B., Perez-Franco, R., & Johnstone, M. (2020). *Advanced Aerial Mobility and eVTOL aircraft in Australia: Promise and Challenges*. Technical report, Deakin University, Australia, 09 2020. https://www.deakin.edu.au/__data/assets/pdf_file/0010/2213794/Deakin-University-Mobility-Whitepaper-Advanced-Aerial-Mobility-and-eVTOL-aircraft-in-Australia.pdf

17. Cureton, P. (2020). *Drone Futures: UAS in Landscape and Urban Design*. Routledge: Taylor & Francis Group.
18. Darragh, M., Ahn, H. S., MacDonald, B., Liang, A., Peri, K., Kerse, N., & Broadbent, E. (2017). Homecare robots to improve health and well-being in mild cognitive impairment and early stage dementia: Results from a scoping study. *Journal of the American Medical Directors Association, 18*(12), 1099.e1–1099.e4.
19. De Lara, S. (2020). *The Driverless City: How Will AVs Shape Cities in the Future?* PhD thesis.
20. Demmel, S., Gruyer, D., Burkhardt, J.-M., Glaser, S., Larue, G., Orfila, O., & Rakotonirainy, A. (2019). Global risk assessment in an autonomous driving context: Impact on both the car and the driver. In B. Mettler (Ed.), *Proceedings of the 2nd IFAC Conference on Cyber-Physical and Human Systems CPHS 2018 (IFAC-PapersOnLine, Vol. 51, Issue 34). Vol. 51. [34 ed.]*, IFAC-PapersOnLine (pp. 390–395). International Federation of Automatic Control (IFAC), France, January 2019.
21. Desai, P., Loke, S. W., Desai, A., & Singh, J. (2013). CARAVAN: congestion avoidance and route allocation using virtual agent negotiation. *IEEE Transactions on Intelligent Transportation Systems, 14*(3), 1197–1207.
22. Duarte, F., & Ratti, C. (2018). The impact of autonomous vehicles on cities: A review. *Journal of Urban Technology, 25*(4), 3–18.
23. Elhenawy, M., Ashqar, H. I., Masoud, M., Almannaa, M. H., Rakotonirainy, A., & Rakha, H. A. (2020). Deep transfer learning for vulnerable road users detection using smartphone sensors data. *Remote Sensing, 12*(21). Article number: 3508.
24. Endsley, M. R. (2019). The limits of highly autonomous vehicles: An uncertain future. *Ergonomics, 62*(4), 496–499.
25. Everett, M., Miller, J., & How, J. P. (2019). Planning beyond the sensing horizon using a learned context. In *2019 IEEE/RSJ International Conference on Intelligent Robots and Systems (IROS)* (pp. 1064–1071).
26. Ferrer, G., Garrell, A., & Sanfeliu, A. (2013). Social-aware robot navigation in urban environments. In *2013 European Conference on Mobile Robots* (pp. 331–336).
27. Ferri, G., Manzi, A., Salvini, P., Mazzolai, B., Laschi, C., & Dario, P. (2011). Dustcart, an autonomous robot for door-to-door garbage collection: From dustbot project to the experimentation in the small town of peccioli. In *2011 IEEE International Conference on Robotics and Automation* (pp. 655–660).
28. Gallacher, D. (2017). Drone applications for environmental management in urban spaces: A review. *International Journal of Sustainable Land Use and Urban Planning, 3*, 1–14.
29. Gambi, A., Huynh, T., & Fraser, G. (2019). Generating effective test cases for self-driving cars from police reports. In *Proceedings of the 2019 27th ACM Joint Meeting on European Software Engineering Conference and Symposium on the Foundations of Software Engineering*, ESEC/FSE 2019 (pp. 257–267). New York, NY: Association for Computing Machinery.
30. Gavanas, N. (2019). Autonomous road vehicles: Challenges for urban planning in European cities. *Urban Science, 3*(2), 61.
31. Gruyer, D., Orfila, O., Glaser, S., Hedhli, A., Hautière, N., & Rakotonirainy, A. (2021). Are connected and automated vehicles the silver bullet for future transportation challenges? Benefits and weaknesses on safety, consumption, and traffic congestion. *Frontiers in Sustainable Cities, 2*, 63.
32. Grych, I., Ben-Aboud, Y., Guermah, B., Sbihi, N., Ghogho, M., & Kobbane, A. (2020). MoreAir: A low-cost urban air pollution monitoring system. *Sensors, 20*(4), 998.
33. Hacinecipoglu, A. (2019). *Human Aware Navigation of a Mobile Robot in Crowded Dynamic Environments*. PhD thesis, The Graduate School of Natural and Applied Sciences of Middle East Technical University, Ankara, Turkey, 2019. http://etd.lib.metu.edu.tr/upload/12624119/index.pdf
34. Hancock, P. A., Nourbakhsh, I., & Stewart, J. (2019). On the future of transportation in an era of automated and autonomous vehicles. *Proceedings of the National Academy of Sciences, 116*(16), 7684–7691.

35. Ivanov, S., & Webster, C. (2019). Robots in tourism: A research agenda for tourism economics. *Tourism Economics*, 135481661987958.
36. Jensen, B., Tomatis, N., Mayor, L., Drygajlo, A., & Siegwart, R. (2005). Robots meet humans-interaction in public spaces. *IEEE Transactions on Industrial Electronics, 52*(6), 1530–1546 (2005)
37. Kellermann, R., Biehle, T., & Fischer, L. (2020). Drones for parcel and passenger transportation: A literature review. *Transportation Research Interdisciplinary Perspectives, 4*, 100088.
38. Khakzar, M., Rakotonirainy, A., Bond, A., & Dehkordi, S. G. (2020) . A dual learning model for vehicle trajectory prediction. *IEEE Access, 8*, 21897–21908. Article number: 8966366.
39. Khambhaita, H., & Alami, R. (2020). Viewing robot navigation in human environment as a cooperative activity. In N. M. Amato, G. Hager, S. Thomas, & M. Torres-Torriti (Eds.), *Robotics research* (pp. 285–300). Cham: Springer International Publishing.
40. Kim, K., Kim, J. S., Jeong, S. S., Park, J.-H., & Kim, H. K. (2021). Cybersecurity for autonomous vehicles: Review of attacks and defense. *Computers and Security, 103*, 102150.
41. Klischat, M., & Althoff, M. (2019). Generating critical test scenarios for automated vehicles with evolutionary algorithms. In *2019 IEEE Intelligent Vehicles Symposium (IV)* (pp. 2352–2358).
42. Kruse, T., Pandey, A. K., Alami, R., & Kirsch, A. (2013). Human-aware robot navigation: A survey. *Robotics and Autonomous Systems, 61*(12), 1726–1743.
43. Kuhn, C. B., Hofbauer, M., Petrovic, G., & Steinbach, E. (2020). Introspective failure prediction for autonomous driving using late fusion of state and camera information. In *IEEE Transactions on Intelligent Transportation Systems* (pp. 1–15).
44. Kümmerle, R., Ruhnke, M., Steder, B., Stachniss, C., & Burgard, W. (2015). Autonomous robot navigation in highly populated pedestrian zones. *Journal of Field Robotics, 32*(4), 565–589.
45. Kümmerle, R., Ruhnke, M., Steder, B., Stachniss, C., & Burgard, W. (2013). A navigation system for robots operating in crowded urban environments. In *2013 IEEE International Conference on Robotics and Automation* (pp. 3225–3232).
46. Lim, H. S. M., & Taeihagh, A. (2018). Autonomous vehicles for smart and sustainable cities: An in-depth exploration of privacy and cybersecurity implications. *Energies, 11*(5), 1062.
47. Lim, H. S. M., & Taeihagh, A. (2019). Algorithmic decision-making in AVs: Understanding ethical and technical concerns for smart cities. *Sustainability, 11*(20), 1–28 (2019)
48. Liu, S., Li, L., Tang, J., Wu, S., & Gaudiot, J. L. (2017). *Creating autonomous vehicle systems* (2017). https://doi.org/10.2200/S00787ED1V01Y201707CSL009
49. Loke, S. W. (2019). Cooperative automated vehicles: A review of opportunities and challenges in socially intelligent vehicles beyond networking. *IEEE Transactions on Intelligent Vehicles, 4*(4), 509–518.
50. Loke, S. W. (2018). Are we ready for the internet of robotic things in public spaces? In *Proceedings of the 2018 ACM International Joint Conference and 2018 International Symposium on Pervasive and Ubiquitous Computing and Wearable Computers, UbiComp '18* (pp. 891–900). New York, NY: ACM.
51. Loke, S. W. (2018). Are we ready for the internet of robotic things in public spaces? In *Proceedings of the 2018 ACM International Joint Conference and 2018 International Symposium on Pervasive and Ubiquitous Computing and Wearable Computers, UbiComp '18* (pp. 891–900). New York, NY: Association for Computing Machinery.
52. Loke, S. W. (2019). *Achieving ethical algorithmic behaviour in the internet-of-things: A review*. CoRR abs/1910.10241.
53. Loke, S. W. (2019). Towards robotic things in society. CoRR abs/1910.10253.
54. Lupetti, M., & Cila, N. (2019). Envisioning and questioning near future urban robotics. In *Desform 2019*.
55. Macrorie, R., Marvin, S., & While, A. (2019). Robotics and automation in the city: A research agenda. *Urban Geography, 42*, 1–21.
56. Marr, J., Zhang, A., Benjamin, S., & Wall, J. (2020). *Implications of Pavement Markings for Machine Vision (Austroads publication no. AP-R633-20)*. Technical report, Austroads Ltd.

57. Mavrogiannis, C., Hutchinson, A. M., Macdonald, J., Alves-Oliveira, P., & Knepper, R. A. (2019). Effects of distinct robot navigation strategies on human behavior in a crowded environment. In *2019 14th ACM/IEEE International Conference on Human-Robot Interaction (HRI)* (pp. 421–430).

58. McCullough, M. (2004). *Digital ground: Architecture, pervasive computing, and environmental knowing*. Cambridge, MA: MIT Press.

59. Mermiri, M. I., Mavrovounis, G. A., & Pantazopoulos, I. N. (2020). Drones for automated external defibrillator delivery: Where do we stand? *Journal of Emergency Medicine, 59*(5), 660–667.

60. Milakis, D., van Arem, B., & van Wee, B. (2017). Policy and society related implications of automated driving: A review of literature and directions for future research. *Journal of Intelligent Transportation Systems, 21*(4), 324–348.

61. Morgulis, N., Kreines, A., Mendelowitz, S., & Weisglass, Y. (2019). Fooling a real car with adversarial traffic signs. CoRR abs/1907.00374.

62. Mubin, O., Kharub, I., & Khan, A. (2020). Pepper in the library students' first impressions. In *Extended Abstracts of the 2020 CHI Conference on Human Factors in Computing Systems, CHI EA '20* (pp. 1–9), New York, NY: Association for Computing Machinery.

63. Nagenborg, M. (2020). Urban robotics and responsible urban innovation. *Ethics and Information Technology, 22*, 345–355.

64. Noor, N. M., Abdullah, A., & Hashim, M. (2018). Remote sensing UAV/drones and its applications for urban areas: a review. *IOP Conference Series: Earth and Environmental Science, 169*, 012003.

65. Noy, I. Y., Shinar, D., & Horrey, W. J. (2018). Automated driving: Safety blind spots. *Safety Science, 102*, 68–78.

66. Okur, E., Kumar, S. H., Sahay, S., Esme, A. A., & Nachman, L. (2019). Natural language interactions in autonomous vehicles: Intent detection and slot filling from passenger utterances. CoRR abs/1904.10500.

67. Okur, E., Kumar, S. H., Sahay, S., & Nachman, L. (2019). Towards multimodal understanding of passenger-vehicle interactions in autonomous vehicles: Intent/slot recognition utilizing audio-visual data. CoRR abs/1909.13714.

68. Okur, E., Kumar, S. H., Sahay, S., & Nachman, L. (2020). Audio-visual understanding of passenger intents for in-cabin conversational agents. In *Second Grand-Challenge and Workshop on Multimodal Language (Challenge-HML)*, (pp. 55–59). Seattle: Association for Computational Linguistics.

69. Riek, L. D. (2017). Healthcare robotics. *Communications of the ACM, 60*(11), 68–78.

70. Rohi, G., Ejofodomi, O., & Ofualagba, G. (2020). Autonomous monitoring, analysis, and countering of air pollution using environmental drones. *Heliyon, 6*(1), e03252.

71. Sabelli, A. M., & Kanda, T. (2016). Robovie as a mascot: A qualitative study for long-term presence of robots in a shopping mall. *International Journal of Social Robotics, 8*(2), 211–221.

72. Salvini, P. (2018). Urban robotics: Towards responsible innovations for our cities. *Robotics and Autonomous Systems, 100*, 278–286.

73. Sanfridsson, J., Sparrevik, J., Hollenberg, J., Nordberg, P., Djärv, T., Ringh, M., Svensson, L., Forsberg, S., Nord, A., Andersson-Hagiwara, M., & Claesson, A. (2019). Drone delivery of an automated external defibrillator –a mixed method simulation study of bystander experience. *Scandinavian Journal of Trauma, Resuscitation and Emergency Medicine, 27*(1), 40.

74. Seera, H., Loke, S. W., & Torabi, T. (2007). Towards device-blending: Model and challenges. In *21st International Conference on Advanced Information Networking and Applications (AINA 2007), Workshops Proceedings, Volume 2, May 21–23, 2007, Niagara Falls* (pp. 139–146).

75. Seuwou, P., Banissi, E., & Ubakanma, G. (2020). *The future of mobility with connected and autonomous vehicles in smart cities* (pp. 37–52). Cham: Springer International Publishing.

76. Sheehan, B., Murphy, F., Mullins, M., & Ryan, C. (2019). Connected and autonomous vehicles: A cyber-risk classification framework. *Transportation Research Part A: Policy and Practice, 124*, 523–536.

77. Sitawarin, C., Bhagoji, A. N., Mosenia, A., Chiang, M., & Mittal, P. (2018). DARTS: Deceiving autonomous cars with toxic signs. CoRR abs/1802.06430

78. Smith, C. (2016). *The car hacker's handbook: A guide for the penetration tester* (1st ed.). New York: No Starch Press.

79. Stolaroff, J. K., Samaras, C., O'Neill, E. R., Lubers, A., Mitchell, A. S., & Ceperley, D. (2018). Energy use and life cycle greenhouse gas emissions of drones for commercial package delivery. *Nature Communications, 9*(1), 409.

80. Tella, A. (2020). Robots are coming to the libraries: Are librarians ready to accommodate them? *Library Hi Tech News, 37,* 13–17.

81. Thomas, J. (2019). *Autonomy, Social Agency, and the Integration of Human and Robot Environments.* PhD thesis, School of Computing Science Faculty of Applied Science, Simon Fraser University. https://summit.sfu.ca/item/19889

82. Thomasen, K. (2020). Robots, regulation, and the changing nature of public spaces. *Ottawa Law Review, 51*(2), 38.

83. Tiddi, I., Bastianelli, E., Daga, E., d'Aquin, M., & Motta, E. (2020). Robot–city interaction: Mapping the research landscape—a survey of the interactions between robots and modern cities. *International Journal of Social Robotics, 12*(2), 299–324.

84. Tonkin, M., Vitale, J., Herse, S., Williams, M.-A., Judge, W., & Wang, X. (2018). Design methodology for the UX of HRI: A field study of a commercial social robot at an airport. In *Proceedings of the 2018 ACM/IEEE International Conference on Human-Robot Interaction, HRI '18* (pp. 407–415), New York, NY: ACM.

85. Trubia, S., Giuffrè, T., Canale, A., & Severino, A. (2017). Automated vehicle: a review of road safety implications as driver of change. In *Proceedings of the 27th CARSP (Canadian Association of Road Safety Professionals) Conference.* http://www.carsp.ca/research/research-papers/proceedings/2017-toronto/

86. Turner, J. (2019). *Robot rules: Regulating artificial intelligence.* Cham: Palgrave Macmillan.

87. van der Heijden, R. W., Dietzel, S., Leinmüller, T., & Kargl, F. (2016). *Survey on misbehavior detection in cooperative intelligent transportation systems.* CoRR abs/1610.06810.

88. Vandemeulebroucke, T., de Casterlé, B. D., & Gastmans, C. (2018). The use of care robots in aged care: A systematic review of argument-based ethics literature. *Archives of Gerontology and Geriatrics, 74,* 15–25.

89. Wen, M., Park, J., & Cho, K. (2020). A scenario generation pipeline for autonomous vehicle simulators. *Human-centric Computing and Information Sciences, 10*(1), 24.

90. Yu, G., Alvear, O., Zema, N. R., Natalizio, E., & Calafate, C. T. (2017). Using UAV-based systems to monitor air pollution in areas with poor accessibility. *Journal of Advanced Transportation, 2017,* 8204353.

Chapter 4
The Future of the Automated City: Social, Technical and Ethical Perspectives

Abstract The previous chapter discussed particular issues in relation to Automated Vehicles, urban robots and urban drones. This chapter discusses visions, perspectives and challenges of the Automated City more generally, including aspirational visions of future cities, what must be overcome or addressed towards a favourable notion of the Automated City, and issues of governance, new business models, city transportation, sustainability, real-time tracking, urban edge computing, blockchain, technical challenges of cooperation, and trust, fairness and ethics in relation to AI and algorithms in the city—we elaborate on the last two aspects in more detail.

4.1 Visions of Future Cities

There have been many future visions of cities, of what cities in the future could look like, some of which are based on what some cities look like today or what certain cities are becoming.

The previous chapters have looked at upcoming technologies as well as metaphors for the Automated City, including the Automated City as partner and as host. However, beyond the technological trends we considered, clearly, the structure, layout, design and shape of a city can be influenced by a wide range of considerations, including walkability, sustainability, resilience, culture and history, and aspirations of people in a given locality.

Future cities will be designed with social proximity in mind. Proximity could be facilitated by new forms of transport mobility, which can virtually or completely "collapse" the organisation of work and home in space and time (e.g., working from home).

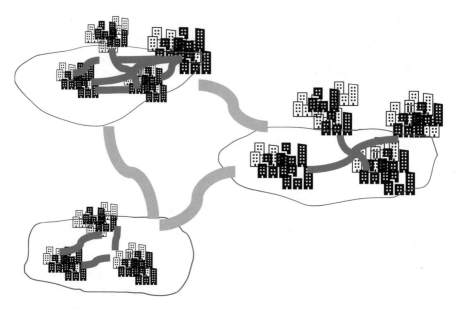

Fig. 4.1 An illustration of walkable urban hubs, where a collection of high density urban areas are inter-connected. Life and work can happen mostly within each hub, with perhaps some travel between hubs. Hubs can form groups of inter-connected groups

4.1.1   The Walkable City and Urban Hubs

Overall, the transportation sector, or "getting around", including the use of planes, cars, ships, and so on, accounts for 16% of total greenhouse gas emissions [28]. Hence, being able to get around without vehicles, where possible, can help.

We consider the National Geographic's discussion on the future of cities.[1] In particular, the notion of *urban hubs*, as illustrated in Fig. 4.1. The idea of high density hubs allows jobs and living areas to co-exist within a walkable range and within scooter or cycling distances, in a largely self-contained hub, thereby reducing the need for commuting over long distances, which in turn, reduces energy and emissions due to transportation. Such high density hubs can also increase opportunities for innovation, increasing the likelihood for cooperation, and enabling convenient social interactions. Proximity plays a role in facilitating interaction, serendipitously or otherwise. Energy, water, sewerage, and other amenities can also be brought to people more efficiently and economically than if they were dispersed or sprawled over large distances.

---

[1]https://www.nationalgeographic.com/magazine/2019/04/see-sustainable-future-city-designed-for-people-and-nature/ [last accessed: 28/1/2021].

In many ways, many current cities have hubs, (Central Business Districts) CBDs, as well as hubs away from the CBD, and town centers that provide a focus of life for disparate groups of people. Small town centers of today might become the CBDs of the future, even as the CBDs themselves grow and develop, with increasing higher density dwellings and offices.

Active transport such as walking, cycling, e-bikes and e-scooters are increasingly popular. There are mounting evidences demonstrating the correlation between physical activities of city occupants and the built environment. Bike paths, parks and streets dedicated to pedestrians are flourishing in modern cities such as Paris or Barcelona. Improving cities' walkability, cyclability, access to green areas, parks and playgrounds, and providing adequate active transport infrastructure are likely to generate positive impacts on health and well beings of city dwellers.

There are notions of the 15 min city[2] and the 30 min city where one can walk or bike to all the places one needs to in a typical day within 15 (or 30) min, e.g., supermarket, workplaces, schools and so on. Walkable cities would reduce dependence on the automobile.[3]

Active transport improves health by increasing the levels of physical fitness. It could reduce the rates of major diseases such as obesity or diabetes. Active transport infrastructure improvements are appealing to the (socioeconomically) group of people leaving in medium to large cities. This is why public policies have actively promoted active transport over the last decades. The city of Pontevedra in Spain has suggested what is possible in an area completely walkable and without cars.[4]

An automated city can provide automated bikes, automated scooters, or similar to allow people to move comfortably within a hub, potentially extending slightly beyond the 15 (or 30) minute reachable range by foot only. Of course, walking itself has implications for health, and with the reduction of energy use for transport, walkability has enormous benefits.

High density busy areas could be a challenge for urban robot navigation, but high density areas would also mean that such robots would only need to work within smaller ranges. Sky highways with drones could then be useful for transport between high rise buildings in high density areas, provided they can be deployed in an adequately safe manner.

---

[2]https://www.fastcompany.com/90456312/pariss-mayor-has-a-dream-for-a-15-minute-city [last accessed: 28/1/2021].

[3]https://www.britannica.com/topic/Our-Future-Eco-Cities-Beyond-Automobile-Dependence-2118409 [last accessed: 22/1/2021].

[4]https://www.theguardian.com/cities/2018/sep/18/paradise-life-spanish-city-banned-cars-pontevedra [last accessed: 22/1/2021].

4.1.2   Trees, Energy, the Green City and Sustainability

Greening the city is becoming high priority in the political agenda worldwide. This fashion did not emerge from a cosmetic necessity or rural nostalgia, but rather a real shift in culture where green is intricately linked to health and well being.

Being green, in different senses of the word, is another key characteristic often mentioned in discussing future cities, but many cities are moving towards this direction.

Singapore was recently noted to be one of the "greenest" cities in the world among a list of major cities,[5] at least from an estimate of tree canopy coverage on Treepedia.[6] Treepedia quantifies urban tree cover in city streetscapes by analyzing Google Street View images based on the amount of green perceived as one walks down a street. One could imagine such an approach being carried out periodically automatically, or as needed, so that estimates can be updated over time. One can extrapolate further and consider how aspects of green planning and planting of trees, and the shaping of greener streetscapes, can be automated—e.g., automated monitoring of tree canopy, computer recommendations of where to green streetscapes and the best placements for tree coverage, as well as even robotic help for planting trees. In addition, one can imagine map-based apps that compute the walking path between A and B with the greatest tree coverage or the best air quality manufactured by green spaces.

There are numerous images of cities saturated with trees and plants, including buildings with rooftop and vertical urban gardens.[7]

Green and sustainability have other aspects, beyond tree coverage, such as the use of renewal energy sources to power cities. A definition of *green city* from [14] is:

> a city that promotes energy efficiency and renewable energy in all its activities, extensively promotes green solutions, applies land compactness with mixed land use and social mix practices in its planning systems, and anchors its local development in the principles of green growth and equity.

With increased automation, and the need for much more extensive computations, as we are imagining for the Automated City, there will be a consequent increase in energy usage. With enormous computing power required, energy is hence a key driver and issue for the Automated City. Hence, to be green in the above sense, renewable or green energy resources become important for the future of the Automated City, including solar, wind, ocean waves, hydro, biomass, green hydrogen, and geothermal. A related question is whether an Automated City can be

---

[5]https://www.renotalk.com/article/singapore-greenest-city [last accessed: 28/1/2021].

[6]http://senseable.mit.edu/treepedia/cities/singapore [last accessed: 28/1/2021].

[7]https://futurereality.wordpress.com/2012/05/10/green-cities-possibilities-of-the-future/ [22/1/2021].

100% powered by green energy sources, yet maintain its operations with no energy-related disruption. Further developments in energy-efficient computing technologies will also help, including new paradigms for computing.[8]

In addition, research towards Green AI [62], where resources (with associated energy costs and GHG emissions) required for AI computations is a key consideration and not just accuracy, will be very important for enabling smart functionality in a more energy and cost efficient manner.

As the urban population grows, there will be a need for sustainable growth, and sustainable continual use of resources, such as materials (e.g., for making chips and computers and batteries, especially with increasing automation), water and energy, and the need to promote and protect biodiversity.[9] The notion of biophilic cities encourages close contact with nature, even for urban living, and looks at how to conserve, celebrate and protect nature in cities (e.g., see [22]).[10] Planning for biodiversity in cities can become a priority [53]. Technologies for tracking cities and biodiversity could be applied, including tracking species and environmental factors that affect them [54].

Built environments will be green, intelligent, connected and automated. The growing demand for green space will allow citizens to grow their own food sustainability. The agriculture sector, at least in part, could move into the city and could no longer be a matter for rural or remote regions and peasants.

---

[8] As noted by Brownell (a previous CEO of D-Wave, a quantum computing company; https://qz.com/1566061/quantum-computing-will-change-the-way-the-world-uses-energy/ [last accessed: 15/2/2021]):

> Most modern classical supercomputers use between 1 to 10 megawatts of power on average, which is enough electricity to meet the instantaneous demand of almost 10,000 homes. As a year's worth of electricity at 1 megawatt costs about $1 million in the US, this leads to multimillion-dollar price tags for operating these classical supercomputers.

Brownell also says:

> In contrast, each comparable quantum computer using 25 kW of power costs about $25,000 per unit per year to run.

The emerging paradigm of quantum computing then becomes a powerful alternative for compute-intensive applications, not only due to potential speed-ups (which could also imply less energy used), but also from the perspective of energy efficiency per unit of computation work done.

[9] https://thedigestonline.com/community-human-interest/sustainable-cities-of-the-future/ [last accessed: 28/1/2021].

[10] https://www.biophiliccities.org/our-vision [last accessed: 28/1/2021].

4.1.3   Other Visions of the Future City

There have been visions of archetype cities to be built from ground up. For example, Tencent's vision is a 2 million square metre city to be built in Shenzhen, China:[11]

> The answer is Net City, built entirely from the ground up to reflect the distributed network of the internet itself. Inter-connected, integrated, organic and welcoming, Net City is designed to be a place where people can dream, come together as a community to connect and create new possibilities for the future.

In the city, public transit, bicycles and pedestrian access are prioritised over general vehicles which are "diverted into the basement around each plot". Sustainability will be central to the city's design, including buildings with solar panels and sensors to monitor the environment.

The Akon City to be located in Senegal, Africa, is resort-style and has inspiring futuristic building designs and layout.[12] To be built from ground up, it will feature smart city technologies, IoT, sensors and communication networks, as well as an education district and technology park.

Toyota plans to construct Woven City—a prototype city located near Mount Fuji, Japan. The new 175-acre urban development will feature "a fully connected ecosystem and be powered by clean energy produced through hydrogen fuel cells" and in particular:[13]

> The Woven City development will function as a kind of living laboratory, where full-time residents and researchers will be able to test and develop technologies such as autonomy, robotics, personal mobility, smart homes and artificial intelligence in a real-world environment.

There are other fanciful visions of the city such as a city in the sky or on the sea concepts.[14]

4.1.4   Impacts of Technology on Citizens and Workforce—What Do We Want City Inhabitants to Become?

Internet and the pervasiveness of mobile technologies have provided real-time access to unlimited information. We increasingly consult the internet before making important decisions.

---

[11] https://www.smartcitiesworld.net/news/news/tencent-unveils-plans-for-futuristic-net-city-in-shenzhen-5362 [last accessed: 28/1/2021].

[12] See https://akoncity.com, and https://www.youtube.com/watch?v=8pff0k_dirE, https://www.youtube.com/watch?v=Tt45h7d6_4Q [last accessed: 22/1/2021].

[13] https://blog.toyota.co.uk/toyota-woven-city-hydrogen-power [last accessed: 22/1/2021].

[14] https://www.arch2o.com/city-in-the-sky-concept-tsvetan-toshkov/ [last accessed: 22/1/2021].

We are flooded with more information than we can consume. In theory, access to information ought to improve the quality of our decision making. Unfortunately, the Internet and especially social media can provide information from countless sources with varying quality.

The Internet is now littered with fake news, oversimplified (summarised in a twit) or alternative facts tinted with conspiracy theories. The Internet has been transformative and it has provided many advantages but it also facilitated ultra-crepidarianism, obstructionism and obscurantism. These "noises" could influence citizens and require them to discern/judge what is wrong from what is right or good. For example, social media can have an impact on perceptions relevant to elections (US).[15]

As Internet can divide or unite the community, and so can automation. Ubiquitous automation, where citizens have instant and effortless abilities to exchange goods and services can change not only our workplace but also the social dynamics.

For example, if the delivery of goods such as food is instantaneous and more economical with the use of robot delivery, it could cause households to move away from cooking or going shopping. Maybe a fridge or even a kitchen would not be necessary white-goods as everything could be delivered for immediate consumption at our doorstep. Over-reliance on automation could have serious health consequences, in this regard. Not exercising (e.g., even walking to the shop) and mental health consequences of not experiencing the serendipity of urban social interactions have been shown to be issues for many during the pandemic.[16]

Of course, this only a very brief discussion on a complex topic and both the positive and negative impacts will need to be considered, and some impacts might only be evident over a long period of time.

4.1.5 Which Vision?

In 1933, during the IV Congrès internationaux d'Architecture Moderne, Le Corbusier stated in the *Charte d'Athenes* that most of the new cities (then) do not address the fundamental needs of its occupants, which are to satisfy their primordial biological and psychological needs.

Automation, AI and algorithms will be part of future cities. For example, in the foreseeable future, AVs would not be able to operate safely without Machine Learning or Deep learning Algorithms. It is wrongly or rightly envisioned as seeking a universal solution to rationalise the complexity or chaos reigning in big cities.

---

[15] A discussion on social media's contribution to political misperceptions in presidential elections in the US is available at https://journals.plos.org/plosone/article?id=10.1371/journal.pone.0213500 [last accessed: 16/6/2021].

[16] A discussion on this issue is at https://www.medicalnewstoday.com/articles/exercise-and-mental-health-during-covid-19-study-explores-link-trends [last accessed: 16/6/2021].

Descartes' "Make ourselves masters and possessors of nature" is appropriate to illustrate the technologisation of modern cities. The City was conceptualised as building an artificial world from which "natural" order is expelled.

However, the design of the city should not be only within the technologist's domain. The design of a city's "fabric" should be a hybridisation of knowledge from different disciplines: philosophy, urbanism, technology, anthropology, mathematics, politics and so on. The ancient Greek philosopher Plato already showed us the way in Greek antiquity when he involved legislators, mathematicians, and dictators as part of the think tank to design the ideal city. The City could be usefully envisioned via a collaboration of minds from multiple perspectives.

One might wonder which vision of the city would dominate in the future. The range of forms of cities is likely myriad due to influences of local culture, government priorities, and local preferences. For example, people who prefer large urban homes sprawled over large areas might hesitate living in high density urban hubs. Most city visions would require the cooperation and willpower of its inhabitants. A combination of the favourable aspects of the above is likely a direction, at least in the short term, i.e., green, sustainable, walkable and technologically supported cities with design aesthetics, with a large degree of automation helping to track, maintain and promote green and sustainability aspects of the city and to facilitate convenient and comfortable living.

4.1.6   The Evolution of Cities: Bottom-Up or Top-Down?

Visions of future cities might emphasize particular ideals and visual forms, and approach city development from a top-down perspective. There are also questions of whether growth might be pre-programmed, i.e., one imagines a machine that continually monitors a population in the city and then automatically modifies or constructs suitable new environments (e.g., new buildings and amenities) to accommodate the increases in population and growth. Such a machine might even compute its output (of new structures) based on inputs from people, inhabitants and planners. The machine might even attempt to persuade people to visit certain places at certain times, use particular roads or paths, or live in certain ways to maximise city objectives (e.g., reduce traffic jams or improve safety). However, such a mechanistic view of urban growth is perhaps too simplified and might not consider the emergent aspects of collective decision-making and actions of inhabitants.

Batty notes that [12]:

> ...real cities grow from the bottom up, as the product of millions of decisions made by individuals and collectives that generate great variety and heterogeneity...

and also that:

> ...the actual invention of the future city is a process dramatically different from the musing of visionaries, since it consists of those millions of individual decisions that in and of themselves must be treated as inventions. It is in this sense that the future city is entirely

unpredictable, full of novelty and surprise. .... This also explains why it is so hard to be certain about the development and autonomous technologies.

Hence, while stereotype cities, visions, ideals and principles can provide a direction, the actual form into which the city evolves will depend on the sum total of its inhabitants' decisions and actions. And if enough of the inhabitants (in terms of number or influence) follow particular ideals or direction, one might then expect to see the emergence of particular features of a city in line with those ideals or direction.

While we have previously outlined a range of technologies for automation in the city, the actual form in which such technologies will manifest and be adapted for use, will be the product of the collective, a combination of the many decisions and actions of the inhabitants.

Batty also considers cities "to be more like organisms than machines", evolving from the bottom-up manner. We previously provided metaphors of cities as machines, as partner and host of their inhabitants, but we further qualify here that the collective, though coordinated, use of a wide range of machines and automation might lead to a more organic evolution of the Automated City, more so in the way that biological systems can be said to be "living machines", than a static mechanical deterministic perspective. Hence, machines might partner with humans in the evolution of cities, or host humans in the city, helping to automate many functions, but it is the cooperation of humans with machines in organic ways, the many interactions of humans with machines and machines with machines, and the many decisions on deployment and operation of automation, that would ultimately determine the form and shape of the Automated City.

4.2 Governance

This section considers the issue of governance for and in the Automated City.

4.2.1 Policies

Different cities will be identified with different areas of immediate and critical importance to their occupants. The Automated City will be built on science and research, with the general aim to increase productivity, facilitate sustainable economic growth, create jobs and improve national well-being.

The emergence of disruptive technologies which will have profound impact on our daily lives requires robust policy making as support—but disruptive technology can take time to be widely accepted—hence, technological innovation can seem like only a part of the picture; the other part is getting users on board.

Such city policies should be agile enough to support and promote innovation to meet the challenges raised by Automated Cities. As an interesting example of the challenge of setting the right policies and incentives, we consider the tax policy on robotics and automation. Bill Gates in 2017 mentioned that robots that take the jobs of people should pay taxes, i.e., a robot tax.[17] This could slow down the pace of automation as society adapts—some countries are indeed exploring the robot tax.[18] This has been discussed from different perspectives—e.g., by Abbott and Bogenschneider in [1],[19] who argued that "existing tax policies encourage automation, even when a human worker would otherwise be more efficient than a machine." Tax is usually on labour rather than capital, and if human workers are replaced by robots, it might result in lost of tax revenue for government and also, of course, lost of jobs. They argued that "tax neutrality between human workers and robots will improve efficiency by allowing firms to select the more efficient worker, robot or human, without tax-based distortions." Hence, getting a suitable tax policy for automation is not easy.

Singapore has an automation incentive package, to support an increase of automation.[20]

How to encourage cities to invest in innovation remains a challenge. While tried and tested technologies could be beneficial with lower risks, technology innovation and early adoption involve substantial risks which might jeopardise the safety of citizens but also might cost crucial votes for policy makers in charge.

Cities need to provide a better understanding of socio-economic, socio-cultural, and socio-political factors and their interrelations with existing and emerging automated technology. Such an endeavour will go hand in hand with research and innovation.

Sustainable energy production, sustainable food and water supply, sustainable transport, sustainable yet widespread use of automation, and building development will likely be the hallmark of future cities. Although cities will grow horizontally and vertically, they will likely remain mostly compact and dense to limit impacts on the ecosystem, and maintain walkability, as discussed earlier.

The relevance and success of automation will depend on its ability to contribute to the city's sustainability (not only in terms of resources like water and energy but also in terms of jobs and welfare of its citizens).

As citizens are increasingly connected, their needs could be gauged in real time with crowd-sourcing mechanisms. Such invaluable information will blur the divide between citizens and decision makers. It could potentially be used by decision

---

[17]https://qz.com/911968/bill-gates-the-robot-that-takes-your-job-should-pay-taxes/   [last accessed: 15/2/2021].

[18]https://www.futureofworkhub.info/comment/2019/12/4/robot-tax-the-pros-and-cons-of-taxing-robotic-technology-in-the-workplace [last accessed: 15/2/2021].

[19]See also the summary at https://clsbluesky.law.columbia.edu/2017/06/06/how-tax-policy-favors-robots-over-workers-and-what-to-do-about-it/.

[20]https://www.enterprisesg.gov.sg/financial-assistance/grants/for-local-companies/enterprise-development-grant/innovation-and-productivity/automation [last accessed: 15/2/2021].

makers to tailor their policies in a very short period. This is the participatory city mentioned earlier in the book.

Other areas of policy, not just policies on innovation, are relevant. Urban planning shapes cities. To our knowledge, there is no comprehensive mechanism on the integration of automation into urban planning policy. For example, there is limited or inadequate policy to support automated drones or automated vehicles in cities. Authorities continue to invest in non automated infrastructure despite the proven benefits of automated systems. Assuming that the right policy is produced, there can still be a big gap in implementation of the policy, undermining global efforts to achieve a true city transformation.

There is a need to develop new knowledge and theory on the status and adequacy of urban planning policy to encourage automation as current knowledge about future automated cities is still in its infancy. Convincing decision makers to establish new policies and persuading citizens to support such new policies are monumental tasks.

4.2.2 Governance by Algorithms

From governance of the the Automated City, we may consider the automation of governance, i.e., governance via algorithms, or algorithmic governance. Decisions affecting city inhabitants, from building permits to parking restrictions, could be made by algorithms. From [72]:

> Algorithmic governance, in general terms, concerns empowering software to take decisions and to autonomously—i.e., without human supervision—regulate some aspects of our everyday human activities or some aspect of the society, according to some algorithmically defined policies.

Algorithms can already play a role in influencing human behaviour, from the news we are allowed to view, our social lives, to our shopping behaviours, e.g., from recommendations for social connections to what to buy and where to go, of course, provided we willingly follow them. Certainly care must be taken with the widespread use of algorithms and automation (even if not for governance).

Insightfully, Bucher [15] discusses the notion of "programmed sociality", the notion that:

> social formations and connections are algorithmically conditioned and governed by the sociotechnical and political-economic configurations of specific media platforms

and, giving Facebook, as an example:

> the ways in which we related to each other as 'friends' is highly mediated and conditioned by algorithmic systems

Indeed, Facebook can be a useful tool to maintain social connections, but also illustrates ways in which algorithms can have a profound influence on life, or in this case, social life, and perhaps in some way, providing an interesting platform-specific perspective on the meaning of "friend".

From the "programmed sociality", can one extrapolate to "programmed living" where the questions of what to study, who to date, who to marry, who to befriend, where to live, when to sleep, when to stand up, when to exercise, who to vote for, what to eat, what to read, what to buy, where to invest, which travel mode to use, which video to watch, what music to listen to, what to wear, when and where to go on holiday, who to hire, and who to keep in jail, might be based on algorithmic recommendations—there is likely an app to provide recommendations for many of these by the time this book is released (or earlier!). To be fair, such recommendations might receive input from people (e.g., collective human opinions aggregated by machines or human experts). Such recommendations are also likely useful, and would be mostly acceptable,[21] provided the recommendations do not become obligations or regulations. As algorithms are increasingly employed to make decisions in our daily life, discussions on algorithmic bias, ethics and fairness of AI, and the governance of AI, also become relevant, which we will discuss further later on.

Automating governance, and governing with the aid of algorithms, can yield greater efficiencies, and improve outcomes, if deployed and employed within the right policy frameworks.

Automation to help manage and govern the potentially vast numbers of deployed automated systems, including automated vehicles, urban robots and drones, in a future Automated City will be required. Thinking of a parallel with traffic lights, which automates the cooperation of vehicles and pedestrians on roads in specific contexts, one can imagine the need for particular mechanisms to coordinate the movement and functioning of large scale autonomous systems in the city. We discuss this further later in this chapter.

4.3   New Business Models

New business models might reflect a more efficient way to allocate and organize resources. It is complex to predict where the constantly evolving digital economy will lead our society in general and cities, in particular. Innovative entrepreneurs (e.g., typified via Silicon Valley) continue to identify new digital opportunities to create new niche markets.

Novel business models tapping on the Internet of Things, big data, Artificial Intelligence, urban robotics, 5G networking, edge computing, 3D printing (of buildings, structures and small objects, even organic materials) and blockchain continue to emerge. New business models are challenging traditional business

---

[21] It is interesting to note the *word-of-machine effect* supported by experiments: "if someone is focused on utilitarian and functional qualities, then, from a marketer's perspective, the word of a machine is more effective than the word of human recommenders. For someone focused on experiential and sensory qualities, human recommenders are more effective."—quoted from https://hbr.org/2020/10/when-do-we-trust-ais-recommendations-more-than-peoples.

models and touching on new untested work practices and norms, especially with developments in smart city technologies.[22] This is not say that future jobs in the city will be performed by robots and Artificial Intelligence only; on the contrary, new technology will empower the city and its occupants to do more things in less time, and it is hoped, lead to the creation of new types of jobs, or aid people in their jobs.

About 40% of existing university undergraduate or postgraduate degrees will be obsolete in a decade (Ernst and Young was reported as saying[23]). This means that we need to have a lifelong learning strategy to adapt to the market. What we have learned today could be obsolete in a matter of possibly a couple of years. Digital literacy is synonymous to being adaptive to constant changes happening in the digital world. There is no escaping the dominance of such a new culture.

Governments and policy makers are catching up with emerging work practices, new skills are required as past practices are being superseded by new approaches powered by digital technology.

A question is how the increasingly Automated City will lead to new business models and opportunities. For example, there could be a fleet of automated vehicles or tour-bots acting as "tour guides" for visitors to a city, who then do not have to worry about finding directions or how to use local public transport (such as buses or trams) or even how to communicate with a taxi driver, as long as the automated vehicle can converse with its passengers in their languages. There could be new connected devices for cities, and their associated services, e.g., from solar bus stops, smart lamp posts, to smart bicycles, or new ways of using city data. A range of urban service robots, drones and automated vehicles might be considered, as well as, a range of automation at home and in local areas.

A Singapore company has been trialling robots to deliver groceries to residents within a part of the city.[24] The robots bring groceries to a pick-up point and inform the residents that their groceries can be collected. For COVID-19 situations, the robots provide a contactless and humanless delivery solution. Recently, in a city in the US, Domino's announced it is using automated vehicles to deliver pizza—it is able to keep food hot and drinks cold while it travels to the customer, and the customer can track it via GPS and needs to pick the pizza up from the vehicle when it

---

[22] As an example, a discussion of smart city technologies and new business models, perhaps starting from informal enterprises, in Sub-Saharan Africa is in https://www.intechopen.com/online-first/orchestrating-smart-cities-new-disruptive-business-models-and-informal-enterprises [last accessed: 17/2/2021]. Other examples of new business models arising from smart city projects are at https://www.capgemini.com/2019/02/smart-cities-emergence-of-new-business-models/ [last accessed: 17/2/2021].

[23] https://www.smh.com.au/education/university-degrees-obsolete-report-ernst-young-20180501-p4zcn5.html [last accessed: 17/2/2021].

[24] See https://www.wionews.com/technology/new-normal-robots-being-used-for-home-deliveries-due-to-surge-in-covid-cases-377223; the robots were developed by OTSAW, http://otsaw.com [last accessed: 20/4/2021].

arrives, at a kerb.[25] It is interesting to note that these vehicles operate on public roads at low speeds, and do not use the sidewalk or bike lane; they are electric automated vehicles with a maximum speed of 25 mph (and so, do not go on highways but stay on neighbourhood roads), and are narrower and smaller than typical cars, not designed to carry people, but designed specially to carry goods (food in the case of Domino's). The vehicles are programmed to choose routes where they remain within their safe operational design domain; when the weather changes, the vehicles can pull over and not continue to operate in a dangerous environment. Sensors on the vehicle detect pedestrians and other objects.

In general, surrounding each type of new technology for the Automated City is an ecosystem of related providers and consumers, with possible new business models. For example, for automated vehicles, one could think of related businesses related to the software for such vehicles, the data collection and processing for such vehicles, the services (e.g., Transportation-as-a-Service (TaaS) or Mobility-as-a-Service (MaaS)) and niche applications of such vehicles, the hardware (mechanical and computer) for the vehicle, the connectivity of the vehicle, the fuel and energy for the vehicle, and supporting infrastructure.[26]

There are companies trialing fleets of robotaxis to serve particular urban areas, though such taxis may not necessarily cooperate in the direct vehicle-to-vehicle communication sense—they can be coordinated centrally.[27]

It is considered that many Automated Vehicles will be shared, including shared ownership, or private vehicles but used as "taxis". There are considerable theoretical studies using psychological construct such as the Theory of Planned Behaviour (TPB) to assess individuals' intentions to use fully automated shared passenger shuttles when they become publicly available [34].

Possibly, owners of AVs, when not using their vehicles, instead of being idle at home, could employ their vehicles for different tasks and to provide services to earn money for the owner.[28] This means that there could be a marketplace where one can query AVs' availability, costs, Quality-of-Service and so on (perhaps using some form of ontology, query-able with a query language). And, payments could be done in a traditional way or using blockchain technology.

We can extend this thinking. Owners of robots might also do the same, depending on the type of robot—where possible, a robot not in use might be loaned out for a fee (or for free for others to use as a community contribution). With

---

[25] See https://dominos.gcs-web.com/news-releases/news-release-details/dominosr-and-nuro-launch-autonor the vehicles are called R2, by a company called Nuro, https://www.nuro.ai/ [last accessed: 20/4/2021].

[26] For example, see https://www.forbes.com/sites/forbestechcouncil/2020/06/24/autonomous-driving-business-models-part-one/ [last accessed: 17/2/2021] for a discussion.

[27] For example, see https://techcrunch.com/2020/08/16/autox-launches-its-robotaxi-service-in-shanghai-competing-with-didis-pilot-program/ and https://techcrunch.com/2020/06/30/momenta-robotaxis/ [last accessed: 13/4/2021].

[28] See https://www.forbes.com/sites/lanceeliot/2019/06/11/making-money-on-self-driving-cars-the-roving-eye-will-be-golden/ [last accessed: 13/4/2021].

ubiquitous robots/IoT, each robots/IoT should be sharable and maybe re-used for different purposes. For example, a LIDAR of an outdoor robot cleaner could be re-used by a surveyor or to detect burglars or even to help check weather in a particular location.[29] They should be re-used because they are often complicated to install and maintain but has the potential to be multiple purpose and provide more cost benefit and return on investment. This means that if robots/IoT could advertise their capabilities, cost of use, quality characteristics and so on, they should be discoverable and accessible via maybe some "contract" negotiation and payment mechanism (perhaps using blockchain again). The scale here is completely different, as potentially we may be talking about millions of devices. A scalable and sustainable mechanism will be needed to make this happen.

Then, there is the notion of drone services, which we have described in the previous chapter, and also the notion of Robots-as-a-Service (RaaS)[30] which is not only about leasing robots for use, but could be much more compartmentalized and specialised, e.g., renting robots on a pay-per-use or similar basis (removing the need for in-house maintenance and update)—say, renting a robot just to help flip burgers twice a week, a robot to help carry goods just 2 h a week, a robot to clean a house once a week, or to mow the lawn once a month.

Of course "new" is relative. What is a new business model for a city may be an already well established model in another city.

4.4   Urban Transportation

Transportation and economic growth are interlinked. A city's transportation infrastructure plays a vital role in ensuring the health and well-being of its citizens. The transport sector is and will continue to be driven by technology. Technological drivers such as automation, connectivity, de-carbonisation coupled with new ride-sharing trends, active transport, and more recently, behaviour changes due to COVID-19, are redefining the city's mobility patterns.

Innovation in mobility technologies often refers to (1) innovation in the vehicles, such as smarter and safer automated vehicles or smarter automated bicycles, and of course, automated trains and smarter scooters (which we discuss further later), (2) innovation in transport systems and supporting cyber-infrastructure (from Mobility-as-a-Service paradigms to multi-modal transportation apps, and vehicle tracking devices, as well as IoT sensing for transport data collection), and (3) innovation in how people integrate mobility technologies into their daily lives.

---

[29]For example, see the role of LIDAR in relation to weather at https://lidarmag.com/2019/12/04/not-just-for-surveying-lidars-big-impact-in-weather/ [last accessed: 17/6/2021].

[30]See   https://www.forbes.com/sites/bernardmarr/2019/08/05/robots-as-a-service-a-technology-trend-every-business-must-consider/   and   https://insights.rlist.io/p/report-robot-as-service-companies.html [last accessed: 17/2/2021].

While we mentioned automated vehicles and drones for transportation, there continues to be innovation in ways of moving around in the city, over the relatively short distances. We discuss the example of micromobility as an emerging form of transport that has recently been gaining widespread usage, and how technology is being used to address some of the concerns of its usage.

Micromobility technology, exemplified by the scooter, or shared e-scooters, refers to the use of lightweight, single or several passenger vehicles, electric or human-powered with relatively low maximum speeds and ranges. It was noted that micromobility "constitutes forms of transport that can occupy space alongside bicycles."[31] Uptake of scooters have led to companies providing shared scooter services in cities around the world,[32] such as Lime[33], Voi[34] and Superpedestrian,[35] which operates as LINK.[36]

The use of e-scooters is not without issues such as safety, sometimes getting in pedestrians' way or scooters being mishandled or left on the streets [5]. Companies have begun to address some of these issues via technology. For example, the Superpedestrian scooter is supported by smart technology and cyber-infrastructure, including (1) geofencing to inform riders of "no-ride", "slow-ride", and "no parking zones", e.g., when the rider is in sidewalk where scooters are not allowed, the rider is informed, and the rider can move to a bicycle lane, and (2) sensors to monitor the condition of the scooter for predictive maintenance and detect vehicle health, and to prevent vandalism and theft.

E-scooter sharing was severely impeded by the pandemic,[37] but generally, provides another complementary form of (micro-)transport. Use of e-scooters can also help to reduce car usage, given that many car trips are short. In a recent online survey of 1640 adults from 17 neighbourhoods [47], it was noted that 21% would consider using e-scooters in their current trips, and a majority would use shared e-scooters in place of their walking and transit trips. Earlier studies indicate e-scooters are favourable [60]. Another recent study suggest that e-scooters are complementing public transit especially in streets around tourist sites, e.g., hotels, and transit stops [46].

However, new technologies alone will not spontaneously make citizens' lives better without adapting our transport systems as a whole and looking at points of complementarity, having the right policies and regulations, and more importantly,

---

[31] See Deloitte report: https://www2.deloitte.com/us/en/insights/focus/future-of-mobility/micro-mobility-is-the-future-of-urban-transportation.html [last accessed: 1/5/2021].

[32] For example, from https://www.bbc.com/future/article/20200608-how-sustainable-are-electric-scooters [last accessed: 1/5/2021], by 2020, there were over 100 cities with e-scooter deployments around the world, with several million e-scooters in use.

[33] https://www.li.me/en-us/home [last accessed: 1/5/2021].

[34] https://www.voiscooters.com/how-to-voi/ [last accessed: 1/5/2021].

[35] https://www.superpedestrian.com/en [last accessed: 1/5/2021].

[36] https://www.link.city [last accessed: 1/5/2021].

[37] See   https://www.theverge.com/2020/3/20/21188119/electric-scooter-coronavirus-bird-lime-spin-suspend-bikes [last accessed: 1/5/2021].

putting the human being at the center of urban planning design to cater for the basic social needs and associated behavior.

Transport is a powerful enabler but can also be dis-empowering. Policy-makers and our society, in general, must ensure that new technologies will make transport more equitable than the current private car-centric approach. For example, public transport is the most efficient means to reduce inequality as it provides access to citizens' fundamental rights: access to jobs and education.

Governments' relentless endeavours towards creating sustainable transport infrastructure by facilitating active travel, use of public transport and creation of attractive public spaces where social interactions emerge are vital for the development of liveable and sustainable cities. Future city designers will have the difficult task of managing the interplay between transport, spaces, and citizen. Predicting the intertwined physical activity, social interactions, and travel mode choice behaviour is a complex modelling exercise.

One of the scientific limitations of anticipating future transport trends involves looking at the future as an extrapolation of the past usage pattern. On one hand, it is often assumed that there will be incremental changes, where existing transport technology will transition to new mobility paradigms and will cope with citizen's need by extending the scale and functionalities of current technology beyond what is currently possible. On the other hand, radical, novel, rare and sudden transport changes are hard to predict scientifically. This makes the science and policy interface extremely hard to bridge as scientists cannot gather convincing past evidence to rely upon and inform policy-makers. Existing travel behaviour theories are based on current practice. There are no comprehensive scientific theories able to predict and model major transportation technology disruptions and to what extent they last in the long and short term.

In this new global world where everyone is connected through technological, economic, geographical and social means, the emergence of new crises, such as pandemics, fake news, financial collapses and natural disasters, create unprecedented uncertainty for policy-makers and scientists. Citizens demand rapid adaptation to often volatile events. The fast-track of COVID-19 vaccines, which should have taken typically several years to create and validate, suggests a "gold standard protocol" to be followed, and is a typical example of how the scientific process had to be adapted and how user perception could be easily confused. Social distancing and the working from home pattern due to COVID-19 have decreased public transport use and increased private car use. We do not know (yet) if such changes of behaviour will persist in the coming years. However, an increase of car traffic in the city will undoubtedly result in gridlock and loss of productivity, and consequently, reduced quality of life. We also do not know if the "Zoom fatigue"[38] will revert citizens to the pre-COVID travel pattern.

---

[38]For example, see https://ideas.ted.com/zoom-fatigue-is-real-heres-why-video-calls-are-so-draining/ [last accessed: 4/4/2021].

4.5   Real-Time Tracking

Knowing the whereabouts of things, services and citizens anywhere anytime is a useful building block for building an Automated City. The Internet of Things begun with the idea of using RFID tags to bridge the cyber and physical worlds. In a sense, an electronically tagged object has a presence in cyberspace and now can be viewed in the computer. Changes in physical properties of the tagged object, e.g., its movement, can be tracked in the computer. As different types of sensors are employed, different properties of physical objects or the physical environment can then be represented in the computer.

As people, objects and places get "connected" to the Internet via some form of sensing, they have a presence in cyber space, and with real-time tracking, or perception, of people, objects and places, algorithms can then react or respond to the changes in their physical properties without human intervention—this ability then enables automation. Hence, the more "pieces" of the world, or situations, that can be tracked, the wider the scope of tasks that can be automated. Sensing and perception are required for effective actuation. Sensing and perception are also useful for acquiring data in order to make predictions and to be proactive.

In [29], the use of public cameras and drones for law enforcement in the US was discussed. Such public cameras have helped police recover stolen vehicles and locate suspects. During police operations, drones can help maintain situation-awareness from a bird's eye viewpoint, quickly scan crime scenes, find hot spots for wildland fires and locate missing persons. As early as the 1990s, the City of London Police has employed Public Space CCTV Cameras to help keep the public safe, and provide images as evidence in court.[39] Even informing the public about such public safety cameras can be a deterrent that can reduce crime rates [64]. Indeed, many cities throughout the world employ such cameras for safety and policing reasons. Not just for policing, cameras in shopping centres and in a range of private/public premises might also be employed.

However, the ability to track and sense people, objects and places can cause privacy concerns, and raise ethical issues about how tracking data should be managed. It is not only about handling of personal data collected via IoT devices, including location data or pictures of persons taken by devices, but also data about objects and places which could be linked to, or associated with, persons. This could range from tracking a device belonging to a person, from vehicles or smart devices, to tracking delivery robots and drones. If such delivery drones or robots are tracked, it could provide some information that someone is receiving a parcel or object, at some frequency, and even variations on that frequency can reveal information about the behaviour or movements of someone. Sometimes, observations by robots of the world, needed for the robot's main functioning, can also capture some aspect of the world that reveals information about persons, even if not intending to do so.

---

[39]https://www.cityoflondon.police.uk/police-forces/city-of-london-police/areas/city-of-london/campaigns/campaigns/2020/secure-city/ [last accessed: 15/5/2021].

People might not be informed that their data are being collected, how their data are being used or how their data can be deleted, or managed—this can result in issues for people in particular contexts and situations.

The Automated City, hence, can increase concerns about data privacy given the need to collect more data, with the central role of data for automation.

A combination of policies accompanied by enabling technologies might be required, e.g., for people to be notified if a connected device is acquiring information about them or when their data is being used, or some means to provide users with control over data and even digital forgetting [36]. However, what is required might depend on context. How people judge machines observing them, compared to humans observing them, can be context-specific. In studies done via obtaining the reactions of people (from the United States) on scenarios with camera systems,[40] people tend to detest machine observers if school children or public transportation is involved, but are indifferent (between machine and human observers) in private-sector venues (e.g., in a hotel or a mall).

4.6 Urban Edge Computing

We have mentioned AI algorithms running on edge computing devices in Chap. 1, and with increasing automation and the need to process data efficiently to enable real-time responses, without the latency of uploading data to the remote cloud or transferring data across organizational and national borders to remote sites, computing at the edge of the cloud could increase.

Gartner predicts that by 2025 as much as 75% of enterprise data could be created and processed outside a centralized cloud.[41] With IoT devices and smart things, and a proliferation of sensors, large amounts of data will be generated, and it would be efficient to process them closer to their points of generation.

The convergence of technologies, including AI, IoT or cyber-physical systems, cloud and edge computing, advanced networking (5G/6G), often associated with Industry 4.0 [2],[42] can apply not only to manufacturing, but to city-scale applications.

The decentralization of data storage and processing to multi-tenant edge and fog computing devices and servers, complements the centralized remote clouds and large data centers, and can lead to a wide-scale deployment of edge and fog servers or hubs in urban areas, with industry beginning to provide local or edge

---

[40]See the book *How People Judge Machines*, at https://www.judgingmachines.com/ [last accessed: 5/4/2021].

[41]https://www.gartner.com/smarterwithgartner/what-edge-computing-means-for-infrastructure-and-operations-leaders/ and https://www.equinix.com.au/resources/analyst-reports/edge-computing-strategies-gartner-2021/ [last accessed: 7/4/2021].

[42]See also https://www.i-scoop.eu/industry-4-0/ [last accessed: 7/4/2021].

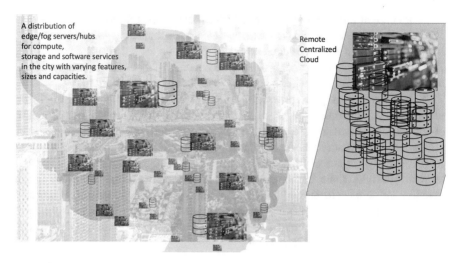

Fig. 4.2 An illustration of edge computing servers or hubs in the city

server computing solutions.[43] Methods to scale up deployments of edge servers will be needed, including optimizing the placements of such servers in the city and the corresponding workload allocation, e.g., the work in [42, 43, 69]. Drones as flying edge servers and autonomous vehicles (or mobile robots) carrying edge cloudlet servers have also been proposed [37, 39] as a dynamic way of deploying edge servers throughout a city. Such urban edge computing hubs or servers distributed over a city might support mobile users, urban robots, vehicles and drones in the city, providing an interesting form of computational infrastructure within a city.

Figure 4.2 illustrates a range of edge computing servers and hubs distributed throughout the city. Such edge servers could be widely varying in terms of services and capacities, ranging from high capacity servers to smaller lower capacity servers. The services can be used to support human users (e.g., smartphone apps) or by urban robots and autonomous systems to support their operations by providing additional compute power, storage, and software services.

---

[43]For example, it was reported that Walmart has plans to utilise its 3500 supercenters (stores) as edge computing hubs—see https://techhq.com/2020/04/why-the-edge-computing-hasnt-taken-off-yet/ and https://techhq.com/2020/01/can-walmarts-supercenter-footprint-fend-off-amazon/, Amazon provides Local Zones to provide cloud computing resources within certain cities—see https://aws.amazon.com/about-aws/global-infrastructure/localzones/, and Microsoft's Cloud Platform Azure provides Azure Edge Zones—see https://azure.microsoft.com/en-us/solutions/low-latency-edge-computing/, and Google provides edge computing solutions, e.g., https://cloud.google.com/solutions/anthos-edge and https://cloud.google.com/edge-tpu [last accessed: 7/4/2021].

4.7 Blockchain for Smart Cities

Blockchain and Distributed Ledger Technology (DLT) have gained tremendous interest in recent years, mainly due to Bitcoin and other popular crypto-currencies. The idea of storing data in a way that is difficult or impossible to be changed by any one party (with limited resources) can be used for many different applications, apart from solving the double-spending problem in crypto-currency transactions.

Blockchain for smart city applications, often used with IoT technology, have been discussed extensively, e.g., as reviewed in [7, 44]—some of the applications discussed are e-commerce transactions without intermediaries, e-voting using one-time-use blockchain tokens, auditable health records management, renewable energy trading infrastructure, supply chain management to record product information throughout its life-cycle, property management (e.g., land registry) and real estate trading, government services (from license renewals to visa approvals and citizen data management), transport related payments and mobility permit trading, and ride-sharing with digital currencies or tokens. An extensive discussion of how blockchain technologies can be used to address the United Nations Sustainable Development Goals, in relation to the smart city functions of city-administration, service delivery, and resource management, is given in [48].

DLT and blockchain-based mechanisms have been employed for swarm robotic systems, e.g., to reach consensus even in the midst of faulty or malicious robots providing erroneous information.[44] There have been several experimental demonstrations. The work in [65] used the Ethereum blockchain framework (in a private network) with smart contracts to provide fault-tolerance in a controlled experimental task of small swarm robots working to estimate the percentage of white squares within a grid of black and white squares; the use of blockchain also prevents Sybil attacks and each robot has a tamper-proof history of events (its own copy of the blockchain) for auditing. The work in [35] demonstrated the use of a DLT consensus algorithm, namely, the Tendermint consensus algorithm, for swarm robots (drones in this case) working together in a simulated search and rescue mission. There are other proposals on how blockchain can be integrated with robotic systems, from payment systems for robotic services in a robot economy [33] to securely logging human-robot interactions [27]. Will blockchain consensus mechanisms be used to coordinate heterogeneous urban robots (together with urban drones and automated vehicles) for particular tasks? This idea remains to be explored and experimentally validated.

Blockchain can also be integrated with edge computing as noted in [56] in order to manage edge resources and services, e.g., blockchain-based identity management,

---

[44]For examples, see the 2019 Symposium on Blockchain for Robotics and AI Systems at https://www.blockchainrobotics.org, and the European Horizon 2020 project "Blockchain: a new framework for swarm RObotic Systems" at https://cordis.europa.eu/project/id/751615 [last accessed: 6/6/2021].

smart contracts for enacting transactions and for resource control and distribution, and blockchain for tracking and auditing.

Many of the above uses are still proposals and experimental—perhaps the future will see wider scale deployments.

4.8 Massive Cooperation

We introduced the *robot standoff problem* in Chap. 3. It may seem far-fetched to imagine robots saturating hallways and walkways and getting into each other's way, and also getting into people's way, but within certain environments, this is a possibility. As discussed in Chap. 3, urban environments will increasingly be spaces for autonomous systems, of which automated vehicles is only one popular type. Modern, but so far less common, forms of transport for people could be Segway type devices such as Loomo[45] and various kinds of delivery robots for goods (mentioned earlier). Robot wheelchairs could be used in public as well other robot-transporters to help the elderly move around in the streets, or to help those who need it (e.g., autonomous wheelchairs in hospitals [8])—now, imagine many autonomous wheelchairs and delivery robots within a hospital environment! Also, indoors, there are robots helping to carry bags in hotels, e.g., Sheraton's robots, robots helping to transfer supplies and lab specimens in hospitals, robot trolleys (and other robots in shopping malls).

For cities with canals and rivers, there can be robots in city canals, and perhaps autonomous ferries, and robots to clean canals. There could also be cleaning robots on pavements and robot-swarms for waste management, occupying walkways and roads, and robots for cleaning and safety monitoring on the streets and pavements. One could automate delivery from shelf to automated car, automated car to doorstep, and in the home, doorstep to cupboard. There could also be advertising robots and tour guide robots in open air malls and streets.

Indeed, such urban robots are not always welcome especially if they occupy valuable walkways and shared spaces intended originally for humans only. With such robots in outdoor and indoor environments and on pavements and walkways, others on cycling lanes and automated cars on roads, a city could turn into a rather crowded space for machines, as mentioned earlier.

Cooperation is also helpful when a collection of robots need to perform complementary functions in dynamic uncertain environments, e.g., cleaning up the roads and malls within the Central Business District (CBD). A collection of cleaning robots need to cooperate with each other, to efficiently clean up the area, either via a centralised controller (which allocates robots to subareas) or robots self-organise (as they observe street conditions, learn from each other and interact with each other about which subareas to go; e.g., in a trivial case, two robots can work things out: "if

---

[45] See https://store.segway.com/segway-loomo-mini-transporter-robot-sidekick.

you clean subarea A, I will clean subarea B", but much more complex cooperation among a larger number of robots would be needed). In Chap. 2, we discussed how multiple machines might work together and cooperate as *one machine* acting as a host for humans in a particular environment.

One can imagine a wide range of phenomena in the city involving machines and/or people requiring cooperation to increase efficiency and scalability—for example:

- a collection of (fully automated) cars trying to get from A to B but coordinating to reduce traffic congestion;
- a collection of (fully automated) cars trying to get out of the way of an emergency vehicle as quickly as possible;
- a collection of (possibly automated) cars trying to find car park (or dropping off passengers) can cooperate to help each other park (or find a drop-off spot) sooner;
- a collection of (possibly automated and human-driven) cars trying to vacate a disaster area, e.g., due to a bushfire or flood;
- a collection of drones trying to serve a given population in an area;
- a large crowd of people (each with smartphones) trying to move as quickly as possible through a building or an area, e.g., evacuating an area due to an incident or disaster;
- a city saturated with a large number of robots or robotic (smart) things interacting and automating city functions;
- a collection of separately owned devices (e.g., smartphones and on-body sensors) attempting to sense a group-based phenomena or collective behaviours;
- a crowd of separately owned devices (e.g., smartphones) working together in an ad hoc manner to compute a global result or search an area;
- a large collection of Internet connected smart things working together to solve an issue, or compute an efficient solution to a problem;
- a very large ad hoc supply chain with numerous independent entities involved and coordinating towards overall goals; and
- a collection of smart things cooperating with each other and humans to provide comprehensive personalised aged care.

The issue is that these entities (or some might say "physical agents") are tangible and will take up physical space in the city, and so, will need to be coordinated with each other and with humans, for efficiency, safety, scalability, and resilience.

In any case, there are already emerging solutions. For example, the work in [25] allows multiple robots to pass each other within a small space without colliding with each other and to make progress through crowded environments, stopping when needed and not getting stuck. The solution uses deep reinforcement learning to first learn a control policy in a simulation environment, which maps sensor readings (i.e., laser scan measurements, the goal position relative to the robot's current position, and the robot's velocity) to actions (i.e., robot movements and direction), and then the learned model is deployed on the robot to work in the physical world. Robots navigate in the physical environment using the LiDAR sensor, which can be simulated with high fidelity—so that training in the simulation environment largely trains (with some fine-turning) the robot for the physical environment. This solution was demonstrated with multiple robots passing through open spaces with objects as obstacles, like in a warehouse. Indeed, readers familiar with swarm robotics, self-organizing systems, and multiagent systems will already see possible approaches to the above issues though, in particular, here, there are issues of heterogeneous nodes, decentralized ownership and control, the need for human and machine collaborations at times, the the need to be protected from cyber-attacks, and the need to tolerate faults and non-cooperative or malicious behaviours.

Regulatory approaches could be a solution to manage the use of shared public spaces by robots. However, another "softer" solution could be greater cooperation. Delivery robots could coordinate with other delivery robots to avoid congesting walkways and pavements. Delivery robots could coordinate schedules and routes with cleaning robots to ensure proper use of shared spaces. While object detection and nearby collision avoidance are important for short-range manoeuvres, robots could also cooperate at a larger geographical level to better use such shared urban spaces—e.g., not just to avoid collisions when they encounter each other, but to choose different routes, thereby reducing "robot traffic" along a route, right from the start. Hence, there are at least two levels of cooperation, the encounter level and at the route level.

4.8.1 Platforms for Massive Cooperation

A possible way to approach this issue is to provide a cooperation platform to enable (mobile) autonomous systems in the urban environment to cooperate in their use of shared spaces.

In many ways, humans already use social media applications on smartphones and the Internet (e.g., email) and the Web to coordinate on a massive scale—as we discussed earlier in the book.

We can also envision a platform where different robots can cooperate on their use of shared spaces in urban environments, e.g., in routing, travel, and for their designed purposes. A range of cooperative protocols can be identified and built into the platform which robots can utilise.

We hypothesise that some cooperation will be better than none, whether centrally orchestrated or decentralised among robots—for example, in the decentralized scenario where there is no central manager prescribing or suggesting routes to robots (central manger only provides rules of cooperation, not the routes themselves), a delivery robot needs to reason about the route it should take, and react if it finds a route too busy yielding inefficiencies (e.g., backtrack in order going down a different lane), but our approach attempts to avoid such a reactive approach by cooperating on routes earlier—e.g., a set of robots (from different companies) at an intersection decide how to distribute themselves along different routes achieving a shortest time for all, even if it means not the shortest path for all. If the robots, even from different manufacturers, are enabled to share knowledge, they can also inform each other of routes to avoid nearby hazards in the vicinity.

Two different types of cooperation approaches can be explored in such a platform:

- *centralised cooperation*: in this type of cooperation, on request from a set of robots, a central controller will allocate routes to robots in order to satisfy particular criteria on use of shared spaces (e.g., number of robots on a certain width of walkways); robots then download their allocations; cooperation is weak since problems will interact with each other but only minimally;
- *decentralised (self-organized) cooperation*: in this type of cooperation, for a certain type of cooperation goal, each robot will download a set of interaction rules (which will pre-defined for each cooperation goal), and via following the rules in their interactions with each other, cooperation among the robots happens, i.e., cooperation is emergent. Stigmergic (analogous to stigmergy used by ants where the cooperation is mediated by the environment and changes made to the environment [32]) and non-stigmergic techniques (e.g., direct inter-robot messaging and signalling, as well as multiagent negotiation protocols [16]) can be considered.

Note that being centralised and decentralised can be dynamic—a system can start off being centralised and then switch to a decentralised mode, and switch back and so on.

A platform can be considered that will enable rules to be downloaded about the use of shared spaces (e.g., as defined by local council or authorities) as a type of contextual information for robot use, that is, relevant behavioural rules are downloaded as needed according to the intended routes and destinations of the robots. For example, local rules could include prohibited traversal of certain areas, even if physically possible, descriptions of geofences, regulations about range of safe speeds for movement in that locality, allowed behaviours (such as sound or light levels for warnings), or rules about what to do when encountering certain obstacles or people). Such rules would be part of a layer in the layered model mentioned in Chap. 3. The API for the platform and the basic reasoning capability required in each robot in order to use the platform will also be defined. It must be noted that such rules should be interpreted based on the local context and constraints of the robot.

Figure 4.3 illustrates what we will call the Cooperation-as-a-Service Platform in the use case of delivery robots running through shared spaces, where the robots send requests to the platform to utilise a cooperation service. Two possible cooperation approaches are illustrated. Note that both approaches download local rules of behaviour for the spaces they utilise.

We mentioned robot societies in Chap. 3, as a means to organize urban robots, and cooperation can happen within such societies each with its own set of rules—however, the cooperation required might need to span such robot societies.

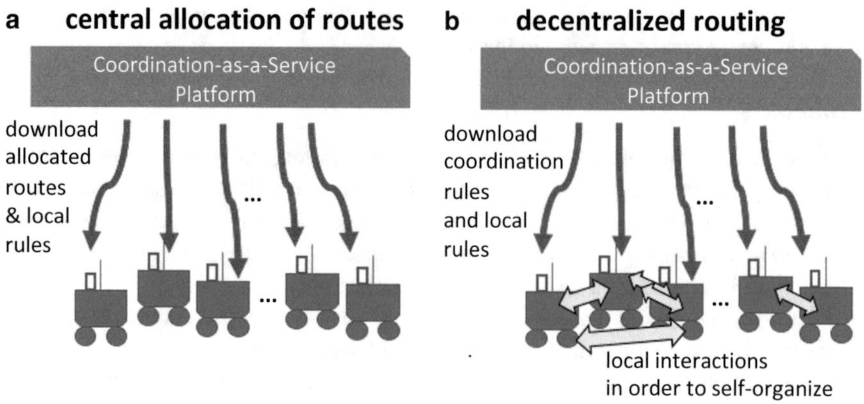

a   central allocation of routes   b   decentralized routing

Fig. 4.3 After notifying the cooperation-as-a-Service Platform of intended usage of public shared spaces, two possible cooperation approaches are: (**a**) centralized allocation of routes for delivery robots; (**b**) decentralized routing where only rules for cooperation are downloaded and interactions between robots lead to self-organized routing. In both approaches, robots download from the platform local rules of behaviour for the spaces they utilise

4.8.2   Cooperative Intelligent Transport Systems (Coop-ITS)

Future automated cities will depend increasingly on concurrent, distributed, parallel, mobile, heterogeneous, adaptive, asynchronous and reconfigurable software and hardware components.

New software architectures and programming languages are necessary to cope with the scale and complexity induced by the insatiable cooperative demands of automated cities.

As explained earlier, automated cities consists of agents-to-agents and human-to-agents cooperative components. Such components need to exhibit distributed problem solving, collective intelligence and adapt to emerging behaviour. Such functions will be supported by the existing platform such as web services, peer-to-peer networks, grid computing/clouds/edge computing.

Cooperative Intelligent Transport Systems (C-ITS) will play a major role in facilitating cities' massive cooperation due to their ubiquity and the amount of transport related information they can provide. C-ITS aims to improve safety, efficiency, comfort and sustainability of surface transportation by using Information and Communications Technologies (ICT).

Although the "C" for ITS stands for Cooperative, the standardisation of C-ITS has focused on the communications aspects such as message formats and communication frequency (e.g., 5.9 GHz). The standard does not specify any form of complex cooperation as we defined it earlier.

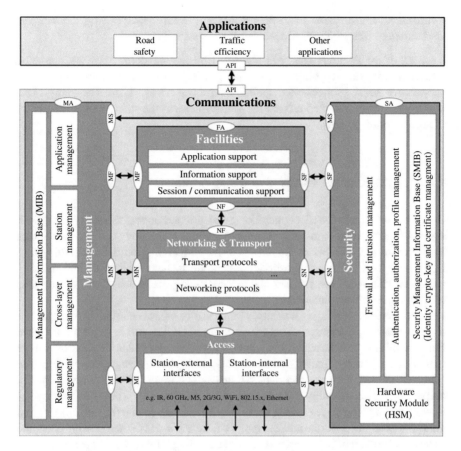

Fig. 4.4 ITS-Stations reference architecture extracted from ISO 21217:2020

The C-ITS standard is based on ISO 21217.[46] It consists of ITS station units compliant with the reference architecture specified in ISO 21217. Figure 4.4 illustrates the ITS-S reference architecture which facilitates combining multiple access technologies, communication protocols and communications approach and secure data exchange and management.

ISO 21217 specifies data exchanges including:

- data collected by the roadside infrastructure and transmitted to traffic control centers, possibly after aggregation,
- roadside equipment configured from the control centers to process a given set of data, or to issue messages to vehicles,
- roadside events reported to control centers, and

---

[46]See https://www.iso.org/standard/80257.html [last accessed: 14/6/2021].

- broadcast transmission of vehicle status and event messages (e.g. Cooperative Awareness Message or CAM) to nearby ITS stations.

A set of applications has been identified by the standard. They are classified into four application groups: active road safety, cooperative traffic efficiency, cooperative local services, and global Internet services. There are many Field Operation Tests conducted around the world to assess the safety and acceptability of such technology [24].

4.8.3 Cooperative Vehicles and Applications

Going beyond basic C-ITS cooperation as mentioned above, there has been work suggesting how vehicle-to-vehicle communications technology can enable vehicles to cooperate in a number of ways [38], from cooperating on the routes they take in order to avoid traffic congestion, cooperating to help each other find parking, to cooperating to increase safety and efficiency, e.g., at intersections, during lane merging, and vehicle platooning.

In cooperative parking [4], vehicles make use of vehicle-to-vehicle communications to exchange messages about where to find parking, and to share information. For example, a vehicle which has gone down particular roads or parts of a large parking area (and say, finding that there is no parking there) can provide information for other vehicles it encounters (which then can choose not to visit those areas with no parking). This can help improve efficiency. Two vehicles which find themselves moving towards the same parking space may coordinate so that the one further from the space need not continue and can target a different space. When parking is not the issue but dropping off passengers is, cars cooperating when dropping passengers off can also be more efficient than every car individually making its own decisions [3].

Groups of vehicles can coordinate and distribute themselves along different routes so that congestion does not happen on the one route, even if its the shortest, so that together everyone could arrive earlier, even if not all travel along the shortest route, or that on average, vehicles save time (even if it could mean more time for some other vehicles) [20].[47] Of course, this would require humans to agree to do so, e.g., to allow oneself some inconvenience in order that everyone, on average, would be better off, and trust that the vehicle taking the longer (by distance) route could actually arrive earlier.

Smart vehicles equipped with sensors, and vehicle-to-vehicle communications, can better utilise roads, and increase traffic efficiency, by being able to safely travel closer together than normal human drivers can, according to a study.[48] Combining

---

[47]See also https://spectrum.ieee.org/cars-that-think/transportation/efficiency/cooperative-route-planning-could-make-driving-slightly-less-terrible-for-everyone [last accessed: 6/4/2021].

[48]https://spectrum.ieee.org/automaton/robotics/artificial-intelligence/intelligent-cars-could-boost-highway-capacity-by-273 [last accessed: 6/4/2021].

the above parts of a journey, from routing, travelling closer together, and finding places to park (drop-off or pick-up), a time reduction of 10–15% for each part, could yield 30–45% reductions in travel time (with consequent reductions in fuel used).

It is noted that while vehicles cooperating can be applied to human-driven vehicles where the human driver receives recommendations from a system—there are possible issues where human drivers might ignore the recommendation and not be involved in cooperative action. With automated vehicles, if left to the vehicle to decide, the choice for cooperating can be built in (though whether the human passengers are allowed to over-ride is another open question).

Apart from coordinated movements mentioned above, there are other ways for vehicles to cooperate.

Vehicles can cooperate to exchange social information. Socialising cars could influence human driving behaviours for the better even in the age of looming automated cars [57].

Another example, when downloading large files, a collection of vehicles can form a micro-cloud via vehicle-to-vehicle communications and collectively download the file, each downloading a segment [31], or when a vehicle receives a part of a big file from a Road Side Unit (RSU), it could receive the other parts from other vehicles [66, 70]. Often, this is called cooperative downloading.

Vehicles can also acts as probes, contributing information to form a knowledge base about some urban phenomena. Crowdsourcing involves aggregating contributions from many to solve problems. In recent times, the idea of crowdsourcing for sensor data has given rise to the concept of crowdsensing, where contributions of mobile sensor data (including geo-tagged pictures, videos, location and other context data) are aggregated to create an overall map or knowledge base of a particular phenomenon. For example, vehicles could collaborate to upload videos to provide a map of where cherry blossoms are in a city [49].

There are many other uses of crowdsensing, from crowdsourcing in order to create maps of 4G/5G bandwidth variations to creating maps of where the crowds are in the city, traffic variations, or temperature [13, 18]. One can imagine machines, whether automated vehicles or urban robots, that roam the streets for their own purposes, but still being able to provide data towards building real-time urban maps for different purposes, i.e. such machines become contributors towards real-time collective urban knowledge. Such crowdsensing can help inform urban design, e.g., as noted in [71].

4.8.4   Cooperative-By-Design

We mentioned above how urban robots and vehicles might cooperate. There are different forms of cooperation involving people and machines. In general, it seems that if the city is to be inhabited by machines with different owners and agenda, where cooperation is the best option, then, the machines should cooperate, rather

Table 4.1 Stag-Hunt Game (Note: $x > v \geq y > u$) and the example on the right has $x = 4, v = y = 2, u = 0$

	Q	
P	Stag	Hare
Stag	x, x	u, v
Hare	v, u	y, y

	Q	
P	Stag	Hare
Stag	4, 4	0, 2
Hare	2, 0	2, 2

than each acting just in its own self-interest, i.e. being cooperative should be built into certain devices from ground-up rather than an add-on feature—in short, machines should be cooperative-by-design. Rather than choosing the best action for itself independently, it could choose the best action in cooperation with other machines—the action chosen cooperatively might be better than the action chosen when trying to maximise their own self-interests independently. An argument from game theory will illustrate this idea.

In game theory, there are various notions of "best" action to take in different situations. One popular game is the *Stag-Hunt Game* illustrated in Table 4.1, where there are two players P and Q, and their respective pay-offs are given in the table in the form (pay-off for row player P, pay-off for column player Q). In the top left cell with (with x, x), the pay-off is x to each if they both catch the stag—in this game, both P and Q must cooperate to catch the stag, but one working independently is always enough to catch a hare. If both do not cooperate, each, working independently, can only catch a hare with pay-off y each; note that with $x > y$, it is more rewarding for both to catch the stag than each catching a hare. In the case where one goes after the stag alone and the other goes after a hare, the one who catches the hare gets a pay-off of v (which is say equal to y, but in general, $v \geq y$), but the one who goes after the stag alone fails (since it is assumed that both cooperating is required to catch the stag), and starves, or gets a pay-off of u (even worse than catching a hare, i.e., $u < y$).

Hence, a machine reasoning above, should choose to cooperate. But note that the Stag-Hunt Game has two Nash equilibria, one where both cooperate to hunt the stag, and one where both do not cooperate, each hunting a hare.

Now consider another the two-player game which we shall call the *Contribution Game*, where each player (the actors) contributes information towards building a "common" knowledge base, which we consider, for this example, to be an urban map of some phenomenon as mentioned earlier. Here, the pay-off to a player represents benefits (minus costs of contributing, if any) to the player of the "common" knowledge base. Note that if no player contributes, there is no knowledge in the "common" knowledge base and the benefits to all players of an empty "common" knowledge base is 0.

Assume that the benefit of this is proportional to the amount of information and the benefit yielded by a "common" knowledge base from one player's contribution is b, and the benefit to each player if both contributes knowledge to the "common" knowledge base is $2b$. The cost of contributing is c, and assume $b > c$. Table 4.2 shows the pay-offs for both players (row player P pay-off, column player Q pay-off). Note that when both contributes, the pay-off for each is $2b - c$, which is the

Table 4.2 Contribution
Game showing pay-offs to
players of the "common"
knowledge base (Note: $b > c$
is assumed)

	Q	
P	Contribute	Don't contribute
Contribute	$2b - c, 2b - c$	$b - c, b$
Don't contribute	$b, b - c$	$0, 0$

benefit from both contributing minus the cost of contributing. If one contributes and
the other doesn't, then the benefit to the one who didn't contribute is b (benefiting
from the contribution of the other), and the benefit from the knowledge base of the
one who contributed minus the cost of contributing is $b - c$. If neither contributes,
then each may have its own knowledge, but no knowledge has been contributed
to the "common" knowledge base, in which case the benefit from the "common"
knowledge base (which is now empty) for both is 0. Note that this is a little different
from the Stag-Hunt Game in the case where the player who tried to hunt for the
stag alone starved (while the other hunted a hare), which is worse than both hunting
a hare; here, the player who contributed still received $b - c$ from the "common"
knowledge base, even when the other didn't contribute, which is better than both
not contributing. Also, in the case where one player contributed while the other
didn't, the player who didn't contribute basically freeloaded from the effort of the
other.

Suppose the probability of the row player P contributing is p, and the probability
of the column player Q contributing is q. The game is symmetric and the (expected)
pay-offs for the players are given as follows; for P:

$$V_P(p, q) = pq(2b - c) + p(1 - q)(b - c) + (1 - p)qb + (1 - p)(1 - q)0$$

and for Q:

$$V_Q(p, q) = pq(2b - c) + q(1 - p)(b - c) + (1 - q)pb + (1 - p)(1 - q)0$$

respectively.

Note that when both adopt the same strategy, $p = q$, then, for $i = P$ and $i = Q$:

$$V_i(p, p) = p^2(2b - c) + p(1 - p)(b - c) + (1 - p)pb + (1 - p)(1 - p)0$$
$$= 2pb - pc = p(2b - c)$$

which is maximised when both players contribute with certainty, i.e. $p = 1$ and
$q = 1$.

Note in this case that "contribute" is a dominant strategy for both players;
whether the other party contributes or not, it is better for a player to contribute.
Generalizing to n players (potential contributors), we would have all contributing,
with $nb - c$ as the pay-off for each player, that is, supposing that the benefit of the
"common" knowledge base to each player from n players' contributions is nb (and

Table 4.3 Contribution Game showing pay-offs to players from their own knowledge and the shared "common" knowledge base (Note: $b > c$ is assumed)

P	Q	
	Contribute	Don't contribute
Contribute	$2b - c, 2b - c$	$b - c, 2b$
Don't contribute	$2b, b - c$	b, b

c is the cost incurred when a player contributes). The larger n is, the more benefit it is to each player, since the cost to each player is fixed.

Note that with two players, the social welfare (here, defined to be the sum of the pay-offs of all the players) is $2(2b - c)$ when both contribute, $2b - c$ when only one contributes and 0 when both do not contribute. So, social welfare is maximised when both contribute. With n players, with $m \leq n$ contributing, the benefit to every player of the knowledge base is mb. Now, for each contributor, the pay-off is $mb - c$ (due to the cost of contributing), and for each non-contributor, it is mb. So, the social welfare is $m(mb - c) + (n - m)mb = m(nb - c)$, which is maximised when all $m = n$ contribute (since $nb > c$).

When one can benefit from one's own knowledge without sharing, another way to view the case of both not contributing is the pay-off (b, b) (instead of $(0, 0)$), i.e., each just benefit from its own knowledge, and in the case where one player contributes and the other does not, the player who contributes gets a pay-off of $b - c$ while the other player benefits from its own knowledge and knowledge from the other player, i.e., a pay-off of $2b$. In this case, a player does not want to contribute since the player is worse off by contributing when the other player contributes and when the other player does not. Table 4.3 illustrate this situation, and the result is that both players would not want to contribute (e.g., from P's perspective, suppose Q doesn't contribute, and P contributes, then the pay-off to P is $b - c$, which is less than b if P does not contribute, and suppose Q contributes, and P contributes, then the pay-off to P is $2b - c$, which is less than $2b$ if P does not contribute; similarly with Q). This situation is comparable to the *prisoner's dilemma* in game theory.

Note that in this case, the social welfare is $2(2b - c) = 2b + 2(b - c)$ when both contribute, $2b + (b - c)$ when only one contributes and $2b$ when both do not contribute. So, social welfare is also maximised when both contribute. Hence, society in general is better off when both contribute even though each might not want to. With n players, with $m \leq n$ contributing, for each contributor, the pay-off is $mb - c$ (with mb from the "common" knowledge base which includes the contributor's own contributed knowledge, and c is the cost of contributing), and for each non-contributor, it is $mb + b$ (with mb from the "common" knowledge base and b from the non-contributor's own knowledge which is not part of the "common" knowledge base). So, the social welfare is $m(mb - c) + (n - m)(mb + b) = nb + m(b(n-1) - c)$, which is maximised when all $m = n$ contribute (since $b(n-1) > c$, for $n > 1$).

Table 4.4 Contribution
Game with thresholding

	Q	
P	Contribute	Don't contribute
Contribute	$2b - c, 2b - c$	$-c, 0$
Don't contribute	$0, -c$	$0, 0$

More generally, instead of "contribution" to a "common" knowledge base, one can think of the above analysis for "cooperation", where the decision is whether to cooperate or not.

Now, suppose there is thresholding, so that only if both players cooperate can the benefits of $2b$ be extracted whereas one cooperating (in this case, contributing) yields inadequate "common" capability (in this case, knowledge) for anyone to benefit, which means that if one player contributes and the other didn't, the contributing player has wasted effort, that is, the pay-offs are as in Table 4.4. Note that this is a Stag-Hunt Game with $x = 2b - c, v = y = 0, u = -c$.

This means that there are two Nash equilibria (i.e., (Contribute, Contribute) and (Don't Contribute, Don't Contribute)), and so, reasoning along this line, it is possible that no one wants to cooperate in this case, since (Don't Contribute, Don't Contribute) is a Nash equilibrium, i.e. P has no better strategy than "Don't Contribute" in response to Q's strategy of "Don't Contribute", and Q has no better strategy than "Don't Contribute" in response to P's strategy of "Don't Contribute".

At this point, we can introduce a different type of equilibrium, called Kantian equilibrium from [59]. Instead of asking what is the best strategy or action to take given the possible strategies of the other player, one could ask both players to reason in a Kantian manner (which will be elaborated below) and ask the same question: "what strategy would I want both of us to play?" Then, the answer is to definitely to cooperate, i.e. for both to contribute. And this also leads to a Pareto efficient outcome. The simple Kantian equilibrium in this case is (Contribute, Contribute) and not (Don't Contribute, Don't Contribute). The simple Kantian equilibrium considers strategy profiles of the form (A, A), i.e., the same action taken by both players. This generalizes to finding $(A, \ldots, A)$ which is the action A best played by all players.

To elaborate on this, the Kantian equilibrium is based on the the philosopher Kant's ideas. The work in [55] discusses ethical rules for machines, i.e. the notion of *Kantian machines*. Kant's categorical imperative as described in [55] is:

> Act only according to that maxim whereby you can at the same time will that it should become a universal law.

or in other words:

> Kant tells the moral agent to test each maxim (or plan of action) as though it were a candidate for a universalized rule.

Indeed, one can justify that a maxim such as "try to cooperate first where possible" should very well be a rule for a machine under this test, especially when cooperation is beneficial. If a machine has this rule of behaviour, we say that *the machine is cooperative*. If this was universal (a maxim adopted by machines), many scenarios of cooperation could materialise, towards outcomes that are better for everyone (or every machine) where cooperation is better than non-cooperation, as we showed above. However, the machine needs to be designed so that this maxim is built-in, that is, as a general rule, by design, a machine should indeed try to cooperate first where possible, when cooperation is the best option for the collective. A machine that has this maxim, by design, as its rule of behaviour could be viewed as one aspect of a machine behaving ethically, even if not necessarily so. Cooperative machines could maximise social welfare (and its own utility), and perhaps one tends to think of an autonomous entity that is cooperative as more favourable, perhaps even more "virtuous" than a machine that is non-cooperative and acts selfishly, when an option to be cooperative is present, especially if that option actually benefits every party concerned more.

This view is, however, not without its issues and remains an open line of investigation. For example, there could be non-cooperative situations, i.e. situations where one tries to cooperate while others do not, which is severely damaging to the one that is trying to cooperate. In a situation where the cost c in Table 4.4 is very high, then it may be too dangerous to be predisposed to cooperating, just in case others don't cooperate. In general, say q is the probability of Q cooperating (contributing), and suppose the probability of P contributing is 1 (it is predisposed to cooperate), then the expected pay-off for P is:

$$V_P(1, q) = q(2b - c) + (1 - q)(-c) = 2bq - c$$

That is, for $V_P > 0$, we need $q > \frac{c}{2b}$, and in the case $b = c$, then $q > \frac{1}{2}$. If $b >> c$, then we may not need q to be too large, i.e., the benefits of being predisposed to cooperation outweigh the risks. If both P and Q are predisposed to cooperate (say, by design), then the Kantian equilibrium and the benefit $2b - c$ is achieved for both, i.e., $V_Q(1, 1) = V_P(1, 1) = 2b - c$.

While we consider that machines should reason in a Kantian manner and try to cooperate as much as possible (i.e., in principle, a machine should be cooperative-by-design), considerations of the risks are required, and would be application specific.

4.8.5 Cooperative Internet of Things

We discussed the Internet of Things in Chap. 1. The idea of connecting people, places, and things to the Internet in different ways has led to the Internet of Things of today. Such things are embedded with networking capabilities in order to be part of the Internet. When things are inter-connected, there is then the potential of these things to not only communicate but also cooperate and coordinate their behaviours, i.e., to be "social".

Machine-to-machine communication is not new, and is facilitated by the Internet of Things. As things become "smarter" and integrated with more AI and autonomous decision-making capabilities (denoted by "Smart/AI"), they might also be able to communicate intelligently and cooperate with other things in their operation, i.e., one might call a type of "social-AI". Two "equations" attempt to capture the ideas of autonomous or smart things and cooperative autonomous/smart things:

$$Smart\ Things = Things + Connectivity + Smart/AI$$

$$Cooperative\ Smart\ Things = Things + Connectivity + Smart/AI + Social\ AI$$

These things that cooperate might be owned by different parties and have their own goals, but yet might need to cooperate to best perform their function—recall the notion of cooperative automated vehicles mentioned above. Also, the cooperative or "social" behaviour of things here is more than just connectivity—two devices might be connected via Bluetooth or WiFi, but a high-level protocol is carried out using this connectivity for the devices to cooperate (e.g., to exchange cooperation messages, or cooperative sensing where shared sensor data or context data is exchanged, or cooperative actions), i.e. there is a *cooperation layer* of protocol above the *networking layer* of protocol.

We spoke of vehicles cooperating with each other, urban robots cooperating with each other, or swarms of drones working together, but cooperation can occur, when useful, among vehicles and urban robots, or urban robots with drones, and drones with vehicles, and so on. In general, the ability to cooperate across different types of devices can be useful in the future Automated City.

4.9 Trust and Ethics in AI and the Automated City

4.9.1 Trusting Machines

Our society is flooded with information. Information about virtually everything is becoming pervasive and accessible. Our daily life is increasingly dependent on complex interconnected systems which provide the information we require for our consumption. Such information is either pushed to us or available with a mere mouse click. This is a fundamental societal shift from the pre-Internet era, when users have to physically go to places of knowledge such as a library or universities to acquire knowledge, to the modern era, where information is nowadays pushed to us sometimes even without even asking.

Software analyses and personalises information for us to help us make daily decisions. Such information gives us the impression that we are making data-driven, evidence-based informed decisions. Lately, the rise of fake news have started to plant the seed in everyone's psyche that what you read or see on the Internet is not necessarily true. Even photos and videos can be faked, the so-called deep-fakes [50].

Moreover, the use of deep learning have started to uncover biases due to the nature of data used to train the algorithm (e.g., "racist algorithms").[49] Deep learning has somewhat blurred the separation between data and algorithms—good algorithms can still do badly with poor data. The quality of data used for training a deep learning algorithm has been shown to have an effect on whether or not significant biases will be introduced into the learnt model used for decision making (e.g., in the case of "racist algorithms"). Such algorithmic bias could affect IoT device behaviours if the algorithms are embedded into (or are used via an API by) devices [40]—for example, if a device (e.g., a smart door) uses facial recognition that is biased in that it is less reliable for people of certain racial origins than others. As another example, it was also noted that for more than a decade, it was known that oximeters may not be so accurate for people with darkly pigmented skin [26, 63].[50]

We increasingly require information to make decisions. Even our devices will use such information to function. While we considered cyber-physical systems for the Automated City in the previous chapter, the Automated City is one where its inhabitants will be aided by information achieved via automated means. We are increasingly dependent on the availability of such information (e.g., weather report, traffic report, pandemic information). The quality and quantity of the required information are of utmost importance as it has direct impact on the results and trust in an algorithm. Reliable and trustworthy AI systems are important in mission critical applications (from recommendation systems to automated vehicles that need to make decisions in the physical world).

As mentioned, a particular area of AI, namely Deep Learning is increasingly used to build systems that make decisions on behalf of humans due to the complexity of inputs. Machine learning algorithms have invaded all layers of our society. Machine learning algorithms are often seen as black boxes in the sense that one can open the box but it can still be very hard to explain how an algorithm arrived at a given result. Explainability of machine learning, or for AI technologies in general, (or popularly known as XAI, for eXplainable AI) has emerged as a fundamental functional and ethical issue brought about by AI. The authors in [9] proposed the notion of *Responsible Artificial Intelligence*, "a methodology for the large-scale implementation of AI methods in real organizations with fairness, model explainability and accountability at its core." The idea is that to win the trust and confidence of human users or a human audience, AI explainability, tailored according to the users or audience, can play a key role—of course, explainability could have other purposes beyond winning trust.

In *Rebooting AI: Building Artificial Intelligence We Can Trust*, Marcus and Davis noted that:

---

[49]For an overview in relation to facial recognition, see https://www.nature.com/articles/d41586-020-03186-4.

[50]See also https://emcrit.org/pulmcrit/racism-oximetry/ [last accessed: 27/5/2021].

> The core problem is trust. The narrow AI systems we have now often work—on what they are programmed for—but they can't be trusted with anything that hasn't been precisely anticipated by their programmers.

It seems that present day AI systems can be trusted to work within narrow or enveloped domains (as mentioned earlier in the book), if carefully engineered, but perhaps should not be thought of as reliable outside their anticipated domains of operations. For AI to work more broadly in the world, Marcus and Davis stated that:

> Trustworthy AI, grounded in reasoning, commonsense values, and sound engineering practice, will be transformational when it finally arrives, whether that is a decade or a century hence.

There seems a need to equip AI with commonsense reasoning and knowledge (or if they could learn them), in order to function in the real-world, apart from the ability to learn. In summary, our expectations of the Automated City might need to be toned down for the short term as AI continues to improve in the decades to come.

Indeed, a reason for the humility and caution with AI and robotics is that technology can still fail, and it could be that people might *overtrust* machines (even those that do not have a 100% successful track record), against their own commonsense judgement.[51]

4.9.2   Can AI and the Automated City be Dangerous?

We discussed governance by algorithms earlier in Sect. 4.2.2. Here, we acknowledge that there are other possible dangers, sometimes more subtle. For example, there could be a dependency of humans on devices or machines for many aspects of life, which in some ways, already is the case (e.g., smartphones). Such a strong dependency can cause issues when the machine does not work as intended.

Also, a robot owned by someone might do something unexpected, and the issue of accountability then arises—whether the owner, robot manufacturer, the robot itself, or some combination of parties, would bear the responsibility. The circumstances of such situations might also have an influence on who should share the responsibility.

We used anthropomorphic metaphors of partnership and host in thinking about the Automated City in Chap. 2. The problems of anthropomorphism of machines have been noted by others [75], from creating too high expectations of machines to requiring them to follow human norms. Emotional attachment to home robots, and the question of whether a company might exploit that, can also be an issue as noted

---

[51] See the discussion on trust in technology at https://www.technologyreview.com/2021/05/13/1024874/ai-ayanna-howard-trust-robots/ [last accessed: 15/5/2021]. In a study done, people trusted robots to lead them out of an emergency situation rather than use their own judgement of exiting safely where they came in [58].

by Darling in *The New Breed* [19]. And can such machines be used to manipulate or trick humans into doing certain things? Drawing parallels with how humans have related to animals over millennia, as both "tool" or aid, and as pets, Darling outlined a possibly new category of relationship, which is that of humans with robots that is based on thinking less about robots as humans, and more about how humans relate to animals. Indeed, this can be a fruitful way of thinking about how humans relate to machines, including how to assign liability when a robot owned by someone does something wrong, and thinking about how humans should treat urban robots on the street.

Hence, with each tool, from the humble kitchen knife to the camera, there are dangers of misuse and abuse, but carefully thought-through integration of technology in society, with appropriate metaphors and mental models, can bring benefits, while allaying the concerns and worries about them.

4.9.3   Ethical Algorithms in the Automated City

Research on the ethics of algorithms has received substantial attention from the media over the past decade. Programming a massive amount of cooperating components in an Automated City requires the utmost attention. The effect of decision-making by machines at the micro and macro levels can have profound ramifications. The use of massively distributed and opaque algorithms to improve individual and social welfare comes with significant ethical risks. For example, allocating mobility priority to a large group of transport users may be socially detrimental to another minority group.

Not every human makes decisions in the same way. Furthermore, humans might program automated systems in different ways using various decision rules based on various information to achieve their goals. During the design of an automated system, the designer faces a multitude of choices. Some of the choices are ethically relevant, e.g., choosing what design requirements and criteria to formulate, what trade-offs between design criteria are socially and individually acceptable, what risks would arise, which secondary potentially unanticipated effects of a design to accept, and what control to enable for the user.

Ethical theories provide a framework for understanding the foundations and goals of a decision. These goals might adhere to a set of ethical principles such as non-maleficence, least harm, beneficence, health maximisation, efficiency, respect for autonomy, and justice, as also used in [61]. The ethical theory that a decision-maker chooses to apply is guided by ethical principles. Four broad categories of ethical principle include deontology, utilitarianism, rights, and virtues.[52] For example, utilitarianism is often upheld by transport managers who think about the good of

---

[52]A quick reference is at https://www.dsef.org/wp-content/uploads/2012/07/EthicalTheories.pdf [last accessed: 15/5/2021].

society as a whole. Utilitarianism holds that the most ethical choice is the one that will produce the greatest good for the highest number road users.

Ethics of fairness, accountability, and transparency is now increasingly scrutinised due to the exponential use of AI such as deep learning algorithms to solve our problems, shape our city, fulfill our societal needs and create our future.

4.9.4   Ethical Algorithmic Behaviour for Smart Connected Things

With the deployment of connected IoT devices with autonomous capabilities, a range of ethical concerns arises. For example, ethical concerns involving such devices include the following:[53]

- Devices lacking security mechanisms built-in, or which are easily hackable, e.g., un-encrypted communications, pre-set default passwords, and unprotected access, can pose a threat to individuals but also to society as a whole, if such devices proliferate. While many IoT device manufacturers are indeed adding security to devices, and guidelines have been issued, legislation is also emerging. In the US, the IoT Cybersecurity Improvement Act[54] was signed into law in December 2020. The Act requires any IoT device bought using government funds to meet minimum security standards set by the NIST.[55]
- Devices will need to be updated and serviced, and maintained, e.g., to avoid problems due to faults or malfunction, and to update security. For consumer devices, constant upgrades can be cumbersome and cause interruptions for the user. For hard to reach devices (e.g., embedded in urban infrastructure), such updates need to be remotely managed, and any resulting down-times considered.
- Handling and control of data collected by IoT devices, e.g., data collected via user interaction with the device or via a device's sensors, microphone or camera, will be important; in particular, medical devices might collect data about a user (e.g., physiological data or sensitive private health data), when used by the user, or as proactively collected by a device (e.g., a robot); providing users who want it control over their data, e.g., perhaps along the lines of the European General Data Protection Regulation (GDPR), including minimising data collection and the right to be forgotten, will be important, though not easy to achieve everywhere— e.g., data anonymization might be done at the local device, via a third-party service or at the manufacturer's end, depending on the user's trust of third-party

---

[53]This is also discussed in [41] in connection with the convergence of automation with Internet connected things.

[54]https://www.congress.gov/bill/116th-congress/house-bill/1668 [last accessed: 15/5/2021].

[55]https://www.iotworldtoday.com/2021/02/02/new-iot-cybersecurity-improvement-act-creating-a-floor-for-iot-security/ [last accessed: 15/5/2021].

services or manufacturers [11], and many stakeholders could be involved with IoT data [23].

- Algorithmic bias that might be incorporated into a device, as already mentioned, e.g., a device that uses facial recognition might not be trained adequately on certain categories of people and so has poorer performance for those people. Algorithmic bias is a concern in itself, apart from IoT devices, but such bias can find its way into smart devices that utilise those algorithms in making autonomous decisions.
- Devices might cooperate with each other over the Internet, and share information, thereby complicating the management of data, and possibly reducing control over data that is now duplicated among multiple devices and stakeholders.
- Smart devices that take action autonomously will need to be transparent (and accountable, e.g., to their owners). This is related to explainability in AI mentioned earlier but with smart devices that inhabits the physical world, such as urban robots and drones, the ability to log and trace actions and impact on the physical world will be useful.
- Devices might take action autonomously and so, the user feels a lost of control or choice. Users, should be respected, that is, given adequate control over their devices, even while a device (e.g., a robot) might be expected to act autonomously—this delicate balance of autonomy and control will need to be negotiated with the user, or at least, the extent of autonomy and control available for a given device should be understood by users.

  There is another issue with machines working with people; we used the metaphor of machines as partner and host in Chap. 2, but their design and deployment should be aligned with human capabilities and preferences—e.g., if a human worker has to work dangerously fast in order to keep up with a machine, or feel forced to behave in certain ways due to the machine's imposition, then the value and role of the machine might need reconsideration.
- Devices such as urban robots that use public spaces might need to be protected, not just from physical harm and malicious actions hindering their operation, but also cyber attacks. Indeed, given that the devices act in the physical world and in public, as mentioned, there can be complex liability issues, e.g., devices that might be harmed due to a misinterpretation of a device's actions, a device being misled into doing damage (e.g., by changing a street sign temporarily), or more subtle issues of a device being hindered or slowed-down in its operation deliberately, even if not actually being damaged.
- Devices might make decisions in critical situations, based on the ethical values of its developers, which might not be aligned with those of their users—for example, an automated vehicle that decides what to do and who to save based on a utilitarian basis. Such dilemmas have been discussed in the popular study on the moral dilemma of the automated vehicle [6].
- Automated entities needs to have a good representation of the surrounding world and a comprehensive assessment of risks in order to navigate safely. A robot senses its environment through a set of sensors to create a representation of the world. The result is a map obtained from fusing data from multiple sensors. Once

a map is created, the automated entity needs to localise itself and other objects within such maps, identifying their whereabouts and the risks they pose. There are many techniques such as Simultaneous Localisation and Mapping (SLAM) or Structure From Motion (SFM) to achieve such mechanisms. These techniques are well advanced—however, they assume that the environment they sense is static, and therefore, they might not perform well in complex highly dynamic environments [73].

Indeed, building devices that behave ethically might require rethinking of the

- *processes* via which a device is developed from inception, requirements analysis, design to implementation and testing,
- *developers* and what their values are and how their values might or might not influence the design and development of the device,
- *the artifact itself*, including the features and capabilities of the device, and implications of what it can and cannot do,
- *post-deployment support and validation*, including what happens when something goes wrong, how to maintain and update the device, and how to support users with the device, and certification and verification of ethical algorithmic behaviour might be needed, and
- *context of operation*, including not only the safe operation domain of the device, but how to manage expectations about what the device can and cannot do, and the regulations around the devices operation. It must be noted that ethics can also be culturally rooted and social context dependent, so that an acceptable ethical behaviour in one context might not be acceptable in a different context, and conversely (see, for example, the study on culture and AI ethics in [30], calls for cross-cultural cooperation on AI ethics [51], and suggestions for anthropological and ethnographic approaches to understanding the social and cultural contexts for AI[56]).

In was noted in [74] that a way to operationalize AI ethics is to include appropriate ethical principles as part of the requirements of a system. Design patterns related to ethical principles, continuous validation and monitoring for ethical principles, governance based measures such as certification of "ethical maturity" and reviews of the ethical impact of systems can be helpful. These ideas can be applied to the development of smart devices, and the algorithms therein. Further development is still required on processes, developer guidelines, artifact validation and testing, regulations and certifications, and post-deployment support that is context-aware. Given the wide range of AI ethical guidelines and principles, tools such as the "Dynamics of AI Principles" toolbox[57] developed at the AI Ethics Lab can be useful for developers of smart technologies to think through the complex

---

[56] See *The Short Anthropological Guide to the Study of Ethical AI*, at https://montrealethics.ai/the-short-anthropological-guide-to-the-study-of-ethical-ai/ [last accessed: 27/5/2021]

[57] https://aiethicslab.com/big-picture/ [last accessed: 28/5/2021].

ethical considerations in the systems they built [17]. A deeper discussion of AI ethics (also called Responsible AI) can be found in [10, 21].

One more factor is a device's *end of life considerations*, including how it might be disposed when no longer in use, re-purposed, or recycled, i.e. considerations of the entire life-cycle of the device with sustainability goals in mind. A science-fiction scenario is where a robot, knowing the near end of its own operational life, goes back to its manufacturer in order to be recycled and re-purposed. A more realistic or nearer term scenario is where a device is not only designed with reuse in mind,[58] but also designed to operate in such a way that it facilitates being re-used and re-cycled—for example, a robot that is designed with modular components, where parts which can wear out faster are separated from other parts.

4.10 Summary of Chapter

This chapter has attempted to capture some of the broader challenges of the Automated City, broader in the sense of going beyond specific technologies (as we did in Chap. 3) and going beyond technical difficulties, while having an impact on how technology is developed. We consider the many different visions of the Automated City, how cities (including the Automated City) evolve, the issue of governance for Automated Cities, new business models in the Automated City, city transportation, issues of trust in AI as they are employed in the city, the challenges and opportunities that real-time tracking yields, emerging computational infrastructure such as edge computing servers in urban areas, blockchain applications for the smart city and robotics, the need for cooperation among the many machines expected in the Automated City, and ethical challenges for a city full of smart devices and automation.

We have outlined challenges and also sketched a number of ideas (on the information and communication technology aspects), much research and multi-disciplinary thinking are still required for these issues, towards careful, beneficial, and ethical integration of AI-incorporated smart devices in the Automated City that would align with aspirational visions of cities.

Certainly, the above list is not exhaustive. However, they hopefully indicate that the challenges of the Automated City are not only technical, but socio-technical and span disciplines, requiring inputs from many different perspectives.

Moreover, the world trends such as increasing urbanization, population aging (in some countries, in particular), climate change, and pandemics, will continue to be influential factors shaping cities. The role of automation to help address issues arising from these trends will be increasingly important, including questions

---

[58]The following white paper proposes component reuse for robotics: https://www.researchgate. net/publication/251871874_The_Use_of_Reuse_for_Designing_and_Manufacturing_Robots/ stats [last accessed: 15/5/2021].

about how automation can help people better utilise shared spaces in the city, how automation can help the disabled and the elderly live better in the city, and how to effectively deploy automation as an aid in disaster and emergency situations. For example, IoT devices can be helpful for the elderly at home, but also when they go outside in the city, e.g., for navigation, continual health monitoring and remote care (see also the extensive review in [52, 67]), and urban robots can help the elderly as they go about in the city. Indeed, many ideas about creating an age-friendly city (or even an *aged*-friendly city) consider utilising appropriate technology,[59] but also requires careful design and planning, e.g., in terms of transportation, housing and making spaces accessible and socially inclusive [45, 68].[60]

References

1. Abbott, R., & Bogenschneider, B. (2017). Should robots pay taxes? Tax policy in the age of automation. *Harvard Law and Policy Review, 12*. Available at SSRN: https://ssrn.com/abstract=2932483 or https://doi.org/10.2139/ssrn.2932483
2. Aceto, G., Persico, V., & Pescapé, A. (2019). A survey on information and communication technologies for industry 4.0: State-of-the-art, taxonomies, perspectives, and challenges. *IEEE Communications Surveys Tutorials, 21*(4), 3467–3501
3. Aliedani, A., & Loke, S. W. (2018). Cooperative autonomous vehicles: An investigation of the drop-off problem. *IEEE Transactions on Intelligent Vehicles, 3*(3), 310–316.
4. Aliedani, A., & Loke, S. W. (2019). Cooperative car parking using vehicle-to-vehicle communication: An agent-based analysis. *Computers, Environment and Urban Systems, 77*, 101256.
5. Almannaa, M. H., Ashqar, H. I., Elhenawy, M., Masoud, M., Rakotonirainy, A., & Rakha, H. (2021). A comparative analysis of e-scooter and e-bike usage patterns: Findings from the city of Austin, TX. *International Journal of Sustainable Transportation, 15*(7), 571–579.
6. Awad, E., Dsouza, S., Kim, R., Schulz, J., Henrich, J., Shariff, A., Bonnefon, J.-F., & Rahwan, I. (2018). The moral machine experiment. *Nature, 563*(7729), 59–64.
7. Bagloee, S. A., Heshmati, M., Dia, H., Ghaderi, H., Pettit, C., & Asadi, M. (2021). Blockchain: The operating system of smart cities. *Cities, 112*, 103104.
8. Baltazar, A. R., Petry, M. R., Silva, M. F., & Moreira, A. P. (2021). Autonomous wheelchair for patient's transportation on healthcare institutions. *SN Applied Sciences, 3*(3), 354.
9. Barredo Arrieta, A., Díaz-Rodríguez, N., Del Ser, J., Bennetot, A., Tabik, S., Barbado, A., Garcia, S., Gil-Lopez, S., Molina, D., Benjamins, R., Chatila, R., & Herrera, F. (2020). Explainable artificial intelligence (XAI): Concepts, taxonomies, opportunities and challenges toward responsible AI. *Information Fusion, 58*, 82–115.
10. Bartneck, C., Lütge, C., Wagner, A., & Welsh, S. (2021). *An introduction to ethics in robotics and AI*. Cham: Springer Nature.

---

[59] See https://theconversation.com/this-is-how-we-create-the-age-friendly-smart-city-152973 and https://ec.europa.eu/eip/ageing/file/2624/download_en%3Ftoken=1Em_qTx7 [last accessed: 13/6/2021].

[60] See also https://theconversation.com/ageing-in-neighbourhood-what-seniors-want-instead-of-retirement-villages-and-how-to-achieve-it-138729 for a case in Australia [last accessed: 14/6/2021].

11. Bastos, D., Giubilo, F., Shackleton, M., & El-Mousa, F. (2018). GDPR privacy implications for the internet of things. In *Proceedings of the 4th Annual IoT Security Foundation Conference*.
12. Batty, M. (2018). *Inventing future cities*. Cambridge, MA: The MIT Press.
13. Ben Messaoud, R. (2017). *Towards Efficient Mobile Crowdsensing Assignment and Uploading Schemes*. Theses, Université Paris-Est, July 2017.
14. Brilhante, O., & Klaas, J. (2018). Green city concept and a method to measure green city performance over time applied to fifty cities globally: Influence of GDP, population size and energy efficiency. *Sustainability, 10*(6), 2031.
15. Bucher, T. (2018). *IF... THEN: Algorithmic power and politics*. Oxford: Oxford University Press.
16. Calvaresi, D., Appoggetti, K., Lustrissimi, L., Marinoni, M., Sernani, P., Dragoni, A. F., & Schumacher, M. (2018). Multi-agent systems' negotiation protocols for cyber-physical systems: Results from a systematic literature review. In *Proceedings of the 10th International Conference on Agents and Artificial Intelligence - Volume 2: ICAART, INSTICC* (pp. 224–235). Setúbal: SciTePress.
17. Canca, C. (2020). Operationalizing ai ethics principles. *Communications of the ACM, 63*(12), 18–21.
18. Capponi, A., Fiandrino, C., Kantarci, B., Foschini, L., Kliazovich, D., & Bouvry, P. (2019). A survey on mobile crowdsensing systems: Challenges, solutions, and opportunities. *IEEE Communications Surveys Tutorials, 21*(3), 2419–2465.
19. Darling, K. (2021). *The new breed: How to think about robots*. London: Penguin.
20. Desai, P., Loke, S. W., Desai, A., & Singh, J. (2013). CARAVAN: Congestion avoidance and route allocation using virtual agent negotiation. *IEEE Transactions on Intelligent Transportation Systems, 14*(3), 1197–1207.
21. Dignum, V. (2019). *Responsible artificial intelligence - How to develop and use AI in a responsible way. Artificial intelligence: Foundations, theory, and algorithms*. Cham: Springer.
22. Downton, P., Jones, D., Zeunert, J., & Roös, P. (2017). Biophilic design applications: Putting theory and patterns into built environment practice. *KnE Engineering, 2*(1), 59–65.
23. El-Gazzar, R., & Stendal, K. (2020). Examining how GDPR challenges emerging technologies. *Journal of Information Policy, 10*, 237–275.
24. Elhenawy, M., Glaser, S., Bond, A., Rakotonirainy, A., Demmel, S., & Masoud, M. (2020). A framework for testing independence between lane change and cooperative intelligent transportation system. *PLoS One, 15*(2), e0229289.
25. Fan, T., Long, P., Liu, W., Pan, J. (2020). Distributed multi-robot collision avoidance via deep reinforcement learning for navigation in complex scenarios. *The International Journal of Robotics Research, 39*(7), 856–892.
26. Feiner, J. R., Severinghaus, J. W., & Bickler, P. E. (2007). Dark skin decreases the accuracy of pulse oximeters at low oxygen saturation: The effects of oximeter probe type and gender. *Anesthesia & Analgesia, 105*(6 Suppl.), S18–23.
27. Ferrer, E. C., Rudovic, O., Hardjono, T., & Pentland, A. (2018). Robochain: A secure data-sharing framework for human-robot interaction. CoRR abs/1802.04480.
28. Gates, B. (2021). *How to avoid a climate disaster: The solutions we have and the breakthroughs we need*. Allen Lane.
29. Gerety, R. M. (2021). Neighborhood watch. *MIT Technology Review, 124*, 30–40.
30. Hagerty, A., & Rubinov, I. (2019). Global AI ethics: A review of the social impacts and ethical implications of artificial intelligence. CoRR abs/1907.07892.
31. Higuchi, T., Rabsatt, R. V., Gerla, M., Altintas, O., & Dressler, F. (2019). Cooperative downloading in vehicular heterogeneous networks at the edge. In *2019 IEEE Globecom Workshops (GC Wkshps)* (pp. 1–5).
32. Hlldobler, B., & Wilson, E. (2018). *The superorganism: The beauty, elegance, and strangeness of insect societies* (1st Ed.). New York: W.W. Norton and Company.
33. Kapitonov, A., Lonshakov, S., Berman, I., Ferrer, E. C., Bonsignorio, F. P., Bulatov, V., & Svistov, A. (2019). Robotic services for new paradigm smart cities based on decentralized technologies. *Ledger, 4*.

34. Kaye, S.-A., Lewis, I., Buckley, L., Gauld, C., & Rakotonirainy, A. (2020). To share or not to share: A theoretically guided investigation of factors predicting intentions to use fully automated shared passenger shuttles. *Transportation Research Part F: Traffic Psychology and Behaviour, 75*, 203–213.
35. Khawalid, A., Acristinii, D., van Toor, H., & Ferrer, E. C. (2019). Grex: A decentralized hive mind. *Ledger, 4*. https://doi.org/10.5195/ledger.2019.176
36. Kolias, C., Seliem, M., Elgazzar, K., & Khalil, K. (2018). Towards privacy preserving iot environments: A survey. *Wireless Communications and Mobile Computing, 2018*, 1032761.
37. Liyanage, M., Dar, F., Sharma, R., & Flores, H. (2021). GEESE: Edge computing enabled by UAVs. *Pervasive and Mobile Computing, 72*, 101340.
38. Loke, S. W. (2019). Cooperative automated vehicles: A review of opportunities and challenges in socially intelligent vehicles beyond networking. *IEEE Transactions on Intelligent Vehicles, 4*(4), 509–518.
39. Loke, S. W. (2015). The internet of flying-things: Opportunities and challenges with airborne fog computing and mobile cloud in the clouds. CoRR abs/1507.04492.
40. Loke, S. W. (2019). Achieving ethical algorithmic behaviour in the internet-of-things: A review. CoRR abs/1910.10241.
41. Loke, S. W. (2019). Achieving ethical algorithmic behaviour in the internet-of-things: A review. CoRR abs/1910.10241.
42. Lovén, L., Lähderanta, T., Ruha, L., Leppänen, T., Peltonen, E., Riekki, J., & Sillanpää, M. J. (2020). Scaling up an edge server deployment. In *2020 IEEE International Conference on Pervasive Computing and Communications Workshops (PerCom Workshops)* (pp. 1–7).
43. Lähderanta, T., Leppänen, T., Ruha, L., Lovén, L., Harjula, E., Ylianttila, M., Riekki, J., & Sillanpää, M. J. (2021). Edge computing server placement with capacitated location allocation. *Journal of Parallel and Distributed Computing, 153*, 130–149.
44. Majeed, U., Khan, L. U., Yaqoob, I., Ahsan Kazmi, S. M., Salah, K., & Hong, C. S. (2021). Blockchain for iot-based smart cities: Recent advances, requirements, and future challenges. *Journal of Network and Computer Applications, 181*, 103007.
45. Marston, H. R., Shore, L., & White, P. J. (2020). How does a (smart) age-friendly ecosystem look in a post-pandemic society? *International Journal of Environmental Research and Public Health, 17*(21), 7701–8291.
46. Merlin, L. A., Yan, X., Xu, Y., & Zhao, X. (2021). A segment-level model of shared, electric scooter origins and destinations. *Transportation Research Part D: Transport and Environment, 92*, 102709.
47. Mitra, R., & Hess, P. M. (2021). Who are the potential users of shared e-scooters? An examination of socio-demographic, attitudinal and environmental factors. *Travel Behaviour and Society, 23*, 100–107.
48. Mora, H., Mendoza-Tello, J. C., Varela-Guzmán, E. G., & Szymanski, J. (2021). Blockchain technologies to address smart city and society challenges. *Computers in Human Behavior, 122*, 106854.
49. Morishita, S., Maenaka, S., Nagata, D., Tamai, M., Yasumoto, K., Fukukura, T., & Sato, K. (2015). Sakurasensor: Quasi-realtime cherry-lined roads detection through participatory video sensing by cars. In *Proceedings of the 2015 ACM International Joint Conference on Pervasive and Ubiquitous Computing, UbiComp '15* (pp. 695–705). New York, NY: Association for Computing Machinery.
50. Nguyen, T. T., Nguyen, C. M., Nguyen, D. T., Nguyen, D. T., & Nahavandi, S. (2019). Deep learning for deepfakes creation and detection. CoRR abs/1909.11573.
51. ÓhÉigeartaigh, S. S., Whittlestone, J., Liu, Y., Zeng, Y., Liu, Z. (2020). Overcoming barriers to cross-cultural cooperation in ai ethics and governance. *Philosophy & Technology, 33*(4), 571–593.
52. Ollevier, A., Aguiar, G., Palomino, M., & Simpelaere, I. S. (2020). How can technology support ageing in place in healthy older adults? A systematic review. *Public Health Reviews, 41*(1), 26.

53. Parris, K. M., Amati, M., Bekessy, S. A., Dagenais, D., Fryd, O., Hahs, A. K., Hes, D., Imberger, S. J., Livesley, S. J., Marshall, A. J., Rhodes, J. R., Threlfall, C. G. , Tingley, R., van der Ree, R., Walsh, C. J., Wilkerson, M. L. , & Williams, N. S. G. (2018). The seven lamps of planning for biodiversity in the city. *Cities, 83*, 44–53.
54. Pimm, S., Alibhai, S., Bergl, R., Dehgan, A., Giri, C., Jewell, Z., Joppa, L., Kays, R., & Loarie, S. (2015). Emerging technologies to conserve biodiversity. *Trends in Ecology and Evolution, 30*, 10.
55. Powers, T. M. (2006). Prospects for a kantian machine. *IEEE Intelligent Systems, 21*(4), 46–51.
56. Queralta, J. P., Qingqing, L., Zou, Z., & Westerlund, T. (2020). Enhancing autonomy with blockchain and multi-access edge computing in distributed robotic systems. In *2020 Fifth International Conference on Fog and Mobile Edge Computing (FMEC)* (pp. 180–187).
57. Rakotonirainy, A., Schroeter, R., & Soro, A. (2014). Three social car visions to improve driver behaviour. *Pervasive and Mobile Computing, 14*, 147–160. Special Issue on Pervasive Education Special Issue on The Social Car: Socially-inspired Mechanisms for Future Mobility Services.
58. Robinette, P., Li, W., Allen, R., Howard, A. M., & Wagner, A. R. (2016). Overtrust of robots in emergency evacuation scenarios. In *The Eleventh ACM/IEEE International Conference on Human Robot Interaction, HRI '16* (pp. 101–108). New York: IEEE Press.
59. Roemer, J. E. (2019). *How we cooperate: A theory of Kantian optimization*. New Haven: Yale University Press.
60. Sanders, R. L., Branion-Calles, M., & Nelson, T. A. (2020). To scoot or not to scoot: Findings from a recent survey about the benefits and barriers of using e-scooters for riders and non-riders. *Transportation Research Part A: Policy and Practice, 139*, 217–227.
61. Schröder-Bäck, P., Duncan, P., Sherlaw, W., Brall, C., & Czabanowska, K. (2014). Teaching seven principles for public health ethics: towards a curriculum for a short course on ethics in public health programmes. *BMC Medical Ethics, 15*. Article number: 73.
62. Schwartz, R., Dodge, J., Smith, N. A., & Etzioni, O. (2020). Green AI. *Communications of the ACM, 63*(12), 54–63.
63. Sjoding, M. W., Dickson, R. P., Iwashyna, T. J., Gay, S. E., & Valley, T. S. (2020). Racial bias in pulse oximetry measurement. *New England Journal of Medicine, 383*(25), 2477–2478.
64. Socha, R., & Kogut, B. (2020). Urban video surveillance as a tool to improve security in public spaces. *Sustainability, 12*(15), 6210.
65. Strobel, V., Castelló Ferrer, E., & Dorigo, M. (2018). Managing byzantine robots via blockchain technology in a swarm robotics collective decision making scenario. In *Proceedings of the 17th International Conference on Autonomous Agents and MultiAgent Systems, AAMAS '18* (pp. 541–549), Richland, SC: International Foundation for Autonomous Agents and Multiagent Systems.
66. Tang, X., Chen, X., Geng, Z., & Chen, W. (2020). Cooperative content downloading in vehicular ad hoc networks. *Procedia Computer Science, 174*, 224–230. 2019 International Conference on Identification, Information and Knowledge in the Internet of Things.
67. Tun, S. Y. Y., Madanian, S., & Mirza, F. (2021). Internet of things (IoT) applications for elderly care: A reflective review. *Aging Clinical and Experimental Research, 33*(4), 855–867.
68. van Hoof, J., Marston, H. R., Kazak, J. K., & Buffel, T. (2021). Ten questions concerning age-friendly cities and communities and the built environment. *Building and Environment, 199*, 107922.
69. Wang, S., Zhao, Y., Xu, J., Yuan, J., & Hsu, C.-H. (2019). Edge server placement in mobile edge computing. *Journal of Parallel and Distributed Computing, 127*, 160–168.
70. Wu, D., Bi, Y., & Liang, J. (2014). Cooperative downloading by multivehicles in urban vanet. *International Journal of Distributed Sensor Networks, 10*(2), 319514.
71. Xiang, S., Li, L., Lo, S. M., & Li, X. (2017). People-centric mobile crowdsensing platform for urban design. In G. Cong, W.-C. Peng, W. E. Zhang, C. Li, & A. Sun (Eds.), *Advanced data mining and applications* (pp. 569–581), Cham: Springer International Publishing.

72. Zambonelli, F., Salim, F., Loke, S. W., De Meuter, W., & Kanhere, S. (2018). Algorithmic governance in smart cities: The conundrum and the potential of pervasive computing solutions. *IEEE Technology and Society Magazine, 37*(2), 80–87.

73. Zhang, J., Henein, M., Mahony, R. E., & Ila, V. (2020). VDO-SLAM: A visual dynamic object-aware SLAM system. CoRR abs/2005.11052.

74. Zhu, L., Xu, X., Lu, Q., Governatori, G., & Whittle, J. (2021). AI and ethics - operationalising responsible AI. CoRR abs/2105.08867.

75. Złotowski, J., Proudfoot, D., Yogeeswaran, K., & Bartneck, C. (2015). Anthropomorphism: Opportunities and challenges in human–robot interaction. *International Journal of Social Robotics, 7*(3), 347–360.

Chapter 5
Conclusion

Abstract We conclude this book by discussing several questions on the city that are on a more philosophical tone.

5.1 The City in Physical Space and in Cyber Space

We have discussed a range of technologies and concerns with respect to the development of the Automated City. It seems that technological advancements in IoT and AI will continue to have a profound impact on future versions of our cities. Accompanying the physical structure and architecture of cities are the cyber structure and architecture of cities, which is becoming increasingly sophisticated. The overlay of social networks, data communications traffic, and cyber space interactions among people and devices over the physical city are not independent of the dynamics, i.e., the physical movement of people and things, and events, in the city. Interactions in cyber space affect the physical space, and conversely, things occurring in the physical world would effect changes in cyber space. City inhabitants inhabit both those spaces—the physical space and the cyber space, and thus, are affected by, and affect, developments in both spaces. We see this inter-play of interactions between these two spaces in many different phenomena.

5.2 What Use Will the Automated City Have? Reflections on the Post-Pandemic City

Viruses infect both the cyber world and the physical world, though they are of totally different kinds. Computer virus attacks on cyber-physical systems impact both the computer systems, and the physical world so inter-weaved with such systems. Careful consideration must then be given to the potential physical impact of computer virus struck cyber-physical computer systems, especially in the design of such cyber-physical systems. Biological virus attacks on humans clearly affect the physical world, whose behaviour changes might then be detected and reflected in computer systems and in activities in cyber space.

COVID-19 has radically changed our lives. It has disrupted the way we work, communicate, shop and move. As pointed out earlier, the movement restrictions and social distancing have unexpectedly forced the entire community, regardless of age or tech-literacy to adopt communication technology such as Zoom, Microsoft Teams, Skype or Google Meet;[1] in a very short period, many more people went online and understood how to do things online more than before (what has been called a *digital surge* [2]). Scalability of computer systems, especially based on the cloud model, allowed rapid scaling up of computer resources to support this.

The ubiquity of video conferencing services facilitates communications. Such use of technology also saves travel time, costs and reduces transport pollution. At the peak of the pandemic in certain countries, GHG emissions decreased by 26% on average [4].

It is also interesting that sensors that normally detect pedestrian and vehicular traffic, and air pollution, captured the impact of the changing behaviour of cities, in some ways, throwing out what has been previously detected "normal patterns of city behaviour". It remains to be seen what new patterns of city behaviour would look like, post-pandemic.

This pandemic is unprecedented. New knowledge of COVID-19 is starting to emerge at a slow pace despite the tremendous global efforts of the international health community. Such new knowledge will continue to re-shape our lives. One thing is that this pandemic has taught us the necessity to re-build the foundations of our society on altruism. All levels of our society, be it family, community or country level has shown an unprecedented degree of solidarity to combat this scourge. Individuals are asked to keep social distancing or wear a mask so that society is safer, the virus is not passed on to the elderly or to alleviate the workload of healthcare staff. States and countries are working together, and control their borders to limit the spread of the virus. Technologists have scrambled to assemble solutions to a range of problems resulting from the pandemic, as we saw in Chap. 1.

COVID-19's impact on cities has been drastic, and as we write the concluding chapter of the book, while some cities are bouncing back and "new normals" are becoming commonplace, there are also cities experiencing worsening conditions.

For many, COVID-19 has changed permanently the way we work and live, for example, the way we travel.The increased number of push bikes is here to stay and it is a new normal [3].[2] Encouragingly, this growth of active transport suggests the potential for positive impacts on health and a fundamental societal

---

[1] https://cloud.google.com/blog/products/g-suite/keeping-google-meet-ahead-of-usage-demand-during-covid-19 [last accessed: 20/5/2021].

[2] See also the BBC report at https://www.bbc.com/future/bespoke/made-on-earth/the-great-bicycle-boom-of-2020.html, the Forbes report at https://www.forbes.com/sites/carltonreid/2020/05/01/bicycling-booms-during-lockdown-but-theres-a-warning-from-history/ and for Australia, https://www.bicyclingaustralia.com.au/news/lockdown-leads-to-surge-in-cycling [last accessed: 19/5/2021].

shift. However, an increase in active transport might disadvantage social groups, with long commuting distances, e.g., rural and remote regions, or the disabled—a question is then how automated technologies, such as those we have seen in Chap. 3, can help ameliorate this issue.

This pandemic has tested the resilience capacities of different socio-political systems. Authors have claimed that COVID-19 has made Australians more conservative, care less about others, and less open to new ideas.[3]

The restrictions imposed by the health crisis such as lock-downs, behavioural and movement restrictions, social distancing, the need to wear facial masks, separation from families and missing loved ones might have contributed to such a general pessimism. Nevertheless, one could wonder about what will happen to our lifestyle habits post-pandemic. And, would the economy take a protectionist path, and sound the death knell of globalization? Would the current globalization be significantly altered and turn into extreme withdrawals into one's own national space?

As we are concluding this book, the latest statistics about the rate of vaccination from Our World in Data[4] reports:

- 22.2% of the world population has received at least one dose of a COVID-19 vaccine,
- 2.8 billion doses have been administered globally, and 40.5 million are now administered each day, and
- only 0.9% of people in low-income countries have received at least one dose.

Such a vaccination rate (indeed some might say not high enough!) could be seen as an incredible demonstration of solidarity between citizens as it is mainly about protecting others, especially, the vulnerable. Furthermore, community based solidarity initiatives are multiplying worldwide, especially to help the poor and vulnerable people hard hit by the pandemic.

In visions of the post-pandemic city, Fulton speaks of areas with *place amenities*, i.e. parks, restaurants, walkability, and charm, that cities are known for. The city might then be "not as concentrated, more varied and more balanced. And the urban amenities that have characterized big cities up to now are likely to spread out to smaller cities and suburbs across the land as urban refugees find new places to live."[5] Parks have become more important than ever as public gathering places.[6] Hence, inclusive public spaces have become increasingly important in cities, with greater decentralization of such amenities. Perhaps such changes in the shape of cities will be accompanied by relevant adoptions, adaptations, and innovations of technologies.

---

[3]See   https://theconversation.com/our-research-shows-covid-has-made-australians-more-conservative-and-care-less-about-others-161500?utm_medium=Social&utm_source=Twitter#Echobox=1624260292-1.

[4] See https://ourworldindata.org/covid-vaccinations [last accessed: 24/6/2021].

[5]From https://kinder.rice.edu/urbanedge/2021/03/15/6-post-pandemic-predictions-how-cities-will-change [last accessed: 20/5/2021].

[6]See   https://theconversation.com/post-pandemic-cities-can-permanently-reclaim-public-spaces-as-gathering-places-150729 [last accessed: 20/5/2021].

The use of automated technologies will continue to develop further for a range of city applications, ranging from dealing with waste management, helping to grow food, cleaning areas, to transporting people and goods. A combination of cooperative devices can be employed, from driverless vehicles to urban robots for automation we described in Chaps. 1 and 4. Automation can be employed to engineer greater resilience for city systems, e.g., for transport or supply chains, and enable easier adaptations and greater flexibility to cope with changes in patterns of city life, by partnering with humans and amplifying human abilities. Perhaps when humans cannot play their roles temporarily, machines that would normally partner with the humans can detect this and step up, in order to keep vital activities going and "hold the fort", until the humans return, wherein the machines return to their role of partner and amplifier. Moreover, the machines that host the human city inhabitants sense and detect the changing patterns of human behaviour and adapt to them accordingly.

5.3   Its Not All About the Technology

It might be odd that, after describing, and at many points, advocating for more and better technology, that the book might end with this section. Indeed, as we noted in Chap. 4, technology in itself can only be part of the answer, and it is its effective integration into society and into user's lives that will make a bigger difference.

Clark, a professor of city and regional planning, in *Solving for the City* [1] made this observation:

> After a decade of pilot projects and flashy demonstrations, though, it's still not clear whether smart city technologies can actually solve or even mitigate the challenges cities face. A lot of progress on our most pressing urban issues such as broadband access, affordable housing, or public transport could come from better policies and more funding. These problems don't necessarily require new technology.

and later, also said:

> A viable future for smart city technology would mean engaging with tough questions that the tech sector has often avoided questions about what advances would best serve cities as such.

What technological advances would best serve cities is indeed a question that we asked ourselves, and while we work on particular technologies and explore their benefits, it is a question that we plan to come back to often. Hence, while we outlined a range of exciting trends for the Automated City, it must be that any bold vision of the Automated City should be accompanied with a dose of humility and caution.

How a robot driven by AI algorithms reaches a balanced compromise between what is ethically justifiable, technically possible, socially acceptable and legally defensible is a fundamental question requiring a paradigm shift in the way we conduct multidisciplinary research in this field. For example, violating road rules is not allowed but it is legally defensible to do so in order to save a life. Such a dilemma makes the task of the Automated Vehicle programmer extremely difficult.

For any form of advanced automation (e.g., a robot) to be an integral trusted part of our city life, there will be an increasing need to consider them as entities with agency (perhaps a new category of agents next to persons and animals), endowed with very specific rights, responsibilities and duties, including that of repairing any physical, economical or moral damage caused to a third party.

What Is an Ideal City?

Another question is: what is the Ideal City? In the *Republic*, Plato describes the *Ideal City* (*polis*) as a place mirroring the harmonious *kosmos* and the individual, based on justice and virtue. This might be considered ideal—to quote London:[7]

> It (the ideal city) was a form of social and political organization that allowed individuals to maximize their potentialities, serve their fellow citizens, and live in accordance with universal laws and truths.

Hence, the Ideal City is not necessarily simply a city full of amazing technology for technology sake but a city that is humane, resilient and responsive, as supported by technology. Consider the Automated City as a response to an aging population using automation to create age-friendly cities, the Automated City as a response to climate change using automation to facilitate energy-smart living and the Automated City as a response to increased urbanization by enabling smarter city governance, city management and city resource utilisation. Time will tell how the Automated City can be a step towards the Ideal City. We hope this book can be part of this discussion.

References

1. Clark, J. (2021). Solving for the city. *MIT Technology Review, 124*, 9–11.
2. De', R., Pandey, N., & Pal, A. (2020). Impact of digital surge during COVID-19 pandemic: A viewpoint on research and practice. *International Journal of Information Management, 55*, 102171. Impact of COVID-19 Pandemic on Information Management Research and Practice: Editorial Perspectives.
3. Doubleday, A., Choe, Y., Busch Isaksen, T., Miles, S., & Errett, N. A. (2021). How did outdoor biking and walking change during COVID-19?: A case study of three U.S. cities. *PLoS One, 16*(1), 1–13.
4. Le Quéré, C., Jackson, R. B., Jones, M. W., Smith, A. J. P., Abernethy, S., Andrew, R. M., De-Gol, A. J., Willis, D. R., Shan, Y., Canadell, J. G., Friedlingstein, P., Creutzig, F., & Peters, G. P. (2020). Temporary reduction in daily global CO2 emissions during the COVID-19 forced confinement. *Nature Climate Change, 10*(7), 647–653.

---

[7]https://scott.london/articles/idealcity.html [last accessed: 19/5/2021].

Index

Symbols
5G, 21
6G, 21

A
Age-friendly city, 151
AI explainability, 144
Air quality monitoring, 20
Akon City, 114
Algorithmic bias, 148
Algorithmic-decision making, 79
Algorithmic governance, 119
Alibaba, 56
Amazon, 24
Anthropomorphic metaphors, 145
Anthropomorphic robots, 54
Array of Things, 20
Art, 61
Artificial Intelligence (AI), 22
Australian Government, 10
Austroads, 75
Automated City, 38, 43, 62, 65, 66
Automated Driving Systems (ADS), 80
Automated hotels, 59
Automated scooters, 72
Automated vehicle, 33, 50, 70
Automated Vehicle Safety Consortium, 80
Automated wheelchairs, 72
Automation, 15, 25
Autonomous cities, 43
Autonomous systems, 19
Autonomy, 15, 146
AutoX, 70

B
Batty, M., 116
Beacons, 9
Beneficence, 15, 146
Blockchain, 129
BlueTrace, 9
BMW, 80
Brownell, 113
Bucher, T., 119
Business models, 120

C
Charging stations, 75
Chatbots, 26
City policies, 118
Civic participation, 30
Clark, J., 160
Cleaning robot, 81
Commonsense reasoning, 145
Community ownership models, 85
Compositionality, 93
Contact tracing, 9
Context-awareness, 15
Contribution Game, 139
Cooperating machines, 58
Cooperation, 48
Cooperation-as-a-Service Platform, 133
Cooperative automated vehicles, 71
Cooperative-by-design, 138
Cooperative downloading, 137
Cooperative Intelligent Transport Systems, 72, 134
Cooperative parking, 136

© The Author(s), under exclusive license to Springer Nature Switzerland AG 2021
S. W. Loke, A. Rakotonirainy, *The Automated City*,
https://doi.org/10.1007/978-3-030-82318-4

COVID-19, 4, 158
Crowdsensing, 137
Crowdsourcing, 137
Cyber-physical infrastructure, 52
Cyber-physical systems, 18
Cybersecurity, 78

D
Data-centric city, 37
Delivery robots, 6, 81
Digital divide, 89
Digital twins, 21
Distributed Ledger Technology (DLT), 129
Drones, 7
Drone station, 97
Dystopian, 64

E
Ethical considerations, 15
Ecosystem, 122
Edge computing, 127
Envelope, 25
E-scooter, 124
Ethical principles, 146
Ethical rules for machines, 141
Ethics of algorithms, 146
eVTOL, 102

F
Farm robots, 84
Floridi. L., 23

G
Gates, B., 118
Geo-fencing, 8
Geo-hazard monitoring, 20
Green city, 112

H
Hackable city, 31
Halegoua, 55
Healthcare robots, 82
Health maximisation, 146
Humane Automated City, 64
Humanoid, 52
Human-robot interaction, 88
Hyperautomation, 66

I
Ideal City, 161
Intelligent Transport Systems (ITS), 32
Internet of Robotic Things, 18, 52
Internet of Things (IoT), 17, 52
IoT Alliance Australia (IoTAA), 37

J
Justice, 15

K
Kant, 141
Kantian equilibrium, 141
Kantian machines, 141

L
Layers of behaviour for urban robots, 95
Learning effects, 27
Least harm, 146
Le Corbusier, 56, 115
Levels of autonomy, 49
LoRaWAN, 18
LTE-M, 18, 19
LwM2M, 18

M
Machine Learning (ML), 76
McCullough, M., 93
Metaphor, 49, 60
Micro-cloud, 137
Mobility-as-a-Service, 122
Mobility choices, 80
MQTT, 18
Multi-sided platform, 26

N
Nagenborg, M., 87
National Institute of Science and Technology,
    36
Navya, 33
NB-IoT, 18, 19
Net City, 114
Network effects, 27
Non-maleficence, 15, 146
Norman, D., 61

O
Operational Design Domain (ODD), 76

P
Pandemic, 15
Participatory city, 37
Participatory city-making, 31
Pervasive computing, 18
Platform, 28
Platform urbanism, 28
Programmed living, 120
Programmed sociality, 119
Proximity sensing, 9

Q
Queensland's Cooperative and Automated
      Vehicle Initiative, 70

R
Recommenders, 120
Radio-Frequency Identification (RFID), 17,
      126
Responsible Artificial Intelligence, 144
Robot, 5, 59
Robotaxis, 70
Robotic Process Automation (RPA), 25
Robot societies, 93

S
SAT42M, 19
Satellites, 19
Scale for drone autonomy, 98
Schneier, B., 55
Self-actioning, 66
Self-organizing city, 45
Self-repairing cities, 45
Sensing, 15
Service robots, 82
Sigfox, 19
Situation-awareness, 15
Six levels of Driving Automation, 70
Smart bookshelves, 52
Smart city, 3, 35
Smart city standards, 34
Smart devices, 148
Smart furniture, 52
Smart park benches, 52

Smart sculptures, 52
Smart street signs, 52
Social-AI, 143
Social distancing, 13
Social inequality, 89, 91
Social mobilization, 31
Society of Automotive Engineers, 70
Space IoT, 19
Stag-Hunt Game, 138
Sustainability, 112
Symbiotic, 47
Symmetrical vehicle, 70

T
Task entropy, 50
Technology acceptance, 86
Telehealth, 14
Tesla, 33
Thomasen, K., 90
Transportation-as-a-Service, 122
Trolley problem, 79

U
Ubiquitous computing, 18
Urban hubs, 110
Urban operating system, 28
Urban robots cooperating, 143

V
Virtual counterpart, 18
Visions of cities, 109
Volkswagen, 75

W
Walkability, 111
Waymo, 33
Web of Things, 18
Wooldridge, M., 23
Woven City, 114

Z
Zoox, 70

Printed in the United States
by Baker & Taylor Publisher Services